Through the Heart of Africa

Also from Westphalia Press
westphaliapress.org

The Idea of the Digital University

Criminology Confronts Cultural Change

Eight Decades in Syria

Avant-Garde Politician

Socrates: An Oration

Strategies for Online Education

Conflicts in Health Policy

Material History and Ritual Objects

Jiu-Jitsu Combat Tricks

Opportunity and Horatio Alger

Careers in the Face of Challenge

Bookplates of the Kings

Collecting American Presidential Autographs

Misunderstood Children

Original Cables from the Pearl Harbor Attack

Social Satire and the Modern Novel

The Amenities of Book Collecting

Trademark Power

A Definitive Commentary on Bookplates

James Martineau and Rebuilding Theology

Royalty in All Ages

A Short History of Medicine

The Man Who Killed President Garfield

Chinese Nights Entertainments: Stories from Old China

Understanding Art

Homeopathy

The Signpost of Learning

Collecting Old Books

The Boy Chums Cruising in Florida Waters

The Thomas Starr King Dispute

Salt Water Game Fishing

Lariats and Lassos

Mr. Garfield of Ohio

The Wisdom of Thomas Starr King

The French Foreign Legion

War in Syria

Naturism Comes to the United States

Water Resources: Iniatives and Agendas

Designing, Adapting, Strategizing in Online Education

Feeding the Global South

The Design of Life: Development from a Human Perspective

Through the Heart of Africa

Being an Account of a Journey on Bicycles and on Foot from Northern Rhodesia, past the Great Lakes, to Egypt, Undertaken While on Leave in 1910

by Frank H. Melland & Edward H. Cholmeley

WESTPHALIA PRESS
An imprint of Policy Studies Organization

Through the Heart of Africa
All Rights Reserved © 2016 by Policy Studies Organization

Westphalia Press
An imprint of Policy Studies Organization
1527 New Hampshire Ave., NW
Washington, D.C. 20036
info@ipsonet.org

ISBN-13: 978-1-63391-388-2
ISBN-10: 1-63391-388-0

Cover design by Taillefer Long at Illuminated Stories:
www.illuminatedstories.com

Daniel Gutierrez-Sandoval, Executive Director
PSO and Westphalia Press

Updated material and comments on this edition
can be found at the Westphalia Press website:
www.westphaliapress.org

THROUGH THE HEART OF AFRICA

THE KALAMBO FALLS.

THROUGH THE HEART OF AFRICA

Being an Account of a Journey on Bicycles
and on Foot from Northern Rhodesia,
past the Great Lakes, to Egypt,
undertaken when proceeding
home on leave in 1910

BY

FRANK H. MELLAND
F.R.G.S. F.Z.S., F.R.A.I.

AND

EDWARD H. CHOLMELEY
F.R.A.I.

"*Africa, in relation to world politics, is but an annex of Europe, geographically as well as, now, by pre-emption*"—CAPT. MAHAN

LONDON
CONSTABLE & COMPANY LTD.
1912

TO

OUR MOTHERS

WE DEDICATE

THIS ACCOUNT OF OUR JOURNEY

ACKNOWLEDGMENT

WE owe our thanks to all who on our journey answered our numerous questions and supplied us with information, to many friends who by their sympathy and encouragement have helped us to write this record of our travels, and to Mr. L. A. Wallace, Administrator of Northern Rhodesia, but for whose kindness, in allowing us time to work at it after our return from leave, this book could not have been written.

F. H. M., E. H. C.

LIVINGSTONE, NORTHERN RHODESIA,
June 1911.

CONTENTS

I

TO THE GERMAN BORDER

Introductory—Reasons for journey—Preliminary preparations—Method of travel—The start—Kasama—Abercorn—Kawimbe Mission—Mishap to one bicycle—Kalambo Falls . . . 1

II

BISMARCKBURG AND LYANGALILE

Lake Tanganyika—Bismarckburg—Life in a German fort—Journey to Mwazye—The French Fathers—Notes on the Watwaki rulers in Lufipa—Religious beliefs of the Wakuluwe . . 10

III

RUKWA

A steep descent—Attractive native dance—The horrors of the buffalo-bean—Meeting with the Mutwaki ruler Sa—Tribal characteristics of the Wakwa—Simba Mission—Negro nuns—Curious customs and beliefs of the Wakwa 26

IV

RUKWA TO TABORA

Game on the Kavu River—A long stalk—Euphorbia-stockaded villages—Unintentional change of route—Reception by Muchereka, Mulungwa chief—And by Kasamia—"Tembo" architecture—Prevalence of tsetse fly—Sport on the Ugalla River—Kalula, chief of the Wagunda—Belt of good timber, with sawpits—Arrival at Tabora 42

V

TABORA

Cordial reception by the officials—Engagement of carriers—The market—The mission—Description of the town—Absence of any form of recreation grounds—Herr Siegel, the Distrikts Kommissar—Transport viâ the Uganda Railway—Curious contention of the Germans—The effect of the German railway from Dar-es-Salam on this traffic and on Tabora . . . 59

VI

TABORA TO MWANZA

Encounter with party of missionaries—Curious rock formation at Ngaya—Notes on the Wanyamwezi—Game on the Mbala Plain—Soap and oil factory at Salabwe—Scenery on Mwanza Gulf—Carriers on road—Arrival at Mwanza 69

VII

MWANZA AND THE ADMINISTRATION OF GERMAN EAST AFRICA

Description of Mwanza—Perambulations and perplexities—Protracted negotiations with the Customs department—General impressions of German East Africa—The country, natives, markets and small coinage, climate—An examination of the old régime and the new 84

VIII

THE VICTORIA NYANZA AND THE UGANDA RAILWAY

The s.s. *Sybil*—Our fellow-passengers—Bukoba—Baganda canoes—Bukakata—Entebbe—The raising of the game licence—Definite choice of itinerary—An impression of the beauties of Entebbe—The police sports—Kind reception and hospitality—The ill-fated bicycle—The Ripon Falls—Meeting with Dr. Milne—Port Florence—Scenery on the railway . . . 103

IX

BRITISH EAST AFRICA

Nairobi—The derelict bicycle is repaired—Visits to dentist, photographer, and other business—Journey to Punda Milia by motor—View of Mount Kenia—Attack of fever—A sisal farm—Sport—Return to Nairobi—Hospitality of the residents—The race-meeting—Lottery night at the Club—Meeting with Wawemba soldiers—Return to Port Florence—Impressions of the country and of the natives—Prospects for intending settlers . . 116

X

RETURN TO ENTEBBE AND BY MOTOR TO MUBENDI

Across the lake on the s.s. *Clement Hill*—The Entebbe Customs—Botanical Gardens—Preparations for journey north—The golf-links—Further impressions of Entebbe—Departure by motor-waggon—Rain at Kampala—Wonders of the motor road—Its maintenance—" Mosquito Camp "—Our fellow-passengers and the prospects for settlers—Mishap to the car and other incidents—Mubendi—Meeting with the Acting Governor . . 136

XI

MUBENDI TO HOIMA

Our new carriers—A chief's house and garden—The civilisation of the Baganda—System of feeding carriers—Rate of pay—Agricultural development—The cotton industry—A native market—Bukumi mission—Elephant grass—Our camp—Crossing a swamp—Hoima—Ivory poaching in the Congo—A Nubian wedding at the military camp—Marriage laws of the Banyoro—Land settlement and communications in the Bunyoro province—Missions at Hoima—Start for Bugoma . 154

XII

ELEPHANT HUNTING NEAR THE ALBERT NYANZA

The "Kabaka" of Bunyoro—Heavy rain—The Bugoma forest—Colobus monkeys—Death of our dogs—After elephant in "elephant grass"—Helplessness of the hunter Duawiri—The Albert Nyanza—Our first elephant—A wet night—Example of native stupidity—An important change in our projected

CONTENTS

itinerary—More elephants near the lake—A big one wounded and lost—More blank days in difficult country—The forest hog—A herd of elephants bogged in a stream—Return to Hoima 172

XIII
ELEPHANT HUNTING IN THE MASINDI DISTRICT—I

Sale of our ivory at Hoima—A civet cat—Total eclipse of the moon—Encounter with Captain Tufnell—Masindi—Elephant hunting in a forest belt—Our second elephant—Blank days near Samusoni's and Benjamin's 191

XIV
ELEPHANT HUNTING IN THE MASINDI DISTRICT—II

The Victoria Nile at Kishilisi—Jackson's hartebeeste and steinbok—Back to Kiliandongo's—More blank days after elephants—Risks run by *shamba* dwellers—Our carriers go on strike, but are appeased—Still more blank days—Our third elephant—An evening outing—Crossing the Nile—Palango—Repatriation of our Rhodesian natives—Arrival of Captain Place . . 204

XV
THROUGH THE LANGO AND ACHOLI COUNTRY

The Lango—The system of governing through Baganda agents—Description of the clothing, ornaments, accoutrements, villages, and huts of the Lango—Start from Palango—Our escorts and carriers—Travelling in the Lango country—Two swampy rivers—Mount Moru—Reception at Mwaka's—The Lango at work—Mwaka's "army"—Gulu—The Acholi—A hunting party—Oliya's village—His cadet corps—More trouble with the bicycle—Nimule 218

XVI
NIMULE TO GONDOKORO

Uninviting country—The Assua River—Arrangements for food supply and extra carriers—Christmas Day—Ledju, the rain-maker—Rejaf—Arrival at Gondokoro—Sale of our camp kit—Arrival of the *Gordon Pasha*—Notes on Uganda and its administration 243

CONTENTS

XVII

THE SOUDAN

The *Gordon Pasha*—New Year's Eve at Lado—Mongalla—The Dinka tribe—An old friend—The sudd—The Bahr-el-Ghazal and Sobat—Kodok—The White Nile railway bridge—Khartoum—Omdurman—Khalifa's palace, Mahdi's tomb, and market-place—School and hospital—The Gordon College—The Nubian Desert—Wady Halfa 260

XVIII

EGYPT

Down the Nile to Shellal—Philæ and the Dam—Asswân—Luxor—The temples of Thebes and the tombs of the kings—Karnak and Luxor temples—Abydos—Cairo—Tura—The Pyramids in sleet—Port Said—End of our journey—Retrospect—Notes on clothes, rifles, cameras 273

XIX

SOME AFRICAN PROBLEMS

The rapid opening up of Africa by rail and river, and some reflections on the problems that this development is presenting . 288

LIST OF ILLUSTRATIONS

The Kalambo Falls .	*Frontispiece*
	FACING PAGE
A Mambwe village .	6
Magistrate's Office, Abercorn	6
Mwazye Mission	12
Kifanyula, our Munyampala, Gun Boy, Bicycle Boy, and other German East African carriers .	12
Old Mufipa Man	14
Kiatu, the Mutwaki Chief of the senior branch of the Wa Fipa	14
"A magnificent tree . . . under which we pitched our camp"	28
The Community of Black Nuns	32
"The composure of her bearing . . . sadly marred by ill-fitting dress, straw sombrero, and ammunition boots".	34
"A fine church was in the course of construction" .	34
"Two solitary fangs in a mobile and humorous mouth ".	44
Making native beer .	44
Another photo of little Mbaula .	44
Native utensils, "bellows, ladles, and trays" .	48
Drawing water from a water hole in a village near the Ugalla	48
One of the Authors in his travelling Clothes at Kelula .	52
"We bagged a leopard" .	52
A Tembo village (to right of background). Beehives in trees in the foreground .	54
In a Mugunda village. In the foreground is a native bed	54
"The Mission House is a fine specimen of an old Arab dwelling".	62
"The soap vendors . . . sitting . . . sedulously working specimens of it into a lather" .	62
A fine old Arab carved doorway at Tabora (in an Arab house)	64
Chief's house at Kahama .	72
Natives threshing Kafir Corn .	72
A balanced rock at Mwanza .	84
View from our camp at Mwanza .	84
A memorial to Bismarck near our camp .	86

LIST OF ILLUSTRATIONS

	FACING PAGE
At Bukoba, Victoria Nyanza, the "Sybil" and Baganda canoes	104
"Red, green-edged roads"	104
Ripon Falls	112
Port Florence civilisation: the Quay	114
The Uganda Railway	114
Nairobi Station	116
Government House, front view	116
Suburban houses on "The Hill"	118
Nairobi Races: the Grand Stand	118
Breaking up the land on an East African farm	124
Two-year sisal at Punda Milia	124
Mr. Alison Russell and his Bougainvillea-covered porch	140
The Uganda Government motor-car on the road	140
"The finest bit of engineering on the road"	152
Mr. Stanley Tomkins, Acting Governor of Uganda	152
Fencing Yekula's Garden	156
Allotting our loads to carriers at Mubendi	156
Bukumi Mission	158
The Dwelling-house, Bukumi	158
Resting in a "Banda"	164
Ferrying our loads across a swamp on Papyrus rafts	164
Looking for elephants on the Albert Nyanza	174
The Kabaka's Dancers	174
Our First Elephant	178
Bargaining	178
In Camp	196
The D.C.'s House at Masindi	196
Our Second Elephant	202
"The stripping and uprooting of several large trees"	202
Chumamaboko standing by a Jackson's hartebeeste	204
Preparing to cross the Nile	216
Fish basket on the Victoria Nile	216
Ferrying cattle on the channels abutting on the Victoria Nile	218
Borassus Palms	220
Weighing our third pair of tusks in camp	220
"Costume consisting chiefly of tattoo marks, a small girdle round the waist, from which hangs, in front, a miniature apron . . . of iron chain-work . . . or strands of hair, and behind . . . a long tail hangs down to the ground"	222

LIST OF ILLUSTRATIONS

FACING PAGE

"The men . . . of fine physique, occasionally wear a skin loin-cloth, but more often a small skin apron is suspended from . . . a corset of . . . grass"	224
Mwaka's Army	226
"The doorways are more or less circular and very low"	226
Old Lango Woman	236
"There were some lounges . . . of most original design"	236
"Young Acholi Bloods . . . even more tightly laced than their Lango neighbours"	238
"Oliya's son, clad in a goat-skin and a walking-stick"	240
"A Headman of the Lango Chief and one of Mwaka's sons who came through to Gondokoro with us"	242
Looking across the Nile to Rejaf	248
The D.C.'s House at Gondokoro	248
Gondokoro Post Boat going upstream	264
Inland Dinka hut	264
Ash-covered Dinka	266
Dinka woman making mats	266
Primitive irrigation on the Nile	268
White Nile Bridge, the centre span swinging	268
Map of the Route	*At end.*

"One of the pleasantest things in the world is going a journey."—HAZLITT

THROUGH THE HEART OF AFRICA

I

TO THE GERMAN BORDER

Introductory—Reasons for journey—Preliminary preparations—Method of travel—The start—Kasama—Abercorn—Kawimbe Mission—Mishap to one bicycle—Kalambo Falls.

THE question that probably first suggests itself to the majority of readers of books of travel in Africa or in any uncivilised quarter of the globe, namely, what was the object of the journey and what was to be gained by it, is not a difficult one to answer to the satisfaction of those, now growing year by year more numerous, who know first hand the call of Africa, and the peculiar fascination of life and travel in the so-called inhospitable or savage interior. The motives that have inspired others to undertake journeys through latitudes that to the uninitiated may seem uninviting, are almost as numerous as the travellers themselves. That of many has been exploration, of others commercial enterprise, of many the extension of missionary work, of others the pursuit of scientific investigation, while for some it has been merely for sport or in the spirit of adventure. Of ourselves we need merely say that, after years of residence in the Northern and least known province of Rhodesia, with a thorough acquaintance with the ordinary ways of reaching and leaving the continent, inspired by a craving to know something more of what lay beyond us, we decided to travel home by the countries to the North of us, instead of by the more beaten tracks. The probability that our acquaintance with a similar country would enable us the better to observe and more justly appreciate what we saw than the traveller or sportsman paying perhaps his only visit to the continent, helped to encourage us in the hope that a journey that was bound to occupy at least the greater part of our vacation leave would not be without result as a useful and educative experience. Moreover, the somewhat conflicting, though interesting, nature of the accounts of such countries from the pens of temporary residents and other travellers, as well as from visitors with whom we had come in contact, formed to us, interested as we were both in the African native and the possibilities and development of his country, an extra incentive to a first-hand study of the conditions in the neighbouring territories.

It was as early as 1907 that we definitely decided to go home through German East Africa to the Victoria Nyanza, and thence to proceed either through Uganda to the Soudan, and down the Nile to Cairo, or, after a short tour in Uganda, to travel down through British East Africa to Mombasa, halting at some of the more interesting places *en route*, and seeing what we could of the surrounding country. The final choice of routes had to remain undecided until we could be quite sure that circumstances, such as time and health, would permit of our first plan being carried out. In the meantime, besides acquiring and perusing a few of the works and official publications that deal with the conditions prevailing in some of the countries through which we intended to pass, we devoted ourselves to the collection of such various information and data as could be of use to us during the journey.

In addition to the published works, and information kindly furnished us by the various Government secretariats, we had the advantage of the notes and itineraries compiled by our friends Messrs. A. De L. Long and P. K. Glazebrook, Mr. J. B. Don, and the late Mr. George Grey, whose tragic death is deeply and universally regretted in those parts of Africa in which he spent so many years of

TO THE GERMAN BORDER

his life. The two first named had in the course of two of their visits to the continent travelled through German East Africa, and from Entebbe to Gondokoro; Mr. Don had a little more recently bicycled from King Williamstown to the Albert Nyanza; while Mr. Grey had made a careful cyclometer record of the direct route from Abercorn through German East Africa to the Victoria Nyanza; but there were, as a matter of fact, but two short stages during which we followed the route taken by any of these travellers, as our object was rather to avoid than follow the beaten tracks, but their itineraries were useful as a stand-by, and enabled us at least on one occasion to contradict the exaggerated estimate of the distance between camps that our carriers would have had us believe.

As for method of travel and transport, the journey from Rhodesia to the Soudan would, we knew, have to be performed in the manner to which we had been accustomed in the course of our duties: complete equipment and a large supply of provisions would have to be carried by native porters, while we ourselves went partly on foot and partly on bicycle.

In those parts of Central Africa where the existence of tsetse fly renders the use of all transport animals impossible, the usual method of personal conveyance has been for some years the *machila* or hammock, slung on a pole and carried on the shoulders of natives, but this is now becoming largely superseded by the use of the bicycle; and we had long since learnt, what will probably come as a surprise to many, that really a very considerable proportion not only of the cleared tracks, but also of the native paths in Central Africa provide almost as good a surface for cycling as could be desired. The fact that we used bicycles has perhaps given rise to an erroneous idea that our intention was simply to get through the country travelling as quickly as possible from point to point, and accompanied by few if any native carriers or impedimenta. As a matter of fact, though this can be and has been done, our machines were never meant to provide anything more than a relief from the fatigue and monotony of foot slogging. To this extent their use in Africa is considerable, but it must not be supposed that it enables one to travel any greater distances, or affects the fact that the day's trek has to be entirely regulated according to the capacity of one's carriers.

The problems that remained to be solved were to what extent, and where, we could rely on obtaining carriers *en route*, and how far we should have to carry provisions to last us for the whole journey.

For a journey straight through to Gondokoro, the latter would have been a matter of no great difficulty, as it could be performed in something like two months, but as we intended to see something of the countries on our way, to spend some five or six months in doing so, it was not so easy of solution. Even for a short trip of three or four weeks, it is difficult to travel in any comfort with less than thirty carriers ; tents, beds and bedding, cooking utensils, crockery, provisions, lamps, guns and ammunition have to be taken, and in loads averaging at the most fifty lbs. in weight.

For a journey therefore of six months, during which we knew but vaguely to what extent we could re-stock such provisions as tea, coffee, flour, sugar, and other necessities, and as we were also obliged—since we were after all proceeding on leave to England—to carry a certain quantity of respectable clothing, a caravan of sixty porters, which included the carriers of drugs, carbide, cameras, books, five loads of spirit tanks, and other apparatus for the preservation of zoological specimens, was, for two travellers, by no means an excessive allowance.

Experience in African travel, moreover, shows that, without indulging in luxuries, it is a mistake, especially when a tent has to be one's home for half a year, to deprive oneself of a few creature comforts for the sake of lessening one's impedimenta by two or three loads. An extra table or two and a few books add considerably to one's comfort, and anything that tends to alleviate the inconveniences of camp life is worth considering in its effect on temper and health.

As personal attendants we took with us a couple of boys each, including a cook, with two gun-bearers, one of whom knowing Swahili would be useful as an interpreter, and a hunter, especially experienced in spooring elephants. All had been in the service of one or the other of us for some years, and expressed their readiness to accompany us to any point from which they could be safely repatriated. All except two were Wawemba, the exceptions being natives who had lived for some years in the Wawemba country.

We left our stations in the middle of July, and met at Kasama towards the end of the month, after journeys of no particular incident. The difficulties of starting on any sort of expedition from an out of the way corner of Africa are of course considerably greater than when starting from England, and the vagaries of local transport were sufficiently brought home to us by the delay of nearly a month in the arrival of one of our machines.

After a pleasant sojourn with old friends at Kasama, enlivened by tennis and golf,—an interval which was spent re-sorting our baggage and reducing the number of our caravan—we left at 3 P.M. on July the 26th, and cycled easily to our first camp six miles out, whither our loads had preceded us, accompanied by Mr. R. A. Osborne (Inspector of Labour Recruiting), whose way thus far lay with ours.

The journey to Abercorn was not remarkable, except as affording us an example of a rather extraordinary bit of scenery, of a really impossible bit of road, of the utter hopelessness of relying on the evidence of raw natives as to the size and accessibility of a herd of elephants, and being the scene of the first bicycle breakdown.

The impossibility of the road was simply due to the fact that it had been recently banked up and re-made, and that its surface was so much like half-frozen plough that the only parts that were rideable were the gutters at the side.

The unusual scenery was the saltpans which lie some six miles south of Abercorn. These are two huge natural hollow amphitheatres lying side by side, one of them being remarkably symmetrical in shape, separated by a narrow neck of land on which runs the road. When the grass is burnt they are the resorts of large quantities of game.

The elephant episode occurred about half-way, took us off our line, and occupied us a couple of days. There were two beasts still due on one of our licences, and a herd being reported close to the road it was a chance not to be lost. Crops and grain stores had been annihilated, and we were assured that the marauders were the largest of bull elephants, and, when we got to the scene, that they could not be more than half an hour away. But the natives' accuracy had been affected by a desire to avenge the depredation of their larders and to encourage our aspirations. It took us a little more than half an hour, not to come up with them, but to discover that they were miles away, and that they consisted of nothing but cows and calves, and we lost no time in abandoning the spoor, returning to the main road. When we struck it, fortunately it had not been so newly top-dressed, and the last day or two into Abercorn it was really good riding. The bicycle breakdown might have been a serious one if we had not discovered that a perfect substitute could be made from the end of a Snider ramrod for a chain bolt that was lost—luckily just on reaching the village at which we were intending to camp—and emphasised for the first time the advisability of carrying every possible combination of spare parts.

The last day into Abercorn, twenty-five miles, we left our carriers behind, and got in by ourselves in time for lunch with Mr. Leyer (the Assistant Magistrate) and Mrs. Leyer.

In the next five days we enjoyed ourselves so much that it was quite a wrench to get started on our journey proper. Besides some excellent lawn tennis, we enjoyed the rare luxury of two or three rides on donkey and

A MAMBWE VILLAGE.

MAGISTRATE'S OFFICE, ABERCORN.

horse back; for, with extraordinary skill and precaution, Mr. Leyer had succeeded some twelve months before in bringing up three of the latter through the fly belt between Broken Hill and Abercorn, and two were still living and doing well. The day before our departure we bicycled out to Kawimbe to the London Missionary Society Mission which had been established since 1887. The Principal, Mr. Govan Robertson, was away; but owing to the kindness of Mrs. Robertson and Dr. and Mrs. Wareham, we much enjoyed our visit to one of the oldest missions in North-Eastern Rhodesia. It is beautifully situated in the Amambwe country; its comfortable dwellings and the magnificent rows of gums and cypress make it one of the most attractive and homelike settlements in this corner of Africa. It was on our way out that the catastrophe occurred that was seriously to affect the comfort of our travelling throughout German East Africa. For some inexplicable reason best known to the makers thereof, when three miles from our destination, the two-speed gear of one of our cycles spontaneously and violently refused either to do its own work or let the other parts of the machine do theirs, and proved, on a careful examination, to be such a complete wreck that it was obvious that the machine was no longer of the slightest use until the broken parts could be replaced. It was 5.30 P.M. before we finally despaired of a remedy; but in spite of the approaching dusk, and no small disappointment at the disaster, there was nothing for it but to trudge the twelve miles back to Abercorn on foot. So accompanied by our two dogs, an odd native or two to carry the bicycles and a lanthorn, we arrived at about half-past eight, in time to meet on the outskirts of the township a relief party sent out to find us, feeling ready to do more than justice to the excellent meal that we had kept waiting so long. It was not altogether an amusing walk—chafing as we were at the thought that the conveniences of transport had been reduced for six weeks by 50 per cent., the heels were coming off a pair of locally bought cycling boots, and the roughnesses of the road were almost worse in the flickering gleams of a stable lanthorn than they would have been in the dark; but as we neared the end of it, and began to get used to the situation, we could not fail to enjoy the eerie stillness of the African night and the faint glitter of ten million stars on the waters of Lake Chila down on our left as we turned the last corner and up the hill into Abercorn. The next day a cable was despatched to the makers in London ordering a new mechanism to meet us at Entebbe, and we left Abercorn on the 6th of August prepared to make the best of one bicycle between us until we reached Uganda.

As far as Abercorn, we had taken carriers from our own districts; beyond that the " Epidemic and Contagious Diseases Regulations " forbids them to travel, so a new gang had to be procured to take us to the German border (about 20 miles) and here we were met by our first German East African carriers, whom the Officer in Charge at Bismarckburg had kindly procured for us. These men would not hear of going with us as far as Mwanza, so we had to be content with engaging them for the first section to Tabora only. Close to the west of the point at which the path to Bismarckburg crosses the Kalambo River, which forms part of the boundary with German East Africa, is one of the most striking little waterfalls in the world. The river is but a streamlet, some 40 to 50 feet across, and in the dry season has but a slender volume of water, but the mere depth of the narrow gorge into which it tumbles, 700 feet sheer drop, lifts it out of the insignificance suggested by its size.

For some miles after leaving Abercorn (which is 5000 feet above sea-level) we had been steadily descending, when we reached the end of a long ridge from which, through the wooded clefts to our left, we had really our first sight of the waters of Lake Tanganyika, and saw some 800 or 900 feet below us a little village nestling in a smooth fertile valley hardly a mile broad. It seemed incredible that close at hand there could be room for so huge a drop twixt that and the level of the great lake.

The wooded ridges at either side increased the deception, and gave no clue of what they hid.

The descent of the gorge itself, though possible, is tedious, and as we had no time to make it we contented ourselves by lying flat on a dry spot on the lip of the fall watching the baboons skipping away up the steep cliff sides and the marabout storks circling about like swallows below us, and trying to realise the tremendous depth to the pool below—insignificant enough at that height, but, as a matter of fact, as yet unfathomed. The hills at either side of the gorge rise, just west of the cascade, to a height of some 400 or 500 feet, giving the gorge in some places a total depth of nearly a quarter of a mile. Narrow at first, it widens considerably at the top, and keeps for some distance an average breadth of some 200 yards.

No photograph had been previously taken that will show the whole height of the cascade, and none that lacks colour will ever do full justice to its beauty. Ours was secured at a distance of from half to three-quarters of a mile, from a precarious foothold on the face of a curve in the gorge. It shows the whole 700 feet of the cascade, the pool being just visible beyond the projecting terraces of cliff.

The following morning, after dismissing our Abercorn carriers and allotting our loads to the new gang, we crossed the boundary, and began the journey through German East Africa.

II

BISMARCKBURG AND LYANGALILE

Lake Tanganyika—Bismarckburg—Life in a German Fort—Journey to Mwazye—The French Fathers—Notes on the Watwaki rulers in Lufipa—Religious beliefs of the Wakuluwe.

SOME ten miles along a winding path through waterless forest and over stony switchback hills brought us to the ridge overlooking the blue waters of Tanganyika, and from some rocks by the path, on which we rested, we had a magnificent view of Bismarckburg Bay, and could see across the lake—which is narrow at this point—to the Belgian side. The bay is practically a replica of Torbay : the contour is almost identical, and the general appearance very similar, though on a grander scale, albeit instead of civilisation there is nothing visible but untamed nature, for the fort itself is just hidden round a corner, and even the telegraph wire to Ujiji and the roads leading to that port and to Kilimatinde and Neu Langenburg do not obtrude upon the view.

The descent was precipitous and tiring, and it was fully an hour before we reached the little valley at our feet, which formed a delta of refreshing green fertilised by the waters of a mountain stream whose winding course was traceable for miles away to the north-east. After a wash and brush up at the stream, we turned to the broad macadamised road leading away on our left up to the fort.

This occupies the end of a small promontory which rises some fifty feet sheer out of the lake, and is cut off from the mainland by a loopholed wall stretching right across from cliff to cliff, in the centre of which is the large double gate that gives the only access to within.

At the gate we were held up for two minutes by a pompous native sentry, who with difficulty roused himself from the indolent ease with which he and his colleagues were enjoying the luxury of cheap cigarettes and deck chairs—a peculiar sensation for us—until he received some assurance or other from within that he might let us pass.

Once inside, we were courteously and hospitably received by the Acting Commandant, Lieutenant Wach, with whom we were fortunately able to converse through the medium of French. He kindly provided us with most comfortable quarters within the fort, made us guests at his mess as long as we were there, and two quite pleasant days were spent there with a German journalist for a fellow-guest.

We welcomed the opportunity afforded us by the courtesy of our host of learning something of the details of official life and routine. At a station like Bismarckburg, which now holds the position of a sub-station to Ujiji, the duties are far from onerous. The customs work is not large, the trial of native cases occupies little more than half an hour per week—the consequence of a system under which the greater part of native litigation is dealt with by the *Wali* or Government-appointed district headman, who has the power to grant or refuse to applicants the right to come before the white man's court, just as he pleases.

Postal and telegraph business is conducted by non-commissioned officers and native clerks. But little district travelling is done, and the irreducible minimum required is regarded as irksome. Tennis courts, rifle ranges, and other means of recreation are conspicuous by their absence, and the life of the occupants of Bismarckburg, whose sole form of exercise seemed to be a short stroll at sundown outside the walls of their fort, did not impress us as very exhilarating.

The methods in vogue in this district are those of the old military administration, which is little more than a military occupation, and the lack of keenness amongst the officials is scarcely to be wondered at. They are Officers seconded from the German army for two years duty in Africa, which count as four in their total service ;

they spend some four months travelling between the coast and their stations, and possibly another two on transfer to a different district; so that the average time spent in a country and in duties that are equally strange to them probably averages rather less than more than twenty months. Hence it is not surprising that the majority of them look forward to nothing but the day that they will leave Africa for good to return to the Fatherland.

Before leaving Bismarckburg we took an opportunity of changing part of our English gold into German currency (rupees and heller of which 100 go to the rupee), and found that while the official exchange was Rs.15 the Indian traders were willing, and even anxious, to give us as much as Rs.17 for £1, as English gold was much sought after for purposes of trading principally in ivory in the Congo.

After completing these financial transactions partly by means of Ki-Swahili, but chiefly by signs, and persuading our new carriers that their demand for a month's food allowance in advance was scarcely reasonable for a trip which was probably going to take but three weeks, we left for Rukwa at noon of 10th August. We had decided to make this detour partly on account of the Rukwa Valley being but little known, and partly in the hope of being able to obtain some specimens of the local fish, none of which had hitherto found a place in any European museum. When bidding us farewell, our hosts were deeply concerned on our behalf when they learnt that our next stage was going to be across country, away from the "burra-burra," or main road, and the indispensable conveniences of regular camps.

Between here and Rukwa we were travelling amongst mixed tribes all known merely as "Shenzis" to the local official, to distinguish them from the Swahili or pseudo-Swahili, through whom they are administered; and we were much interested to learn from a Walungu chief named Kaleka, at whose village we camped three days out, that his people were akin to the section similarly named under Chitoshi living at the south-west of Tanganyika in

Mwazye Mission.

Kifanyula, our Munyampala gun boy, bicycle boy and other German East African carriers.

Northern Rhodesia, and recognised Chitoshi as one of their great chiefs. We found too that he was able freely to converse with and understand us in Chiwemba, the language of our Wawemba of Northern Rhodesia. This was an interesting piece of evidence of some forgotten migration of which we could learn no details, for, between this and the other section there is now a considerable wedge of entirely different tribes.

Between this and Mwazye Mission in the Lyangalile hills which was our next objective, the country was dry, badly watered, with a poor clay soil, and clothed with scanty timber and thorn bushes, but gradually improving as we reached the higher altitudes in the immediate neighbourhood of the French settlement; but our otherwise dull passage through this arid region was considerably alleviated by the courtesy and attention paid to us by the natives. At every village at or near which we camped for the night, the headman lost no time not only in pointing out what he considered to be the best spot for pitching our tents, but also in summoning his people, who willingly and cheerfully first cleared a convenient camping ground with their hoes, and then fetched an ample supply of water for ourselves, our staff, and our carriers. We found this kind of reception to be the rule rather than the exception all the way to Tabora, and though one might expect it from one's own natives, it was a pleasant surprise to find it extended to total strangers in a foreign territory.

Among natives of so friendly a disposition we had but little difficulty in finding our way when off the beaten tracks; guides from point to point were provided as soon as asked for, and, although in the true African spirit they occasionally attempted to take advantage of our ignorance of local topography, they did their duty passing well according to their lights.

On nearing Mwazye Mission, we thought it as well to announce our visit by a messenger in advance, and when within a few hours of that post we were agreeably surprised to meet our messenger returning with a cordial note of welcome from an old friend, Père Guillemé, who had been for many years associated with the Nyasa diocese, and had been for some time holding the post of *visiteur* in the Tanganyika District. We arrived at about ten o'clock on Saturday, and rested the whole of the following day.

Our visit was one of considerable interest. This post of the White Fathers of Algiers has, owing to its magnificent position, been adopted as a sanatorium to which members of other branches in need of rest are allowed to repair, in order to recruit their health. And besides the permanent staff there were one or two old African residents from less healthy stations who were benefiting by their sojourn here.

The invalids are by no means entirely free from the discipline of their order, and daily routine imposed upon them is quite in keeping with the spirit inspiring a community that has won such universal regard as much by the simplicity and austerity of its members' lives, as by their wise and patient handling of the difficult problem of grafting Christianity upon heathendom. An hour or two "*temps libre*" is permitted in the course of the day, and the tone of the regulations suggests that it would be the height of impropriety were any of the sufferers to succumb to their ailments at any other time.

The soil is as fertile as the site is well chosen, and we spent an enjoyable afternoon in an inspection of the gardens, fruit plantations, and wheat fields on the slope below the house and buildings, which are finely constructed of stone with tile roofs.

The natives, who are Wafipa, with a few Walungu emigrants, are an unsophisticated lot, and were wildly excited at our elementary gyrations on the bicycle, which was a thing that they had never seen before. Their curiosity at the arrival of strangers was amusing rather than offensive, but grew a little embarrassing at times. For an hour or two after our arrival, they were not content with crowding round on the verandah three or four deep, and peering into the rooms that any of us had entered, but the opening of a door from within generally disclosed the

OLD WAFIPA MEN.

Photo supplied by Père Wyckhaert.

KIATU, THE MUTWAKI CHIEF OF THE SENIOR BRANCH OF THE WA FIPA.

presence of at least one piccanin whose eye had been glued to the key-hole.

The history of the Watwaki, the rulers of the Wafipa people, as well as the customs and religious belief of a neighbouring tribe called the Wakuluwe, presents points of exceptional ethnographical interest, of which owing to the kindness of Père Wyckhaert, Superior of the Mission, we were able to make a careful record, and publish with his approval.

The Wafipa tribe forms with its offshoots one of the most numerous and important in this part of the continent, and covers a large area to the south of Tabora and Ujiji, down to the Saisi River (which, rising in British territory near Abercorn, flows into the south-west of Lake Ikwa). It is chiefly remarkable for the fact that the rulers are entirely distinct in origin to the tribe whom they rule, being of Galla (Gala) or Hamitic stock.

With regard to the inhabitants of Uganda, Sir Harry Johnston says (*The Uganda Protectorate*, 1902, vol. ii. p. 484) that it consists of five main stocks : (1) Pygmy—prognathous type ; (2) Bantu ; (3) Nile Negro ; (4) Masai ; (5) Hamite ; and of the last named he says :—

"The fifth and last among these main stocks is the Hamitic, which is negroid rather than negro. This is the division to which the modern Somali and Gala belong, and of which the basis of the population of ancient Egypt consisted. These Hamites are represented by the remarkable Bahima aristocracy of the western portions of the Uganda Protectorate, and possibly by certain tribes at the north end of Lake Rudolph." And again he writes of the "light-coloured Gala race of almost Caucasian stock . . . which in the modified and more negroid form . . . constitutes the aristocracy to-day of all land between the Victoria Nile in the north and Tanganyika in the south." And in the same writer's Introduction to another book (Cunningham's *Uganda and its People*, 1905, p. xi) he says of "the Hamitic invader and civiliser of Negro Africa," "I have also traced this element in lessening potency down the west coast of Tanganyika to regions north of the Zambezi."

Sir Harry Johnston visited Rukwa himself in 1889, and has informed us that he noticed this Hamitic family of Watwaki at the time, but neither in his books nor in any other published documents can we find any record of the Hamite influence at the south-east of Tanganyika, so that ethnographical students will feel grateful to Père Wyckhaert for allowing us to make use of his researches.

Sometime in the middle of the eighteenth century a woman called Unda, accompanied by two daughters and a small retinue, came from some country to the north and stayed with the chief of Lulungu at the south end of Lake Tanganyika. They were of nearly pure Hamitic stock and very light coloured. The chief of Lufipa resided near by at Milanzi, and was acquainted with an ancient prophecy as to the advent of these women, in consequence of which he informed his wife that if any " white " women came to Milanzi they were on no account to be allowed to sit in his royal chair ; as, were they to do so, the sovereignty of the Wafipa would pass from him to them. One day, when he was absent on a shooting expedition, this Hamitic woman Unda arrived with her daughters, and asked the Fipa chief's wife to get her his royal chair. Either without thinking, or overawed by the stronger character of the visitor, their hostess complied with the request, and on the return of the chief from his hunting Unda was discovered by him sitting on the royal seat of state. Immediately he perceived this he abdicated, and Unda became chief of the Wafipa. What the chief said to his wife the legend does not record, but the Wafipa appear to have accepted the change in rulers without question.

Unda belonged to a tribe known as Watwaki, and she found husbands for her daughters from a tribe called Wanika, immigrants from the south reputed to have been driven north by the Angoni. Before she died she gave an order that the descendants of her daughters were never to marry outside their own families, under penalty of death,

BISMARCKBURG AND LYANGALILE

and so for one hundred and fifty years or more the descendants of these two Watwaki and their Wanika husbands have intermarried—first cousins and even brothers and sisters (the analogy to the marriages of the Pharaohs is curious), and there has been no infusion of fresh blood in the family from that day to this, though now that almost all the descendants have embraced Christianity the rule is being broken: and it is none too soon, for the continual in-breeding has led to sterility; though it does not appear to have affected the mental powers of the offspring.

At the time of her arrival in Lufipa Unda carried a stone on her back as a woman carries a child, and this stone was deeply reverenced by the Wafipa. It was placed by Unda on the top of Milanzi mountain, the old chief of Lufipa, who had abdicated, being appointed guardian of the hill, a position which his descendants still hold. The village at Milanzi, moreover, is never moved, as are the surrounding villages, but is kept on the original site as being the residence of the guardian of the sacred mountain; nor are any rectangular huts allowed to exist within its confines.

The country of Lufipa thus acquired by Unda extends from Karema on Lake Tanganyika in the north (about 7° S.) to the Saisi River in the south (between 8° and 9° S.), and from Tanganyika in the west to the border of Rukwa in the east. Some time after the advent of Unda the Watwaki rulers divided into two factions. The split occurred on the death of one of the immediate successors of Msire, who was the first grandchild of Unda's to be born in the country. This chief had two sisters, each of whom was ambitious, and as each had a son the chief foresaw trouble as to the succession, and consequently decided to nominate one of the two as his successor. Unknown to his nephews, he decided to test them, and on different days sent each to herd his cattle, instructing them to watch the animals carefully, as one of the cows was about to calve. The first, known as Wakukatanga, idled and took no trouble to tend the cattle, as his uncle ascertained by means of a spy, and on his return, when asked to fetch a chair for the old chief, picked up the one nearest to him, and passed it in a very casual manner. The second, Wakuire, herded the animals very well, and towards sunset drove them back, and reported to his uncle that the cow had not calved. When asked to fetch a chair, he proceeded to bring the royal seat, and in consequence of his behaviour was nominated as the chief's successor, a choice that was acquiesced in by the tribe.

Wakukatanga's mother, however, formed a faction against Wakuire, and when he succeeded she captured the capital Sumbwanga (in the country called Kanse), and very nearly succeeded in capturing the young chief, who, however, made good his escape to the hills of Lyangalile. After a time his cousin, the usurper, Wakukatanga, heard that he was there, and promptly sent emissaries to capture or kill him; but his friends placed Wakuire in an old hut such as is used as a shelter for the dying, and placed in it some decaying meat and skins, so that when his cousin's messengers arrived they thought, from the smell, that he was very ill and returned to Wakukatanga, informing him that his cousin was dying. On their departure Wakuire went to the chief of the Walungu and asked for help to regain his capital, Sumbwanga, and his country. The necessary assistance being given him, he defeated and drove out Wakukatanga, who, in his turn, fled to Lyangalile, and there founded a new branch of the family, whose descendants rule in that part to-day, the present ruler being Sa (the daughter of Pilula), who succeeded another Sa, who died in 1910. But the senior branch at Sumbwanga is ruled over by Kiatu, the son of Kapufi, a descendant of Wakuire.

There has been nearly incessant warfare between the two branches, but whenever a male in either branch has lacked a bride he has sought and obtained one from the hostile branch rather than break the ordinance of Unda as to marrying outside the family. On only three occasions have the two branches united:—(1) During the Angoni invasion between 1850–60. The Angoni are known locally as the Wa Tuta, after their leader Tuta, and this invasion formed part of the great migration of this tribe, who crossed the Zambezi in 1825 and settled under Mombera and Mpeseni in Nyasaland and North-Eastern Rhodesia, and also penetrated as far as the south-east of the Victoria Nyanza. (ii.) During the raids and incursions of the Wawemba, which took place up to about 1890. And (iii) during the war with Kimaraunga, a filibuster whose meteoric career deserves more than a passing comment, forming as it does a good example of the romance that a strong man inevitably brings to the pages of history.

This remarkable man was the son of a slave who had been a great elephant hunter, and, having acquired considerable wealth from the sale of ivory, purchased his freedom. On his death Kimaraunga and his brother could not agree as to the disposition of their father's property, so the brother went to a country called Luwende or Lukawende, on the east of Tanganyika, between 5° and 6° S., and Kimaraunga settled between Lake Ikwa and Lyangalile. He managed to get together an army of sorts, and captured a considerable tract of land, and then made an alliance with the junior chief of the Wafipa—the ruler in Lyangalile—and, together, they succeeded in defeating the senior chief in Kanse. But shortly after this Kimaraunga and his ally fell out, and the two Fipa chiefs made an alliance and defeated him on the plains of Rukwa.

The adventurer then fortified a stronghold on the west of Lake Ikwa, in which no one dared to attack him, and eventually captured the country of the Wakuluwe on the lower Saisi River, and became a terror to the countryside. But about 1900 a German officer cut short his career by defeating him and making him prisoner. At Sumbwanga, *en route* to Bismarckburg, he was guarded in a hut, but succeeded in getting out, and, knocking down the sentry, made off, but was shot by the officer.

In 1909 the representatives of both sections of the Watwaki were converted to Christianity, and the feud that began with Wakuire and Wakukatanga has come to an end.

The Wakuluwe who have been referred to above as being conquered by Kimaraunga possess remarkably advanced theistic beliefs which are well worth recording as differing in many ways from the superstitions of the neighbouring tribes. These Wakuluwe are a branch of the Wachipeta who live on Lake Nyasa and moved to the Saisi Valley in the footsteps of the Angoni between 1860 and 1870.

They believe, firstly, in a god *Ngulwe*, a creator, and, as is generally the case in this part of Africa, consider that, having created the world, he had not bothered much about it since. The belief is essentially a monotheistic one, as the spirits that are referred to later are not considered divine in the same sense as *Ngulwe*. Secondly, they believe in evil spirits, of which only one has a name, *Mwawa*, of whose origin there are two accounts, some holding that he was always an evil spirit; whereas others contend that *Mwawa* was originally a servant of *Ngulwe's* who got into trouble and ran away. *Cf.* Milton, " Satan, thou wast not ever thus."

To this spirit is attributed the power to enter into people's bodies and possess them, the persons so possessed not being considered as evil in themselves, like *waloshi*, who are in league with the evil spirits. *Mwawa* can take human form, male and female, but generally assumes the shape of a dog and runs about in the villages, stealing and biting, and any one who beats him when in this shape is sure to suffer severely for it. Another favourite form for him to assume is that of a mouse, because in this shape he has the easiest access to the huts. To him is attributed the introduction of smallpox. Next in importance come the *Malesa* (spirits of the dead), also called *Fisingwa* (shades), who are really intermediaries and are not worshipped, but are appealed to convey prayers to *Ngulwe*, who is never prayed to directly. Offerings are made to them which are placed in the usual little spirit huts. The *Malesa* are considered responsible for death because when they are lonely they come back to earth to seek a companion.

There is a drink called *Lukansu*—a narcotic of some

kind—connected with the cult of *Malesa,* which is administered by the witch doctor, and which is supposed to give the drinker certain supernatural powers, such as invulnerability, superhuman strength, and the power to know and see things withheld from ordinary people.

There are two different accounts of the Creation : one being that a man and a woman fell down from heaven together, being provided with an axe, a hoe, bellows, and a few seeds for sowing, everything else having been created previously. These two were provided with a soul (*mwenzo*) which remains with them after death—*i.e.* when they became *fisingwa* and when they revisit the earth (*nkiwa*)—but to start with they were immortal. This original couple, like Adam and Eve, were absolutely innocent, but knowledge did not come to them as the result of temptation and fall.

Nec primo muliere concubare homo concupiebat, at cum non corpori suo illam corpore simili uti videretur, vulnere affligi illam putabat. Itaque vulnus medicare conabatur dum Ngulwe tandem in terram latus errorem demonstravit.

The other version is that the man and woman descended from heaven without the implements and seeds. They too lacked any sexual feeling, so *Ngulwe* caused the woman to bring forth a child, called *Kanga Masala,* from her knee. This child had great wisdom and grew up very quickly, and taught his parents how to make hoes and other implements, and also, feeling in need of a helpmeet, explained to them the relationship between man and wife. By him, too, they were instructed in the weaving of cloth wherewith to clothe themselves.

The "fall" is divided into two parts—woman's fall, which brought work into the world, and the fall of man, to which death is due. The first woman used to take a single grain of millet (about the size of an ordinary pinhead), and put it in a pot covered by a flat basket, and it was turned into sufficient porridge for her needs and her husband's. When her daughter grew up, the mother told her to take a single grain, and, having ground it, place it under the basket ; but the daughter, not knowing that her mother had done this for a long time, thought she must be mad to imagine that one grain could produce the required quantity of food, so she set to work and ground a whole basket of millet. The mother discovered this and cursed her, saying that for the future they would always be obliged to work hard and grind all their flour. The fall of man came about in this way :—*Ngulwe* had told the man that he was not to look for medicines among plants, nor on the ground, nor anywhere else, but that if any illness occurred he would cure it, and that man and his offspring should never die. One day one of the children was ill, but, remembering *Ngulwe's* instructions, the man did not seek any medicine. The following day, however, seeing that the child was not better, he went out into the bush and secured some herbs, which he gave to the child and cured it: but *Ngulwe* was angry, and told the man that since he preferred to find remedies for himself he could do so, but that his immunity from mortal diseases would be removed and that he and his descendants would die.

The classification of sins is rather an elaborate one, and presents many unusual features, one of the most noticeable being that they are divided into two classes —*Mpondo*, crime, and *Tusinza*, petty offences or misdemeanours. Neither kind had anything to do with the soul, and man could be entirely purged of them by confession or punishment, leaving the sinner none the worse for what he had done.

The sins (*mpondo*) are three in number :—

(1) Sorcery, being in league with *Mwawa*.
(2) Procuring abortion.
(3) Adultery, and the desire for incest.

Homicide is not included, as it is not considered a crime in the ordinary sense—that is to say, it is not a matter for trial as for the administration of justice, but simply an affair calling for revenge by the murdered person's relatives. The misdemeanours (*tusinza*) number five :—

(1) Breaking a vow.

BISMARCKBURG AND LYANGALILE

(2) Refusing to take part in public sacrifices, such as take place at the sowing and reaping seasons.
(3) Theft of a tool or implement (but not other forms of larceny).
(4) False testimony.
(5) Ingratitude to parents (*nkota*).

For the *tusinza* there were no punishments, but for the *mpondo*, the chief administers punishment which till recently usually took the form of mutilation. *Ngulwe*, too, frequently brought sickness upon the sinner and his family.

A curious form of public confession is associated with the *mpondo*. This confession, which is a well-established practice in this tribe, is known as *Kupemula mpondo*, which is not easy to translate as the word *kupemula* is not used in any other connection, but it means the taking off of the load or burden of the sins. The confession, which is only practised by men, takes place in the presence of the elders of the village, no women being permitted to attend. The man about to confess stands at the doorway of his hut, facing west, with a basket in his hands, in which are placed some sand and a few pieces of dry grass. Having confessed his *mpondo* aloud, he throws the grass and sand into the air, and the wind carries away the pieces of grass, while the sand falls back into the basket. The man then cries out, "My *mpondo* are now gone like the blades of grass, my *tusinza* are as numerous as the grains of sand in this basket, let them go too," and, suiting the action to the word, throws out the sand. He then says, "I have no more *mpondo*, and *Ngulwe* will cure my sickness" (or "will give me a prosperous journey") or whatever it was that led to the confession: for this public confession is only used in cases of sickness—presumed to be due to *Ngulwe's* wrath at some sin—or when starting on a journey, especially when about to cross the Saisi River in full flood, at which time, near its mouth, it is considered very dangerous.

Perhaps the most interesting part of the beliefs and customs of these Wakuluwe is their idea of the residence of departed spirits. As they do not consider the soul has anything to do with sins, they do not divide this abode into heaven and hell, but have only one residence for all the souls of the departed. On the death of any one it is considered that only half of the person dies; for, when the first man died his descendants buried him near the village, and while they were discussing the advisability of removing to a new site on account of his death, the corpse rose and showed half of his body above the ground and then disappeared again. This was taken as a sign that the soul (*mwenzo*) remains with the shade (*kisinzwa*). These *fisinzwa* are supposed to remain in a village in the centre of the earth; neither *Ngulwe* nor *Mwawa* interferes with them, but they have the power to approach *Ngulwe* and intercede with him. They live a life described as being one continuous night, having nothing to do, and suffer from *ennui* and nostalgia, which is the reason why they come at times to carry off a fresh companion from the earth. When some one dies, the relatives ask the witch doctor which of the *fisinzwa* has called him; and, having told them, he informs them that he must disinter the corpse and burn the remains (for which he charges a heavy fee) and cast the ashes to the winds.

The village inside the earth in which the *fisinzwa* live is said to be lighted by a mightier light than the earth, and spirits wear shining clothes, and the huts are thatched with shining grass—the word used to describe this being *kulelemela*, which is the word employed for the bright shining of the moon.

There exists in the tribe a regular sect or guild of porcupine hunters (*Waleli*), who aver that they visit this village of the *fisinzwa* when they enter the porcupine's burrows, and that there is a mighty river in the near side of it that no living person can cross without a charm, so that they have to wait on the near side till a woman comes down to draw water. They ask her for a charm, which she throws into the water, turning it into sand. The chief of the village is called *Lungabalwa*, and is most hospitable to them, and never lets them go away empty-handed—always giving them a porcupine.

The possible connection in these beliefs and customs with parts of Genesis, the Decalogue, Hades, and the Styx provides interesting speculation for the student of ethnography and folklore.

III

RUKWA

A steep descent—Attractive native dance—The horrors of the buffalo bean—Meeting with the Mutwaki ruler Sa—Tribal characteristics of the Wakwa—Simba Mission—Negro nuns—Curious customs and beliefs of the Wakwa.

ARMED with a passport in the shape of a cordial letter of introduction from Père Guillemé to any of his *confrères* with whom we might come into contact, we left Mwazye for Rukwa in the afternoon of the 15th August, escorted by a cheery troupe of boys and girls, whose curiosity or anxiety to see us safely on our way was not satisfied until they had accompanied us for something over a mile. Seven miles brought us to Mpwi, the village at which Sa resides, standing on the brow of a curving rise towards the eastern edge of a magnificent open plain, with a glorious view of the Lyangalile hills breaking up the horizon to the south-west. Sa herself was away, but her representatives showed but little embarrassment at having to do the honours in her absence; and, with the shelter of the chieftainess's verandah from the afternoon sun and a clear open space near it for our tents, our camp left little to be desired.

A little hampered by the conflicting statements of the local natives as to which of the tortuous paths that lay ahead of us was the most direct route by which to reach Simba in the Rukwa Valley (to them a most uncomfortable objective, for which in common with our carriers they seemed to have considerable difficulty in imagining any sound reason), we reached the edge of the escarpment on the following day, to find the view of valley below us entirely and perhaps mercifully obscured by impenetrable haze that for three parts of the year hangs like a veil over the lake and its environs, and at this time was intensified by the smoke of the bush fires that were filling the air with hoarse crackling from the rocks close to our feet to the parched plain 3000 feet below.

The descent occupied something over two hours; the gradient varied from one in four to something like two in three; and the path, which was generally over rock or loose stones, was in places rendered uncomfortably slippery by the dry grass that covered it like a mat.

The valley at the base consisted of parched and blackened country, dotted with baobabs and thorn trees, with patches of stiff yellow grass that looked as if it never could have been green.

After tramping for another hour through the baking heat, we were relieved to find ourselves at a dried up river bed, choked with masses of reeds that indicated the existence of moisture somewhere, on the opposite bank of which was a fair-sized village, with a magnificent tree at a corner of it, and under this we pitched our camp.

The native dances at the villages through which we had been passing had been neither strikingly interesting nor original; but here, at Ilembwe's when the moon was up, we enjoyed one of a quite unusual type. The first part was in the usual style—a row of men and girls opposite each other, accompanied by singing of a refrain that sounded extraordinarily like "Come along and have another one." Then a change took place, and a professional dancer in costume gave a *pas seul*, accompanied by drums and girls only, singing, the remarkable feature being the fact that not only was the refrain an exceptionally musical one, but the drums, singing, and dancing were all in strict time.

The country through which we tramped for the next few days was more thickly covered with vegetation than the foothills, but it was hot, dry and thorny. We were fortunate, however, in having a well-marked track most of the way, flanked by the hills towering away on our left, which presented a glorious spectacle when lit up at night with sparkling and sinuous terraces of flame from the bush fires creeping along their slopes, but it was on the whole an uninviting stretch.

One of these days will long be remembered. One of us, when leaving the path for a minute, was unfortunate enough to run into some buffalo bean. It is an innocent enough looking plant, the buffalo bean—a humble creeper with a russet-coloured woolly little pod, but of what this woolly little pod is capable, only those who have felt its torture can realise. The woolly appearance is due to a coating of infinitesimal and almost imperceptible hairs. At a touch they become detached, and, floating broadcast, alight or are wafted on to any object that is at hand. Their presence is not immediately detected, as the irritation caused is a little time in taking effect. The victim in this case got pretty well sprinkled on arms, legs, and neck, as well as on the inside of a light overcoat.

The following is a description in his own words: "I had walked several steps before I had a notion of what had happened, and then the fun began. First a slight tickle on an arm, then another at the back of the neck, then at the back of a bare knee, then all over again *da capo* until the spreading torture left me quite bewildered as to where to scratch, but no longer in any doubt of the particular kind of picnic I was in for. From seven o'clock till evening, with two short intervals during which it partially subsided, the intense irritation continued, and though I tried everything I could think of to alleviate it, nothing had more than the slightest temporary effect.

" In despair at the ineffectiveness of my own remedies, I asked one of my natives what they used themselves, and he recommended hot ashes. Even blisters seemed preferable to what I was suffering, and I ordered him to rob the nearest fire without delay. By this time the fiendish things seems to have got through shirt, shorts, and everything, and there were not many square inches of me into which I did not have the stuff rubbed. Fortunately consideration for his own fingers prevented the boy from applying the ashes too hot, but by the time he had finished I was

"A MAGNIFICENT TREE . . . UNDER WHICH WE PITCHED OUR CAMP."

about as much like a dustman before his weekly bath as I ever shall be.

The counter-irritant had a slightly distracting effect, but even that was not permanent, and I had to realise that the only thing to do was to sit as still as possible and let the irritation wear off, which it did, leaving me an exhausted and considerably wiser man between four and five o'clock. Even then I had not heard the last of it. Why or how the tiny hairs that cause the trouble disappear at all, or whether they do disappear, or only lose their poisonous powers, I do not know; but I had an unpleasant reminder of them a few days later when, on donning the same garments again, after a thorough washing and beating, I found that the fine hairs were still there, and the clothes were not yet fit to wear."

The Wakwa, as the inhabitants of Rukwa are named, amongst whom we were now travelling, differ in many interesting features from the tribes that we had left behind us on the Lyangalile highlands. One of the most notable of these is their habit of eating slabs of a sort of unleavened bread, made of maize flour, in the place of the porridge that is the customary diet of the majority of grain-growing natives. They grow but little millet, and that usually high up on the steep slopes of the hills, a habit contracted in the times when concealment from enemies was an important consideration and still maintained, possibly with a view to avoiding the poll tax. They have also a peculiar taste for eating rats, of which they cook large numbers—skin, hair and all, which causes an unpleasant smell in the vicinity of the cooking place. Their principal crops are maize, used for the brewing of beer as well as the making of bread, bananas, tomatoes, chillies, the castor-oil plant, and a good deal of cotton. They weave a coarse, strong serviceable cloth in pieces averaging 7 by $4\frac{1}{2}$ feet on a primitive handloom.

The baskets in general use also present some novel features. In addition to the almost universal "*lupe*," or flat tray-like basket, they have a soft, plaited receptacle, called a "*chiwo*," resembling a massive egg-cup in shape, and which is probably of Swahili origin, while they carry pumpkins, gourds, and other bulky objects in a large open wickerwork crate, suggesting the style of a parrot cage. The flat loaves, while still intact, they ingeniously use as trays and plates. The huts are mostly circular, the walls built of reeds, which are placed vertically, being neither plaited nor laid horizontally, as is usually the case in reed-built dwellings. Owing to the absence of the type of tree from which barkrope can be made, creepers are employed for binding.

They are a well-clothed race, wearing the cloth of their own manufacture, as well as imported blankets and prints; the women wear beads around their necks and their foreheads and metal ornaments inserted at the side of the nostril, while a few affect an ear ornament (worn in a hole in the lobe) of a piece of wood a little larger than a five shillings bit. Brass bracelets and anklets are also common.

The males wear but few ornaments of any kind. Bows and arrows are usually carried, but spears are rarely seen. Small herds of cattle and large flocks of sheep and goats are found at most villages of any size. In place of the usual bark cylinder, crudely hollowed wooden vessels are placed in the trees to act as beehives.

At Sakaliro's village, which we reached shortly after the encounter with the buffalo bean, we had the pleasure of meeting Sa, whom we had missed at her village, and who was returning with a large retinue from a visit to her relatives in Rukwa. Intelligent-looking, with the Hamitic strain plainly visible at close quarters in comparison with the frankly negro type of her subjects, her dignity was unmistakable, but the ease and composure of her bearing were sadly marred by the ill-fitting cheap cotton print dress, the calico-covered straw sombrero, and the ammunition boots which she apparently had learnt to consider inseparable from her dual rôle of queen and convert.

News of our approach had already reached her, and we were expected visitors. Stools for herself and for us were promptly ordered and produced, and for several minutes we sat in a little circle in the middle of the village and exchanged polite greetings and inquiries in Ki-Swahili. The conversation was not animated, for she was obviously exceedingly self-conscious and shy, and the suggestion that she and her suite should sit for their photographs was welcomed as a relief.

Presents were exchanged before we parted, and after the purchase of a piece of native cloth from her, which showed that her friendly relations in no way interfered with her instincts for driving a hard bargain, we proceeded on our way accompanied by one of her henchmen, who was to return, if we had any luck in shooting later in the day, with some meat for his mistress.

At our camp that evening, near which we did succeed in securing a couple of reed buck, we learnt that Sa had thoughtfully sent messengers to the neighbouring villages with orders to bring in supplies of food and beer for ourselves and our carriers. In obedience to these orders the people came in, but almost empty-handed: food, they protested, was very scarce, and they naïvely confessed that they themselves had drunk all the beer there was. We found the demeanour of some of them quite convincing, particularly in the case of one merry crowd that volunteered to accompany us all the way to the Victoria Nyanza, but on the following day, having either forgotten their offer or thought better of it, were nowhere to be found.

On the 19th of August we reached Simba Mission, at the north-west corner of Lake Ikwa, and received a hearty welcome from the Superior, Père Avon, and his colleagues. This post of the French Fathers is chiefly remarkable for the community of black nuns who live there; and who are, we believe, the only native women in this part of Africa who have ever taken the veil. The fact that they have done so is largely due to the initiative of one of the Watwaki family called, like the founder of the dynasty, Unda, who, after receiving an education at Karema Mission—to the south of Ujiji on Tanganyika—

volunteered to found the sisterhood, and persuaded three Bantu friends to join her. Of these, two are Wenemalungu from the west of the lake, and the third is the daughter of a chief of the Bende tribe on the eastern shore. We were much impressed by the demeanour of this remarkable sisterhood, the cleanliness of their house, and everything belonging to them. The Mutwaki (now known as Sœur Agnes) had plenty of natural grace, and the dignity that seems part of the inheritance of this Gala stock; the other three were rather shy in our presence, but are, we gathered, devout members of the Church, and, like their leader, make themselves very useful in attending to the sick women and children in the neighbourhood, besides, doing the laundry work for the Mission. Nor are they without some considerable culinary skill, as we discovered from a sweet and a cake made especially for our benefit.

A fine church which was in the course of construction at the time of our visit pleased us particularly by its simple architectural beauty and its symmetry. Pillars were being purposely omitted from the scheme, as the congregation were so fond of hiding behind them ! Life at Simba must be very trying ; the climate is hot and stifling, and hardly any one ever passes the Mission, which lies a little to the south of the main road from Dar-es-Salam and Kilimatindi to Bismarckburg. We were very much disappointed to find that the whole northern half of the lake was dry, and that it would mean a journey of five days in a southerly direction to reach open water. As this would mean a delay of ten or eleven days, we were obliged to forego it. We managed, however, to collect from the tributaries that are absorbed in the sandy bed which is all that remains of the north end of the lake, a few specimens of fish for the British Museum, one of which proved later to be a new species.

Ikwa is one of those peculiar lakes that has no outlet, so that a study of its fish should prove most interesting. The amount of water in it varies considerably. Up to 1880 it had been generally fairly full, but in that year the northern half dried up owing—so the natives say—

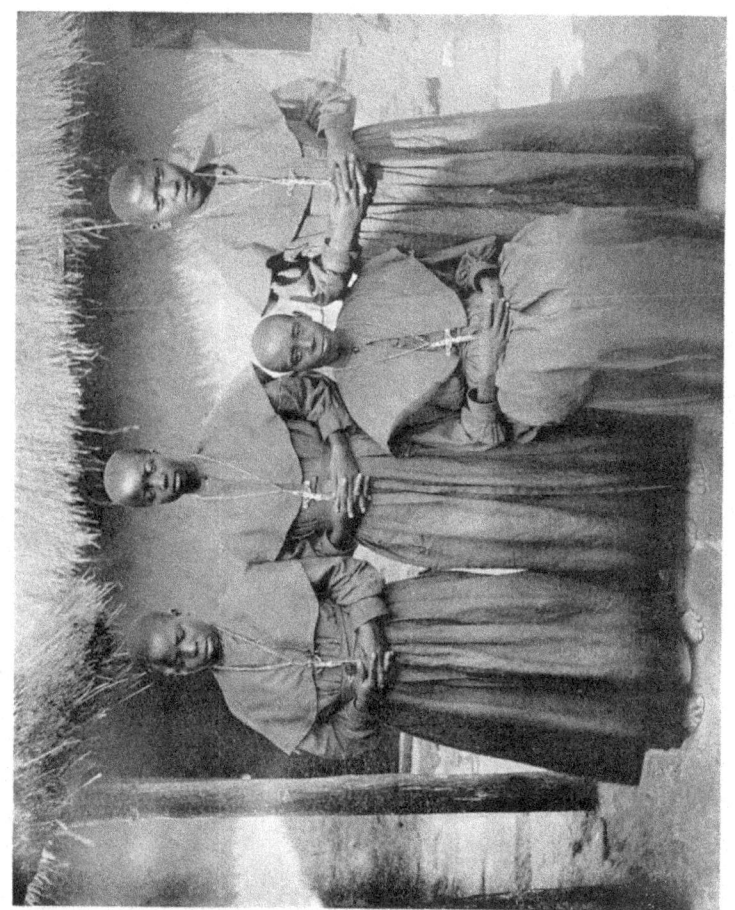

THE COMMUNITY OF BLACK NUNS.
(Sister Agnes is seated.)

to the death of a German explorer, who was interred close by and subsequently drank the waters to quench his thirst. The lake filled up again between 1900 and 1902, but since then has been getting emptier year by year. At the end of the dry season a great wind known as *Kikulwe* springs up, and raises the sand and potash from the dry bed and lake shore to such an extent that the sun is totally obscured and the surrounding country covered with a heavy deposit for some miles round. Mirages are common on and near the lake, and are called *amangisisi* by the natives.

Thanks once more to the courtesy of one of our hosts (Père Teurlings), who had spent many years among them, we were able to collect much interesting information about the customs and religious beliefs of the Wakwa.

There are very few customs observed at the birth of a child. When the woman is *enceinte* she confesses if she has been unfaithful to her husband so as to avoid the risk of dying in childbirth, which is supposed to result if the confession is not made. (This and many other incidents closely resemble those in vogue among many of the Central African tribes.) When the child is born a present is made to the local midwives by the parents, of a ram in the case of a son, and a ewe in the case of a daughter. The father is not allowed to see the child till an interval of three days has elapsed. In the case of twins one was killed, and five sheep (or goats—or occasionally hoes or other tools) given to the midwives. A somewhat similar custom exists among the neighbouring Wafipa, where at the birth of twins ten sheep are presented by the parents to the paramount chief. After the midwives have received their sheep, they and their colleagues from the neighbouring villages collect, and go to the Chief's village to announce the birth of the twins, and then separate to spread the news throughout the surrounding villages. The parents may neither drink nor take snuff on the day of the birth, nor may they eat, except a small bowl of porridge mixed with pieces of a tree called *umnombo*. Should either refuse to partake of this, his (or her) hands are attacked by a violent trembling which lasts till death.

Instead of the choice of wives resting with the Chief or with the parents, the Wakwa boys choose their own, generally starting to choose at about the age of eight. When a youth has finally made up his mind, or thinks he has, he carries a load of firewood to the girl's parents' hut, and if they approve of him they give him some porridge. Having thus committed himself, he goes next to his own father to ask him to provide sufficient of the world's goods to enable him to set up an establishment for himself. The father then, provided that he agrees with his son's choice, goes to the girl's parents, taking a hoe (*nkomo luyi*) to the girl; and asks for her on his son's behalf. Consent on the part of the girl is shown by her keeping silent, but refusal by her saying " No " and leaving the house. Once the young couple are engaged, which is what these preliminaries amount to, they are not allowed to look at each other during the daytime, nor may the youth look at his future parents-in-law till the marriage has been consummated and a child born. The girl may look at her parents-in-law after the marriage ceremony. During the " engagement " each must scrupulously avoid meeting the other's parents, and must turn in another direction if there is any chance of a meeting (the fixed times at which they meet for certain parts of the ceremony are, of course, excepted). Sexual intercourse between the young people prior to the giving of the first present is not considered wrong, but after that it is strictly forbidden till the marriage has taken place; or, strictly speaking, as will be seen, till the fifth day after the marriage.

After the betrothal comes the regular present-giving, which varies from three to fifteen sheep (five being a common number)—the local value of a sheep being about Rs.2. On the eve of the wedding day the young man takes a fowl to the girl's hut, and her parents bring her in crying: a dance then follows, after which the man leaves, returning at first cock-crow on the following morning with his companions, and taking with him some earth and water, with the mud made of which the girl covers his

"The composure of her bearing . . . . sadly marred by ill-fitting dress, straw sombrero and ammunition boots."

"A fine church was in the course of construction."

neck and chest, and he does the same to her. Then they cover each other's bodies all over with the mud. Porridge and meat are then fetched, and he puts some in his fiancée's mouth, and her companions put some in his. About noon they wash. A woman then takes a young child (*kisindi*) to the bridegroom's hut, and he gives her five fowls; after which she sits on a stool between his parents' hut and that of the bride's parents. This woman proceeds to mark out the distance between the huts by hoe-lengths, and if she stops at every hoe-length he presents a fowl at each halt, and if it is every ten hoe-lengths a sheep. All these gifts placed upon the ground go to the bridesmaids. The bride also has a *kisindi*, and both are oiled all over. After this present-giving the bride and bridegroom are oiled, and the bridegroom dons a cloth, a comb in his hair, a belt of beads, and bells on his ankles and on his left side. The bride wears a cloth, beads on her neck and body, and also as a belt, with shells all over her head; and on her forehead paints *usuli* (a decoction of pungent leaves powdered). The bridegroom's *kisindi* goes to the bride, and gets a little of the *usuli* on his finger and brings it to the bridegroom to smell to see if it is good. The man then takes a little thatch from the roof of his father-in-law's hut, and stands with a miniature bow and arrow on his left hand and a stick in his right hand, and looks at the sun for half-an-hour. While he is thus engaged, the village midwives gather round and insult him. The father-in-law then emerges from his hut, and puts an arrow in the bridegroom's hair; this is followed by the bride's appearance, and her husband greets her by putting a wooden "tooth hush" in her mouth and by slapping her on her head—and sometimes on the body as well; the bride's father and mother then address the people; the bridegroom takes another handful of thatch from his father-in-law's roof, and removes the arrow from his hair, which act completes the marriage.

Beer-drinking follows, and the bridegroom goes to his parents' hut, and gives the arrow to his own father. Then his relatives go to fetch the bride, who has a fowl given to her on leaving her parents' hut, and beads and other presents at every landmark or halting place *en route* (*i.e.* on crossing a stream, or climbing a hill), and further presents on entering the bridegroom's hut, on receiving porridge, on undressing, and on lying down. All the bridesmaids and the bridegroom's young friends sleep in the hut with the couple that night.

The next day the bride shows the presents to her parents, and then returns to her husband, keeping her head down and her eyes fixed on the ground for three days so as to see no one. On the fourth day they return to their own parents' huts, and on the fifth day the bridegroom fetches firewood for his parents-in-law and they give him porridge just as was done at his first proposal. He then returns to his own hut, followed by his wife carrying porridge and meat. That night they cohabit, and live together thenceforward as man and wife.

The customs of the Wakwa at death and burial present one or two novel features, though many points of resemblance to those of other tribes will be apparent to any student of comparative ethnography. In the event of sickness, the relatives of the invalid go to the doctor to discover who is responsible for the illness. One of the methods of divination employed by the doctor is to place a string between two upright sticks and affix to it a small pot which he manipulates while asking the relatives leading questions with a view to finding out from them on whom this suspicion rests. Having ascertained this, he accuses the person indicated, and for so doing receives a present of one white fowl. The relatives then request the accused to make some payment, and, if he complies and the sick person recovers, there is an end of the matter.

When a person dies the relatives begin by crying and rolling on the ground, after which they bind strips of bark round their foreheads and chests. The deceased's friends (not his relatives) dig the grave, and the corpse is buried in a sitting position, the calves of the legs tied back to the thighs, and the forearm to the shoulder. On the death of a woman who has not given birth to a child, a burning stick is placed by her side. "This," they say, "shall be as a child to you." Lepers are not buried, but their bodies are thrown into the bush. At the burial all the people of the same totem as the deceased take part. After the digging of the grave and the tying up of the corpse, some relatives (of the same sex as the deceased) enter the grave, and standing upon it receive the corpse, which is handed to them, and then rake in the first earth with their elbows. They then emerge from the grave, and the rest of the earth is thrown in with hands and hoes; every person present must throw in at least one handful as a farewell to the deceased. Finally, a stick is placed at each end of the grave to mark the place. The mourners then return to the village and howl for a spell, while they make a fire, spatchcock a fowl, and purify themselves. The fowl is eaten with porridge. An animal (ox, sheep, or goat) is killed, and all who were present at the funeral receive meat and porridge, the men receiving the hind quarters and head, and the women the fore quarters and back: the following day is a day of rest known as the *wanda wa msio*, on which no work is supposed to be done; and any work done on this day is supposed to be unprofitable.

If the relatives of the deceased had, prior to his death, discovered the individual "responsible for" his illness, he is compelled to undergo a *mwavi* test (ordeal by poison). If the discovery has not been already made, the doctor is consulted after the funeral with the object of ascertaining whether death was due to witchcraft or to a summons by the spirit of some deceased relative (*vide infra* in notes on disinterment). On the third day following the funeral the midwives of the village perform within a hut a dance, concerning which nothing is known except that the performers are in a state of complete nudity, even the *mwele* being removed, and on the fourth day the relatives wash themselves, sweep out the deceased's hut and throw the dust collected into the river and anoint themselves with oil, which completes the obsequies.

Where the death has been attributed to a departed spirit, the doctor has to divine which particular spirit it is that has called for a companion, which he does by taking a piece of *kilolo*, the root of a plant called *milala* and the leaves of another plant called *kavumbe*, chews and spits them out into the palm of his hand, and rolls them thereon with a small stick. Then having already taken the precaution of ascertaining which of the deceased's ancestors' spirits is suspected, he names him as having been selected by his magic. (Another method of "divination" sometimes employed is by the applicant holding the top and the doctor the base of an antelope's horn, which is manipulated while the doctor "divines" the responsible spirit.) For the service of divination the doctor demands but a small fee; but having divined the shade that has caused the trouble, he orders the disinterment and burning of the remains. For this a very high fee is exacted, and no one but the doctor himself is qualified to undertake it. All the relatives of the deceased accompany the doctor to the grave of the person to be exhumed. The doctor sprinkles the grave and its immediate neighbourhood with medicines, and the relatives proceed to disinter the remains. Any bones found are removed and sprinkled with medicines, and then placed on a rude plank. A fire is then kindled inside the grave to consume any remains that may have escaped the notice of the diggers. The bones that have been placed on the plank are taken away and burnt near a river, into which the ashes are then thrown. Ablutions complete the ceremony.

A few notes on the succession laws will complete the description of Wakwa customs. On the death of a married man the eldest surviving brother succeeds to all his wives and divides his other property with the remaining relatives. On the death of a married woman her relatives take possession of her property, but provide the widower with a new wife. On the death of a male, even if his successor (*e.g.* a younger brother or nephew) happen to be immature, he is compelled at least once to cohabit with the wife or wives to whom he succeeds despite any discrepancy in age. Should he fail to fulfil this duty any one else is then at liberty to marry the woman or women on the payment of a price to the youth who has failed to make good his inheritance. After the settlement of the deceased's affairs, the relations shave their heads and indulge in a carouse.

The religious beliefs and superstitions of the Wakwa are particularly interesting when regarded in conjunction with those of the Wakuluwe related in the preceding chapter, for the Wakuluwe and Wakwa are neighbours whose territory is contiguous; but whereas the former have a distinct religious code based on a rather elaborate theistic belief, the latter are frankly pagan—indeed far more so than any of the neighbouring tribes with which we are acquainted.

Beyond a belief in a Creator (*Lesa*), who created the world and did nothing else (the common idea in this part of Africa),[1] no reference is made in their superstitions to any god, but their principal object of worship is the Sun (*Ndaka*), which they consider to be the giver and preserver of life. They believe that the sun had at one time a battle with the moon, in which the latter was badly worsted, the signs of the conflict being still visible upon its face. In consequence of this defeat the moon is not worshipped. The worship of the sun is of a simple nature, being conducted in private inside the worshipper's hut, and has no external ceremony whatever. They merely pray to it for life and health.

Next in importance comes the worship of sundry sacred places—groves, rocks, or trees, in which snakes (especially pythons) are found; and the following is the list of the principal places:—

Name of Place.	*Name of Priest.*
Ushyela.	Kipoma.
Namatata (near Nkoma, where there are many snakes).	Koswe of Nkoma.
Fwaila (a big tree near Lake Ikwa).	Kipoma.
Chandikala (another tree).	,,
Namwela (a small hill near Simba).	Wakulimalungu.
Ngola (a hill at Ntetezi).	Kipoma.
Inkinga (a big stone near Yunga).	,,
Nsovwe (a rock at the top of the hills west of Mayengi).	?
Inkulu (a big tree).	?

[1] *Cf.* Ennius:—"Ego deum genus esse semper dixi, et dicam coelitum;
  Sed cos non curare opinor,
  Quid agat humanum genus."

The control of these sacred places and objects is entirely in the hands of the priests (*kapepa*), and none but the recognised priest can offer sacrifices or conduct worship at any of them; and they have the power to order attendance for worship at any of them at any time they please, which order must be obeyed by all. Moreover, every one, even the chief, has to make a present of beer to the priest before attending. When a priest dies he is succeeded by his son, who has been instructed in the mysteries during the lifetime of his father.

When proceeding to worship, the priest attires himself in a cotton cloth of native manufacture, encircles his arms with large white beads and his neck with small blue ones. He takes with him the chief's sceptre (*iluazi*), and the small bow used in the marriage ceremony (*amakolwe*), and is accompanied by two small girls and a small boy. One of the girls carries his chair (*chamapepo*), the other a basket of flour (*mpanda ya mulimo*), while the boy carries a small drum (*mtumba*), and the whole population of the village follows a little distance behind. Arrived at the sacred place, the priest announces in a loud voice that the ceremony is beginning (*nkuuma akito*), and spills some beer and flour upon the ground. He then drinks some beer from the pot, and hands some round to the others in a calabash. All the people chant, striking the spears which they hold in their left hands with a small stick. The priest then proceeds to the sacrifice, which takes the form of either a black sheep or a white cock, and sprinkles the blood upon the ground. After this they all return to the village, and the people salute the priest by lying down and clapping their hands crying, out "*Monse mukulu tata.*"

The only form of direct worship of snakes, other than that of the rocks and trees where they live, is to carry porridge and place it near their holes for them to eat. This is frequently done.

The spirits of ancestors (*azimu*) are also worshipped inside the huts, near the door, at the side of which is built an altar with a hole in it (*kiloa*). After a brewing of beer, a small quantity is always left on this altar for one night. When about to proceed on a hunting or fishing expedition, birds' feathers are placed upon the altar, and in the event of the expedition proving unsuccessful the altar is broken to pieces. Beyond this, and the allocation of responsibility in cases of death and sickness, already referred to, the people appear to pay no attention to the *azimu*.

The last "deity" in the mythology of the Wakwa is the Lake god, *Mwena* (a word also used by them for waterspout and for smallpox), who is feared and worshipped as causing death by his servants the crocodiles (*ng'wena*).

IV

RUKWA TO TABORA

Game on the Kavu River—A long stalk—Euphorbia-stockaded villages—Unintentional change of route—Reception by Muchereka, Mulungwa chief—And by Kasamia—"Tembo" architecture—Prevalence of tsetse fly—Sport on the Ugalla River—Kalula, chief of the Wagunda—Belt of good timber, with sawpits—Arrival at Tabora.

THE vast open plains into which the Rukwa Valley broadens out to the north along the Kavu River enjoy local reputation as being the feeding grounds of huge herds of game, and we were glad to reach a locality where there was a good chance of sport. Our carriers up to this point had had but little meat, and we ourselves were wondering how soon we should have an opportunity of justifying the expenditure of Rs.200 per licence for shooting ordinary game in German East Africa. We had not, as a matter of fact, been encouraged to take out a game licence by the official at Bismarckburg; he assured us that it was both cheaper and easier to purchase sheep or goats when we were in need of food.

The second day after leaving Simba we reached a village on the edge of the plains, and camped for the night, and on the following morning we rose at half-past four, an hour earlier than usual in this section of our journey, so as to be certain of finding some game before the heat of the day. We had been further encouraged to this unusual energy by the urgent advice of the local natives to start *after* dawn, as there were always lions about at an earlier hour. They admitted on inquiry that the lions so far had proved quite innocent of any hostile intentions towards man, and, as a matter of fact, we saw none at all. It was just light when, on rounding a bit of cover, we sighted our first beast—a topi bull standing in the open at about two hundred yards. There was no time for very careful aim, as he had already seen us; and the first shot, which was a miss, sent him away at a gallop to join a group that we then spied standing about half-a-mile away. The half-burned cane grass was long enough to hide them at times, and we were unable to make out their numbers, but there were then no others in sight, so we decided to try a stalk. The wind, as we stood, was in our favour, but there was no cover within considerable distance on either side between us and our quarry, and it was therefore necessary to make a long detour to the east in order to take advantage of the shelter of a patch of an unburnt grass that lay about a mile to our right front. It was the most tiring kind of walking, the surface of these plains being closely studded with tough little clumps of grass roots rising several inches above the level, against which one is constantly and painfully stubbing the toes or twisting the ankles; the sun was rapidly gaining power, and there was not a square yard of shade for miles. On our getting within a few hundred yards of the grass patch, the topi, which had, after all, been watching our movements, apparently realised that it was time to be on the move, and put another half-mile between us.

This put us on our mettle, and spying a thicker island of grass which offered nearly as much advantage as the first, we set ourselves to reach it, by first walking some distance at an angle in order to have it between us for the rest of the stalk. On reaching it, we found that the herd, still on the alert, had spread out, and that a sentinel in advance of the rest had spied us round the corner. New tactics suggested themselves—we divided, the one, deliberately keeping in sight, moved off to the left, with the object of holding their attention while the other slowly and painfully forced his way through the brake, making as little noise as possible and hoping to find the herd within range on the other side.

Once more disappointment was in store. They had moved on again. Our strategy, however, was succeeding. They had not gone far, and as their attention was riveted on the decoy still slowly tramping away in the opposite direction, and there was a small clump of grass within some eighty yards of them, it seemed as though after all our strenuous efforts would not be unrewarded. The grass clump was not more than four feet at its highest, and only the bottom half was thick enough to act as a screen, so there was nothing for it but a crawl. It lasted perhaps 120 yards, but with all sorts of uncomfortable things scratching one's bare knees and elbows, the burnt grass making a regular sweep of the crawler, and the efforts of carrying an $8\frac{1}{2}$ lb. rifle so as to guard against the muzzle being choked with foreign objects, it seemed like half a mile. It was therefore no small relief to find, on reaching and cautiously peering over the slender screen, that the game had remained in the same spot, and that their attention was still engaged elsewhere. After a short pause to recover the breath, an unusually persistent stalk ended with a very fair bull and an old cow topi lying on the ground, victims to a right and left at about eighty yards. We then turned back towards Kalumbalesa's village at the edge of the plain, where we had directed our carriers to await us. Hundreds of bohor reedbuck were popping up in all directions, and we accounted for half a dozen on our way; and, arriving at the village at about noon, we pitched our camp.

There was a generous supply of beer in the village, of which we purchased about a gallon, and drank nearly all of it. This beverage forms an important item in the native dietary. It is made by pouring boiling water upon crushed and partly fermented grain, and forms a thick fluid, exactly like thin bran mash; the natives like it fairly thick, but if diluted and strained to the consistency of thin cream it provides a refreshing and sustaining drink, containing about as much alcohol as light dinner ale. When there is beer there is generally dancing, and in the evening we made two efforts to obtain a flash-light photograph of the village *en fête;* the effect upon the revellers was so amusing as to justify the experiment, but the photographs unfortunately both turned out to be failures.

Another photo of little Mbaula.

Making native beer.

"Two solitary fangs in a mobile and humorous mouth."

The next day we decided to stay at the same spot, and, trying the plain a little farther north, devoted most of the day to shooting. One large herd of topi that we came upon in the shade of a belt of timber must have numbered close on four hundred, whilst a second seen in the evening was about half the size. They were wary, however, but we succeeded in securing a few heads well up to the average, and a welcome supply of meat for the carriers and our hosts.

The vagaries of an old rifle prolonged the outing for one of us to a tiring day of $11\frac{3}{4}$ hours. First the pull of the trigger, for some unaccountable reason, suddenly increased to 23 pounds (and the gut binding round the broken stock made it impracticable to look inside); then the ammunition, of which he was carrying a very small supply, gave out: he had a fine bull topi lying wounded close by, the natives had not got a spear between them, his spare gun was left behind, and the only thing to do was to send back to camp for another weapon. The first man sent for it lost his way, and arrived at the camp about sundown; and a second, with a better bump of locality, got back to the scene with another battery at about 3.30, and camp was not reached till two hours later.

It was in this neighbourhood that we began to notice the prevalence of the euphorbia-fenced village. The huts in many cases had been built and rebuilt over and over again within the slowly growing rising stockade that in the days of mutual hostility with their neighbours had been found, by reason partly of its denseness and partly of the poisonous properties of its juice, to be so effective a barrier against the intrusion of enemies.

Some of these had grown to such a height and such a thickness that it was quite impossible, except at very close quarters, to detect the presence of the huts within.

In the construction of the huts themselves there was a feature that was new to us; the walls, instead of being composed of reeds, bamboo, or, commonest of all, slender poles, were constructed from large thornwood, split by reason of its greater size into rough lathes. This was, of course, due to the absence of small straight timber.

It had been our intention to travel *via* the French Fathers' Mission at Mpimbwe, but soon after leaving our hunting grounds, our carriers, for some reason best known to themselves, took the right hand of two tracks (leading from our camp at a village called Pantula), which happened to be the wrong one. Near the end of this long day's march, of which 17 miles was through a waterless tract sparsely covered with thorn trees, borassus palms, and baobabs, we discovered that we had gone too far to the east to make it worth while to carry out our original purpose. We decided, therefore, to follow the track that had been chosen for us, consoled by the reflection that it was perhaps a slightly shorter route to Tabora, and led through a less frequented part of the country.

We had now left the Wakwa behind us, and entered a section of the country called Lungwa (also the name of a river running through it), the natives of which call themselves Alungwa. The first of their villages at which we camped was that of one of the principal "Sultans," as they are locally called, a well-preserved, middle-aged woman named Muchereka—with quite as good idea of her position as Sa. She, however, was not embarrassed by the incongruous trappings of civilisation, nor by the self-consciousness of recent accession and youth, and her reception of us was an amusing mixture of dignity, familiarity, and respect. She got in a handshake, when we were off our guard, provided us with stools until our chairs arrived, invited us to pitch our tents close to her own compound, which was enclosed in a 12-foot reed fence, and gave us the use of a comfortable and well-built *nsaka*, or half-open shelter, just outside it.

We tried the experiment of inviting her to have a cup of tea with us when she came round to pay a call in the afternoon. She accepted with alacrity; and, sitting on her chair, which she had brought with her, her husband and court squatting on the ground at her side, showed by her enjoyment of two cups sweetened with plenty of sugar, that it was not an unfamiliar beverage. The tea she consumed entirely herself, but a large slice of cake was discreetly nibbled, and then passed on to her husband and the rest of her household to finish. She had already presented us with a pot of beer, of which we found quantities in process of brewing on our arrival, and later twice repeated the gift, invariably tasting it herself before it was handed to us. It was a little thin at first, but evidently grew mellow within the next few hours, and the penetrating harangue to which she treated her husband shortly after the middle of the following night testified to its potency when taken in sufficiently generous doses. Our second day's halt was mainly with the object of trying to shoot some game, in which our hostess assured us the neighbourhood abounded, but of which it was a long time since she had had a taste.

The evening of the first day was unsuccessful, but the following morning spent in the finely timbered forest belt, spreading for a few miles to the south of the village, resulted in a bag of two mpala and two warthog, one of each of which formed a welcome addition to her larder and ours.

Our next definite objective was the Ugalla River, which forms the administrative boundary between the Ujiji and Tabora districts, and on which we had heard that there were great quantities and several varieties of game. The rocks were changing from granite to conglomerate, and part of our route was over uncomfortably steep and stony hills, through a country so badly watered that even in August the sole supply was from isolated and inadequate holes, sometimes covered with a screen of palm leaves for protection from sun and dust, dug in the beds of dried-up rivulets, which later in the year must with difficulty have afforded a sufficiency even for the barest needs of the population. At the village of a delightful old chief called Kasamia, whose sole clothing consisted of a scanty loin cloth, a bunch of medicine charms round his neck and two solitary fangs in a mobile and humorous mouth, and whose cordial welcome of us and despotic handling of his people were particularly refreshing, we noticed the first example of the change from the ordinary circular to the "tembo" architecture in the native huts. The latter, which is apparently due to Arab influence, was particularly well shown in a village at which we camped the following day, and of which we made a careful plan. The principal features are the flat and almost horizontal roofs, plastered with a thick coating of mud, on which there is generally a large crop of grass, the long narrow compartments into which the huts are divided and the formation by the walls of the huts themselves, of a self-contained and completely closed in fortress. Some of the carved wooden doors, evidently of considerable age, as well as the markedly foreign type of utensils, *e.g.* bellows, ladles, and trays, of which we secured some photographs, also betrayed the influence of Arab settlement or incursions, while a peculiar and probably purely native use of the bark of large trees was seen in the construction of pigeon cotes, corn bins, and even the roofs of open shelters. From Kasamia's, where there were cattle apparently thriving in spite of it, tsetse fly abounded along the whole route, and in some spots were so persistent in their attacks as to be almost unbearable. Among the old spoor of various kinds of game, that of giraffe was far the most plentiful, the track itself and the bush at the side of it being almost continuously dented with it. Little of it, however, was at all fresh, most of it apparently dating from the previous rains. One herd of elephant had crossed our track some two days before; we bagged a jackal and hartebeeste (the jackal a galloping shot with a Greener .310), but saw little other game until within a few miles of the Ugalla River.

Komekeshya's small village, where we camped on the last day of August, was notable as enclosing within its compound the two largest *mitawa* or bark-cloth trees we had ever seen. Round the thinnest part of their trunks (*i.e.* between the swelling of the roots below and the thickening as they branched above) they measured respectively 8 feet 8 inches and 12 feet 10 inches in circumference, whereas these trees are usually regularly stripped of

NATIVE UTENSILS, "BELLOWS, LADLES AND TRAYS."

DRAWING WATER FROM A WATER HOLE IN A VILLAGE NEAR THE UGALLA.

their bark for making cloth, these, besides being evidently of great age, had never been mutilated in any way. It was while resting in the shade of one of the trees that the headman produced a rather rare and remarkable pet in the shape of a scaly manis, which he sold to us for one rupee. Though the natives were mortally afraid of it and declared that it was a vicious biter, we soon found that it was perfectly harmless, quiet, and inclined to be tame. We kept it for three or four days, during which we amused ourselves in the evening by studying its quaint gait and quainter physique as it ambled leisurely about our camp looking for ants and other insects; but one morning we woke up to find to our intense annoyance that, by the carelessness of the boy responsible for its security, the beast had got out of its box and wandered away into the bush, never to be seen again.

On arriving at another village at which we had thought of camping, we were advised by the inhabitants to go a stage farther, because there were two cases of small-pox amongst them.

As they were crowding round us themselves and were obviously taking no sort of precautions to prevent the spread of the contagion, we at first felt a trifle uneasy, but when they assured us that they (a couple of dozen who were standing round) had all had it, and we noticed that not a single one had any traces of the disease, we came to the conclusion that it must have been chicken-pox or some other minor ailment. In choosing our camp that evening we were entirely misdirected by an affable and intoxicated lady of rather distinguished if gaudy appearance, by whose advice we went at least seven miles out of our way. We met her again the following day at the village of a very youthful chief of the Agulu tribe, named Mbaula, who had just succeeded to the position, and found that she, quite old enough to be his mother, was his chief wife thrown in with the position! For amongst most Bantu people an heir invariably takes over his predecessor's wives. She was still a little drunk and more debonair than ever, which suggested that she possibly had sent us out of our way so as to give herself time for a finishing touch to her toilet, and her first consideration was to see that we, too, were generously supplied with beer. As may be inferred, it was the beer season, and the entire population of this neighbourhood seemed for the time to have forsaken all other forms of nutriment.

Before we succeeded in actually reaching the Ugalla River we had still further examples of the utter unreliability of the natives' estimate of direction and distance. In fact, after thinking we had reached it at least twice, we began to despair of reaching it at all, if not actually to doubt of its existence. When we finally crossed it on the 3rd September, the bed was mostly dry, and water only remained in a series of stagnant pools, but its neighbourhood justified its reputation as a haunt of game. For the last ten or twelve miles the bush at either side of our route was full of it, and without making a long halt we saw topi, hartebeeste, roan, sable, reedbuck, and bagged two roan (out of an extraordinarily tame herd at our camp), and a leopard at about 10 A.M., a few hours before getting there. The thick jungle on both banks was full of bird-life, and the woods for miles round were criss-crossed with game tracks running from all directions down to the river; we stayed here two nights and, including elephant and hippopotamus, of which we only saw the fresh spoor, we found no less than seventeen different species of game.

An hour or two after pitching camp a crocodile was reported in the pool at which the natives were drawing water. One of us went to investigate, and at 5.30 a gun boy returning to camp for more ammunition, the other joined him and found he had already bagged six. We spent the rest of the evening sitting on the high bank under the shelter of the thick shrubbery, ruthlessly picking off the noisome reptiles one by one as they came up to the surface for a breath. The attacks of the tsetse fly and of the mosquitoes as the sun got lower were pretty nearly unbearable, but we added another six huge victims to the bag before approaching darkness warned us that it was time to return to camp. On our way back we almost ran into a herd of zebra strolling unconcernedly towards the river for their evening drink, but we left them alone and contented ourselves with bringing down a brace of guinea-fowl out of the dozens that were coming chattering along to roost in the branches of nearly every tree of any size on either bank.

Our night's rest was undisturbed except by the restlessness of the three dogs that we had with us, who kept barking now and again during the night and making occasional rushes into the gloom beyond the firelight. In the morning we found that two lions had been strolling round the camp on their way down to the water, and in passing had evidently stood for a while and taken a good look at us, from fifteen to sixteen paces from our tents.

As this was probably to be our best chance of any good shooting that side of Tabora—and the local natives, two of whose villages were close to our camp, begged us to shoot them some meat to supplement their diminished food supply—we decided to stay another day, and the following morning one made an early start to try the grazing grounds that lay to the north-east, away from the river.

By 9 o'clock and less than four miles from camp a bag of six sable and one mpala had been secured, and roan, reedbuck, hartebeeste, warthog, and giraffe had been seen on the way. The last-named were a huge pair, sighted at about 300 yards, lurching away into the distance. The roan and topi were a little wary, but the sable, mostly young, were extraordinarily tame, and could without much difficulty have been completely wiped out.

Towards evening another visit was paid to the crocodile pools, and four more victims were accounted for—one was a young one, which fell to a ball-and-shot gun as it lay asleep on the bank. The Greener .310 again surprised us by completely perforating the body of a wounded monster as he rolled and twisted about on the surface. Some three or four of them crawled out on to the bank when wounded, and enabled us to realise their hideous bulk; the remainder sank where they were shot, to rise again after a short interval, their tails lashing and churning up the filthy water in their furious contortions, and finally either entirely floating or remaining suspended in the water with a nose, a tail or a gleaming yellow belly protruding above the surface. A skull of a waterbuck and a few horns and bones at the edge of the pools bore witness to the gruesome fate that was awaiting the unwary antelope as he came down to quench his thirst. The danger of approaching too close, as well as the loathsome state of the stagnant fluid, had forced the natives to dig holes in the sand at a discreet distance and wait for the water to filter through, and we felt not the slightest compunction in executing as many of the disgusting brutes as we possibly could.

The sun was already too far below the horizon when we left the scene of slaughter for us to make an attempt to secure any of the numerous wildfowl that were whirring and whistling overhead, so with a couple of pigeons and another guinea-fowl for the pot we hastened back to camp. In the deepening dusk about half-way we espied the form of a fat waterbuck something less than 50 yards away on the opposite bank of the river-bed. It was too tempting to resist; a couple of shots from a .360 knocked him over, and on our arrival in camp just after dark we sent a handful of natives to fetch him in. They were not enthusiastic about it, even when given a lanthorn and a gun, but they went, and in less than an hour they were back again, empty-handed, declaring there was no beast there for them to bring in. We were convinced that there was, for it was certain that the waterbuck hadn't got as much as a kick in him when we came away; and, suspecting that they had been thinking rather too much about lions to make a thorough search, we told off our hunter Chumamaboko to take them back again, and, reinforced by an acetylene lamp and another gun, to be sure of finding the correct spot. Chuma didn't exactly jump at it either, but he obeyed without any express démur. However, he hadn't been gone more than half an hour

"We bagged a leopard."

One of the Authors in his travelling clothes at Keiula.

before he was back with the same story. There was no waterbuck: only unmistakable signs of its having been dragged away in a thick belt of jungle. Some lazy impudent beast of a lion had evidently been hanging round for the chance of a cheap meal, and hadn't been long in picking it up either. There was nothing for it but for us to sally forth ourselves. It was pitch dark and quite impossible for us to find our way through the tangled undergrowth, and, *a fortiori*, to ascertain what had happened without an effective light; so, arming ourselves with a ball-and-shot gun and an ordinary scatter gun loaded with S.S.G., we set out, carrying the acetylene light, which, while likely to spoil any chance of a shot by frightening the beast from its prey, was not to be despised as affording a safeguard against attack.

We might just as well have stayed in camp, however, for Chumamaboko's account had been, we found, a perfectly correct one; and though we found the spot where the waterbuck had fallen, and followed the spoor of the lion and the buck as it had been dragged through the thickets for no little way, we found progress slow, and, not hearing anything of the marauder, came to the conclusion that he must have taken his meal a considerable distance, and we returned to camp.

That night, being fairly certain of another visit from the lions and hoping for the chance of bagging one, we gave orders to our boys to call us immediately should they be detected close at hand. From eight or nine o'clock the dogs were incessantly on the alert. We went to bed at our usual time, and for some time heard nothing except the occasional uneasy barks of the dogs, and the snoring of the natives round the fire. Just after midnight, however, a probably excellent chance was just missed; the boy who was to wake us saw one of the lions at about 12 yards, from just beyond one of the outer fires, and cautiously creeping up with the object apparently of bagging the dog that was barking at him. The boy came and told us at once, but it was too late; by the time we had emerged from our tents, the lion, probably put on his guard, had vanished. Two minutes later, however, we had a rather rare and somewhat alarming experience of hearing him giving chase to a small buck just outside the range of our firelight. The convulsive grunt of the lion as he bounded after his victim, and the frantic squeals of the buck, which did not, apparently, get caught, brought our carriers to their feet in no time expecting all sorts of unpleasant possibilities. Chuma, lifting himself up on an elbow, looked round sleepily and said with some contempt "*Chimbwe*"—which means "hyæna"—and went to sleep again. The lions were not taking any more risks, and we were not disturbed again. Chuma was led round in the morning to inspect the spoor all round the camp—and had to apologise.

It was a tempting place to stop at, but as we wanted to get to Tabora without any further pauses, we had to tear ourselves away. At the end of the next two days' journey, chiefly remarkable for the amount of tsetse fly and giraffe spoor on the way, we struck one of the Bismarckburg and Tabora roads at a village called Kakoma's.

This village presented no features of especial interest, and we would have pushed on a stage farther had we not been told by the local natives that there was no village or water within three hours—although we doubted this, our ignorance of the country made us decide to camp there, and we felt fairly annoyed the next day at finding villages with water at 1, 4, 13, 15, 17 and $18\frac{1}{2}$ miles, the second one being one they had told us was three hours off.

The village at $18\frac{1}{2}$ miles was quite a big place, inhabited by the Wa-Gunda and ruled over by Kalula, a big stout woman, who visited us at our camp outside the village. Carried on a man's shoulders and wearing some gorgeous cheap clothes and a white helmet, she brought her own chair with her, and sat down in the open barn-like shelter allotted to Europeans and conversed with us in Ki-Swahili for some time. She then returned to her quarters and sent the women of the village to fetch water for us, and also told them to bring plenty of food to barter for the meat with which our carriers were plentifully supplied;

A Tembo Village (to right of background). Beehives in trees in the foreground.

In a Mugunda Village. In the foreground is a native bed.

this was a suggestion that was readily enough complied with, and throughout the afternoon the camping was a busy scene of haggling and chattering natives, a thin continuous stream of old hags, buxom matrons, lithe young girls and little children coming with their tiny bowls and baskets of flour and going with their still tinier bits of meat. No one, of course, was ever satisfied with a bargain, but it was all good-natured and seemed to be rather a joke to be cheated than a ground of serious complaint.

As a rule, the women drive a fairly hard bargain, as they know that the porters must have the flour at any price; but at Kalula's the women came in such large numbers and all wanted meat so badly that for once the competition was the other way round, and the carriers obtained good supplies of flour, kasava, beans, &c., without making serious inroads upon their supply of dried meat.

Kalula's village is well built and consists of many fine huts, both round and rectangular, but the outstanding feature was Kalula's own house, a large two-storied building of sun-dried bricks, which at the time of our visit was being more or less reconstructed—the walls and first floor heightened, the roof altered, and a verandah being added.

Originally built in 1907, it measures about 60 by 45 feet and is about 30 feet high. The roof timber, window-frames, bars in the windows, door-frames and doors are all made of massive sawn timber, and the bricks are well laid, though the angles and lines are hardly marked by mathematical accuracy. Nevertheless, considering the fact that it is the work of unsupervised native labour, the result is almost as creditable as the plan is ambitious.

The Germans apparently make a point of placing women in power, in succession to male chiefs who die or are removed, as being less likely to cause trouble. The predecessor of our friend Muchereka was a chief who used to amuse himself by shooting the old men in his village, because, he said, the hawks were hungry. The German authorities got a bit tired of this and deposed him, placing him in a small village by himself. He then appealed for a gun on account of the lions, but received no more comfort than to be told that he had better trap them. However, before long he managed to secure a firearm of some kind from some one and shot the first old man who was rash enough to visit him. After this exploit he was arrested and taken to Ujiji, where he still languishes, and Muchereka was appointed in his stead. Similarly on the execution of Pirula, the Mutwaki chief of the Wafipa, the late Sa (predecessor of the lady of that name whom we met) was put in his place.

Three of our seven Rhodesian boys being a bit seedy, we rested the next day, one going out to get some meat for our hostess and securing a roan, while the other remained in camp writing letters—which was rather difficult, as a tremendous and erratic wind arose which got hold of everything that was not tied down, and blew the lighter articles to the four points of the compass. The spare fly in front of one of the tents was swept away, and while the two tents were still suffering from the attack, a dust devil came along and nearly lifted one of them bodily from the ground. Luckily some of our staff were near and held on to the ropes for dear life, saving it from a violent journey into the clouds. Tents and men were both flapping about in a limp and helpless attitude when the dust devil passed on to wreck the nearest thatched roof.

Anything more uninviting than the country round Kalula's it would be difficult to imagine. How this poor soil, clothed with a wretched scrub, manages to support even the small scattered population that exists here it is hard to guess. It is not apparently even a good grazing country, for since we left the Kavu River a fortnight previously the large flocks of sheep and goats had dwindled down to few or none, and Kasamia's and Kalula's were the only two villages in which there were any cattle. Maize is the staple crop, but as the villages remain in the same places year after year, the soil, which can never have been anything but poor, is so exhausted that but very poor returns are obtained.

The natives are very friendly and respectful to the stranger, and never failed to treat us with courtesy in all their dealings with us. They seem a contented and fairly prosperous community in spite of the poor country in which they have to spend their lives, and there was at any rate no apparent chafing at the German rule.

The only notable features after leaving Kalula's were a fine belt of timber beginning at 30 miles from Tabora, the cessation of tsetse fly, an interesting change of native diet, and the second example of the pretentious palaces which some of these chiefs build for themselves. The timber belt, which extended for some 7 miles, was a refreshing change after the long scrubby stretch of country, devoid of anything worth calling a tree, through which we had been passing. In this belt we found two deserted sawpit-camps and a third in full working, in which we saw several hundred fine straight logs about 25 feet long and from 9 to 30 inches in diameter. The wood was of a good hard type not unlike elm, lighter in colour than the teak-like wood (*malombwa*) so common in Northern Rhodesia, and lacking both the soft white outer edge of the same tree and the red-black core of the *mopani*. This timber, which is locally called *mukula*, is excellent material for general carpentering and cabinet work. The fly belt ended about 12 miles south of Tabora, and at about the same spot we found ourselves among a people whose staple food was no longer maize, but kasava. This change from cereals to roots was rather curious, as at Tabora itself and for a long way to the north of it the natives eat kaffir corn (sorghum).

The "palace," which was built after the same model and on the same scale as Kalula's, but was in a finished state, was the residence of the Itetemia, the chief who rules over the flat bare country covered with granite kopjes that are a striking feature of the environs of Tabora.

The road winds in and out of these rocks without giving any indication of what lies beyond, and on September 11th, on turning a corner, we came quite suddenly on the township of Tabora, lying at our feet, with its fine old mango trees closely dotted over the rolling plains, presenting the appearance of a veritable oasis in the midst of the bare landscape. The morning sun had not yet attained much strength as we came to the first street sign we had seen for a very long time, and found ourselves in "Itetemia Strasse," out of which we turned towards the fort to call on the Commandant, or Governor, of the District.

V

TABORA

Cordial reception by the officials—Engagement of carriers—The market—The mission—Description of the town—Absence of any form of recreation grounds—Herr Siegel, the Distrikts Kommissar—Transport *via* the Uganda Railway—Curious contention of the Germans—The effect of the German railway from Dar-es-Salam on this traffic and on Tabora.

THE Government buildings, just as fort-like as those at Bismarckburg though better and more artistically built, stand on a rocky spur at the junction of the Kilimatinde and Bismarckburg roads and look down upon the township spreading away to the north and north-west. They are constructed of granite with red iron roofs, and consist of a large square, the sides of which are occupied by offices and mess-rooms. On reaching the gates, at which we were agreeably impressed and surprised at our courteous reception by the sentries, we learnt that the Commandant was away on *safari*, and his deputy and assistant had gone out shooting—it being Sunday—but were expected back shortly, and meanwhile, guided by a trooper told off for our escort by the Sergeant of the guard, we proceeded to call upon Herr Siegel, the Distrikts Kommissar — District Commissioner — at his quarters a few hundred yards down Bahnhof Strasse, a fine street leading away from the Fort to the north-west. He met us at his door and gave us a most friendly welcome, from which we learnt with pleasure that he spoke excellent English. On learning that we preferred our tents to the hotel—of the existence of which we learnt with some surprise—he took us a little farther down the Strasse and showed us an excellent spot on the road, and in the shelter of a group of magnificent old mangoes, at which to pitch our camp.

He then invited us to accompany him to the Boma, where we enjoyed a very welcome drink in the official mess. Herren Knach and Busch had meanwhile returned, and presently joined us. Neither was more than slightly acquainted with English, but the sincerity of their welcome to us was sufficiently obvious, and they insisted on us being their guests while at Tabora.

They were hungry after their morning's shoot, and our breakfast we had almost forgotten, so we sat down to a meal of beefsteaks and Guinness and Pilsener. We had done ourselves thoroughly well by the time our hosts rose, saying it was time to shed their bush togs, and it came as a shock to be told that we should, of course, be expected to come and enjoy the warthog at 12 o'clock lunch. It was only 10.30 and the meal we had been sharing was the sportsmen's breakfast! 'Twere ungrateful to shirk it; an effort had to be made, and, though we rather doubted the sufficiency of an hour's rest in camp to produce another appetite at so short a notice, we turned up again at noon, for that warthog-liver lunch, and, what is more, we did it justice.

Dinner at 7.30 was another enjoyable meal, at which we were the same party as at lunch with one addition, but the evening ended early, our host very sensibly remarking at about 9.15 that it was time for bed. A notable feature of the meal was that we were served with the famous black bread, which we, both of us, preferred to the brown, and the brown was equal to any average English loaf.

One of our first tasks now was to collect another gang of men to act as carriers for the journey to Mwanza. We had written some time before our arrival to the Officer in charge at Tabora asking him if he could be of assistance to us in the matter. Knowing of some other travellers who had had to wait over a week at Tabora under identical circumstances, we were a little anxious, even after an assurance that there would be no trouble in raising men, when we learnt that, in compliance with our request, it was intended to send out for men

TABORA

the *following* day. But early next morning we were awakened by the news that three or four of our Bismarckburg gang, however, had decided to come on, ten volunteers had joined us at the Ugalla River, and with some more volunteers that had applied for employment the previous evening, there were now altogether fifty men who were anxious to go with us to Mwanza; so there was after all not much cause for alarm.

The fact was that, owing to the large number of loads arriving at Mwanza *ex* Europe *via* Kilindini, the Uganda Railway and Kisumu for German East Africa, there was constant employment for thousands of carriers at Mwanza. The Wanyamwezi—though nothing will induce them to work in the rains—are in the dry season only too ready to accept any employment that will take them to a distribution centre like Mwanza. By ten o'clock we had all but the required number, when Herr Siegel, who had put himself at our service for a few hours, arrived at our camp and made clear to them, in what we thought the most admirable manner, their conditions of service. They were to get Rs.5.50 for the trip to Mwanza, R.1.50 in advance as food allowance, and Rs.4 on arrival at Mwanza. This was an improvement on the rate at which we had to pay our Bismarckburg men—208 miles for Rs.5.50 as against 280 for Rs.18.

With Herr Siegel as cicerone we then did a tour of the town. First to the Post-Office, where information was given and our business dealt with with courtesy and despatch, and where we learnt the dates of sailing of the Uganda Railway boats at Mwanza; then to the Hotel, which is also one of three principal European stores, where we were able to make quite a number of useful additions to our stock of provisions, then through a fine avenue of old *mitawa* trees, the branches of which met overhead, on to the Indian bazaar, which provided us with a few items, *e.g.* paraffin, flour, and potatoes, that we had not been able to get at the hotel, and so to the native market, which we found in full swing. It is carried on in four large thickly thatched buildings with open sides, each consisting, in fact, of a roof on heavy pillars, and situated in a broad square. Two of the buildings are devoted to the sale of a variety of native produce, *e.g.* snuff, dried kasava, meal and grain of all kinds—maize, millet, sorghum—sugar-cane and soap—manufactured from wood ashes and butter or beef fat—and cheap ornaments of European origin. The soap vendors may be seen sitting with a tray of their wares before them sedulously working specimens of it into a lather to convince intending purchasers of its quality. Of the other two buildings one seemed to be devoted entirely to the sale of meat—mostly beef—which is sold at 5 heller per lb. = 20 lbs. for one-and-fourpence, and the other to native beer. This may be brewed from any of the local grains, *e.g.* maize, millet, sorghum or a grass-like seed known as *wuwere*, and is sold retail at a heller a draught.

We were not a little impressed by the decent order that prevailed in spite of the constant stream of buyers and sellers. A small guard that is always on duty in the market-place itself, as well as the proximity of the subsidiary fort, evidently have no difficulty in keeping things quiet. After buying two rupees' worth of beef—40 lbs.—which we discovered later to be worth just about what we gave for it and no more—we returned to our camp, Herr Siegel proceeding to his quarters.

After lunch we first finished our mails and then we made another brief tour, this time with cameras. At 5 P.M. we called upon Père Schmitt and his colleagues at the French Mission, whose buildings and garden we had passed in the Mission Strasse on the way to and from the market. The Mission house is a fine specimen of an old Arab dwelling, adapted to European needs. It is of a fine height with steep, pitched, thatched roof, a broad verandah supported by the original fluted wooden pillars; the rooms are small but cool. The Church, which stands within 100 yards and is enclosed by the same high wall, is simply built of sun-dried bricks, while the Sisters' residence, constructed of similar materials, lies a short distance off in a separate compound.

"The mission house is a fine specimen of an old Arab dwelling."

"The soap vendors . . . sitting . . . sedulously working specimens of it into a lather."

Tabora as we saw it will soon cease to exist just as the old Arab Tabora of pre-European days has already disappeared, for when the railway arrives early in 1912 the place will change rapidly. Of the old Arab settlement a few traces only remain, the greater part has gone, and in the place of irregularly built and more irregularly placed hovels, straight streets of well-built dwellings are being put up. The groups of mangoes in every direction, avenues of mangoes and *mitawa* and a few palms stand as monuments to the Arab, who always planted where he settled. Père Schmitt had some negatives of the old Arab town and its market, but as neither he nor we had any printing paper we could not get any prints. Nothing remains now but three of the doors, one of which is illustrated in this chapter, a few scattered doorways, and pillars, the best of which are on the front verandah at the Mission.

On this Arab foundation the Germans have built, as usual, regardless of cost. The roads are fairly broad and very well kept, being in every case planted with trees ; some old mangoes and *mitawa* of the Arab days, the majority younger, but carrying the promise of shade in the future—and at Tabora shade is a considerable asset. The *boma* is a fort, which was built to supersede the old fort by the market-place, and is surrounded by a wall above which rise the two-storied buildings, which form the corners, connected at the sides by lower buildings. The officials do not live within the fort, which from one side bears a distinct resemblance to a pagoda, but their dwellings lie on either side of Bahnhof Strasse, and are well built, though too low for iron-roofed buildings and rather small. The older ones have gable ends and verandahs back and front ; the newer ones are octagonal with pavilion roofs and deep verandah rooms on four sides. All the buildings are of stone, pointed with cement and roofed with iron ; but all are more or less spoilt by not having a false upper storey with ventilators.

Apart from the Mission the dwelling-houses and business premises of the non-official European population resemble those of the Government Staff, being equally well built but suffering from the same defects as to insufficient height.

The population throughout the town, as in the market-place, is orderly and the place far quieter than one would expect. During our stay we saw no rowdiness, and the cleanliness of the town is remarkable considering the number and nature of the community. This order and cleanliness is obtained without undue parade of force in the shape of either military or police.

The European population consists of two officers and two sergeants (in charge of 200 police), perhaps a dozen civil officials, including clerks, and fourteen traders and missionaries; and with a population of this size—no inconsiderable township for Central Africa—it seems extraordinary that there is absolutely no recreation ground of any kind; though Tabora lies on what can best be described as gigantic and perfect golf links, which would also give room for several race-courses, or even ærodromes, and tennis courts could be made anywhere.

In the evening we dined once more at the fort, and enjoyed some two hours' conversation with Herr Siegel after his *confrères* had withdrawn. He was charmingly hospitable, genial, sympathetic, and we felt that we might have been talking to a colleague. The country, the natives and native administration as well as Anglo-German polities, were freely dealt with. He showed the same broad-minded and intelligent grasp of international as of local questions which charmed and impressed us, and made one feel that with men of his type in the service the conduct of affairs in German East Africa is in capable hands. We had already had an opportunity of seeing his methods of handling the natives, with whose own language as well as the official Ki-Swahili he was well acquainted. He showed a wide knowledge of as well as sympathy with the many interesting tribes of the country; he had spent eight and a half years in German East Africa; the last four in Tabora itself, and he expressed himself as quite content to end his days there. In contrast to the concern expressed in other quarters at our choice of route, he keenly appreciated the spirit of

A FINE OLD ARAB CARVED DOORWAY AT TABORA (IN AN ARAB HOUSE).

our journey and said, on learning of our detour to the Rukwa valley, "of course, knowing the natives, you find it much more interesting travelling along the less beaten tracks and as far as possible away from the *burra burra.*"

More striking, perhaps, than our agreement on the majority of subjects on which we touched was a peculiar difference of opinion apparently common to all the officials on the question of the completion of the railway from the coast to Lake Tanganyika and its effect on existing transport routes and transport receipts. We had already had ample evidence that large quantities of the goods imported into German East Africa and the Belgian Congo from Europe were being carried by the Uganda Railway and its steamers to Mwanza and thence distributed by native porterage. Even before reaching Tabora we had met numbers of carriers whose loads bore the Kilindini Port (Mombasa) marks, and the French Fathers at Tabora had informed us that this was the route by which the missionaries and traders on both shores of Lake Tanganyika and the Western Districts generally of German territory,[1] almost without exception imported their goods. Mr. Don, too, who had cycled through the country at about the same time of year, had told us that between Tabora and Mwanza he had met about 1000 loads on each of the three days which he occupied on this section. We were aware that the German Government, for reasons of its own, invariably imported by Dar-es-Salam, even though this meant using a route which, in the infancy of the railway, was more dilatory and expensive, and that all officials, except those of the Victoria Nyanza districts, were forbidden to enter or leave the country by the British route. It was, however, a little astonishing to be assured that we were actually quite mistaken in supposing that there was, or ever had been, any considerable tendency among the importers of German East Africa, except those on the shores of the Victoria Nyanza, to make use of the Mombasa and Port Florence system. It seemed to us a curious instance of a desire to minimise by sheer denial an unpalatable fact.

[1] Viz. Ruanda, Urundi, Ujiji, Tabora, Bukoba, Mwanza.

Surely this was the logic that inspired in the ostrich the belief that, if his face were covered, his pursuers could not see him. We had not long to wait for still further evidence of the fallacy of the German official contention. Between Tabora and Mwanza, travelling on but one of three possible routes, we met a constantly increasing stream of natives with loads for the interior whose marks plainly betrayed their port of entry, and in the course of ten days must have seen not less than 5000 such loads, and finally we learnt on the s.s. *Sibyl* that, besides the cargo carried by the Arab dhows, the Uganda Railway boats were discharging on an average 250 tons per month at Mwanza. Mwanza itself can scarcely absorb more than a third of this, if as much; but reckoning its consumption at that rate, we are left with a total of 80,000 carriers' loads per annum for Tabora and beyond, discharged by the steamers at Mwanza. The dhow-borne cargo is by no means inconsiderable, including as it does not only bulky goods of small value, but all the paraffin imported by this route—the steamboats refusing to carry it—of which we met some hundreds of cases going south.

Whether the loss of the greater part of this freight will affect to a serious degree the receipts of the Uganda Railway with its already considerable and rapidly increasing local traffic in goods to and from British East Africa and Uganda, we were hardly in a position to judge, but that it will have some effect seems as obvious as the German attitude is perplexing. Another more natural but less innocuous mistake seems to be being made by those who are anticipating that the arrival at Tabora of the railway from Dar-es-Salam will mark the beginning of a big local boom.

That there will be the temporary increase of business inseparable from the presence of railway construction works, there can be no question, but before a belief in its permanent future can be justified, an examination of the basis of its present degree of prosperity is advisable.

There are three principal stores which keep a varied stock of European goods, but by far the greater portion of the trade is in the hands of Indian traders, and consists in the sale to natives of cloth and cheap goods, and therefore depends not only upon the wage-earning capacity of the native population, but on the point at which this population receives its wages. At the present time besides the Government employés (native troops, &c.), whose monthly wage-bill amounts to some £400 or £500, the wage-earning class consists *almost entirely* of the crowds of carriers who are paid off after bringing loads from Mwanza and the coast. Now it is sufficiently obvious that on the completion of the line to Tabora this carrier work will, except to a limited extent for distribution to outgoing parts, practically cease to exist. Once the railway construction has passed there will be a large local population in search of employment. Employment will not be lacking, but it will be on the farms and plantations nearer the coast, where the workers will not only be paid their wages, but will probably also have plenty of opportunity of spending what they earn at the stores that will be erected or now exist in that neighbourhood. Thus not only will the railway take the place of the native carriers' transport, but the quantity of the actual goods to be carried will *ipso facto* considerably diminish.

There will be, in fact, a redistribution of labour, in which Tabora seems likely to suffer the most. In the days of Arab predominance Tabora was the main depôt between the lakes and interior on the one side and the coast on the other, and up to the present it has more or less maintained this position under German rule. Once deprived, as it will be by the railway, of its importance as a transport centre, it is difficult to see on what will rest the prosperity of a large town in a practically non-productive stretch of country in the heart of tropical Africa.

It can boast of nothing in its immediate neighbourhood but its herds of cattle, and they are within a very few miles of tsetse-fly belts on every side.

The farmers and settlers will scarcely be tempted to invest their capital in a bleak, waterless and, except for one strip, timberless country with a rather poor soil and obviously risky if otherwise suitable for the raising of cattle.

On the other hand, there is a faint possibility of Tabora taking the place of Dar-es-Salam as the administrative capital of the territory. If this should occur, there is of course no doubt that the town will enter upon an era of prosperity which, if not prodigious, will at any rate be stable. There are at present some 200 officials of all grades at Dar-es-Salam, and as probably not more than a third would be needed at the port, the transfer of the seat of Government would mean the accession of a considerable population to the town. Failing this, it looks very much as if, with the advance of civilisation and the iron road, the penultimate chapter in the history of this old Arab metropolis is being written.

The requisite number of carriers had been made up without any difficulty, and at two o'clock on the 13th September, after bidding our hosts farewell, we continued our journey north. Our personal staff from Rhodesia was still with us, with the exception of one, who was returned to his home from Tabora, travelling as far as Bismarckburg with the carriers whom we had engaged from there.

VI

TABORA TO MWANZA

Encounter with party of missionaries—Curious rock formation at Ngaya—Notes on the Wanyamwezi—Game on Mbala Plain—Soap and oil factory at Salabwe—Scenery on Mwanza Gulf—Carriers on road—Arrival at Mwanza.

It is always difficult to make an early and punctual start after a stay at a civilised centre, and taking the west of the three routes to Mwanza along which the telegraph line runs, and which we had chosen, partly as offering the best opportunities of sport, we made a short trek of $5\frac{1}{2}$ miles.

The country that we were now going through was barer than ever. The grass that bordered our track for the first 4 miles was thin and close-cropped by cattle; trees, except in small isolated groups, were conspicuous by their absence. The grass presently gave way to native gardens on both sides, and at the place where we camped the road itself was the only possible place on which to pitch our tents; dry sorghum stalks were the only available fuel, and with the added discomfort of a small hurricane, which kept us on the *qui vive* most of the night, and all but swept our tents from their bearings, it was small wonder that the morning found us but poorly refreshed and disinclined to get up till a little after half-past six. Our usual practice during this section was to rise at about 4.30 A.M. and, breakfasting at once, to send most of our carriers ahead, and get off about an hour later. Except during the three or four days following the full moon, an earlier start was hardly practicable; nor indeed did we find it necessary, for though we averaged more than 20 miles a day between Tabora and Mwanza, we never failed to reach camp before the noonday heat. By a simple method of sharing our remaining machine we were both able, if necessary, to do half of each day's journey on foot and half on bicycle, *e.g.* if the journey were one of 20 miles, the first of us could take the machine, ride 10, and leave it on the path for the other. As a matter of fact, we always began the day by both walking an hour or so, and rode and walked roughly half and half of the rest of the way. A native, picked for the purpose, always accompanied the bicycle while it was being ridden, wheeled or carried it where it was not in use, and was generally, though not always, in charge of it when it was left by the roadside.

At about 8.30 A.M. on our second day we met a party of three French missionaries on their way from Mwanza. All were on bicycles, and were taking advantage of a smooth stretch of path to do a double days' journey into Tabora, which they hoped to reach about noon, having camped some seven hours back.

These were the advance-guard of a party of thirteen, consisting of eleven Fathers and Brothers and two Sisters, of whom we had heard from Père Schmitt, and the balance of which we found an hour later at a wayside camp. All except the Father in charge were newcomers to Africa, and all were bound for various posts on the Belgian as well as on the German side of Lake Tanganyika. As they reported that there was no water within another six hours, we decided to go no farther, and bivouacked under the lea of a hill a few hundred yards from their camp. Later the Père Superieur paid us a visit, and after a cup of tea took us back with him to return the call, which was celebrated with a bottle of wine.

Shortly after dark our carriers amused and surprised us by getting up a party to go out and kill birds. Armed with sticks and knob-kerries and torches of burning grass they sallied forth quite confident of returning in an hour or so with a few guinea-fowl or partridges, which they said they would find on the roost. We promised to put sixpence on every bird they killed, but we were not called upon to pay.

Two hours through timbered but stony hills brought us to flat, thinly-wooded and scrub-clothed country with no water for 16½ miles. About the middle of it we came across an interesting example of the commercial spirit of the German East African natives in the shape of a wayside stall at which half a dozen of the inhabitants of the nearest villages were sitting, with pots of beer for sale to passing caravans. There was a quantity of spoor on the way. Giraffe, eland, hartebeeste and topi, all but the first being fresh, but no game, barring a single duiker, was seen. The next three days were dull treks of 20, 24½, and 19½ miles, the last of which brought us to the French Fathers' mission at Ngaya. At the end of the first our carriers came in a deputation to protest against the rate at which we were travelling. They were completely exhausted, they said, they had had no time to buy food on the way, and they must have a rest the next day. As the majority of them were Wanyamwezi, who enjoy the reputation of being about the best carriers in Africa, this tickled us not a little. We were sorry, we told them, that they were unable to live up to their reputation, but they must stick to it, for the morrow's trek was going to be longer still —24½ miles. This much alarmed them, and they declared there was no *sokoni* (market or stall at which to buy food), no game, and little or no water on the way. However, with a little threatening, to the effect that if we loitered we should miss the steamer at Mwanza, and that if we missed it there would be nothing for it but to spend another fortnight in the bush before they got paid off; with a little chaff, and a promise that we would make an early start and that they should buy food on the way, we got round them, and did our 24½ miles—to find a *sokoni*, a small Indian store, and plenty of game, all quite close to our camp.

Our boys from Rhodesia had naturally had a little difficulty in adapting themselves to the local coinage of the heller and the one-and-fourpenny rupee. Even when they knew that 100 heller went to the rupee, which took them some time, as they never troubled to count, they seemed unable to dissociate the heller from the penny.

For instance, when one of them bought a small handful of ground nuts for 3 heller, he firmly believed he had been swindled, and it was in vain that we demonstrated to him that, taking the local price of a yard of calico (calico and beads forming the small coinage of his country) at 25 heller, the ground nuts he had bought (being, as he admitted, about one quarter of a yard's worth in his country) had really cost him but half as much as they did in Rhodesia. Similarly it was almost equally vain to attempt to convince them that the meal they were buying was, comparatively, as cheap, and that anyway, they could buy as much as they could possibly eat with their allowance of 10 heller per day. They understood the calculation in the end, but whether they believed our statements is another matter. Moreover, the last argument never is convincing to a native; he is quite incapable of realising that he can only eat something less than 2 lbs. of meal a day (which has been proved by experiment), and thinks that under some circumstances there is no limit at all.

The third day to Ngaya, first over a huge bare undulating plain, dotted here and there with villages and herds of cattle though humming with tsetse fly, then through a patch of thirsty bush consisting entirely of straight long-thorned saplings, and then out again into the open, was not remarkable except for the big village of Kahama in the first plain and the curious rocky ridge formation of the second.

At Kahama's was the highest developed native market that we had seen; with its "pitches" for the sellers of native produce, two or three Indian shops and a butchery, it almost amounted to a bazaar. We bought some excellent lentils here at a heller a handful, which formed a useful basis for the next two days' potage. The house of the village chief was quite a notable one. Not so large as either Kalula's or Tetemia's, it showed, with its high-pitched roof with pavilion ends and creditable attempt

Chief's house at Kahama.

Natives threshing Kaffir corn.

at gable windows, a higher standard of architecture than either.

It was towards Ngaya that the peculiar granite boulders were first seen—the plains here are broken up by low ridges running roughly north and south, their long summits strewn and embattled by curiously regular rows of granite masses—while here and there are huge outcrops rising clear and solitary out of the flat surface of the plain itself.

These latter, split horizontally by the same weathering that has given the hill ridges the look of hewn blocks, form sometimes a series of pillars, arches and colonnades that by their huge bulk and grotesque arrangement suggest the handiwork of some ambitious architect of the gigantic age.

The village of Ngaya, from which the camp derives its name, consists of some dozen huts nestling, like many of its fellows, at the foot of a group of these mighty monoliths, from under which bubbles a little stream of cool clear water spreading out and down to irrigate the pasturage and gardens of millet and sugar-cane on the lower slopes of the plain. We found the villages almost solely occupied by women folk, the men apparently being employed on transport or railway construction work away from their homes. Those whom we saw struck us as being of a good type, with bright, intelligent faces, and we were particularly struck by the action of one young girl who, noticing one of our dogs as he lay panting with the heat when we were making a short halt in her village, spontaneously fetched him a bowl of water to quench his thirst—an act of kindness rare enough in any native : here prompted perhaps by a fellow feeling, for the Wanyamwezi look on their women folk as an animal so much lower in the scale of creation than man that they habitually refer to them as " cows that cannot be milked."[1] Here for the first time during the journey

---

[1] Cf. *The East African Protectorate*, by Sir Charles Eliot, p. 125 : "Wives are the recognised sign of wealth, and girls are regarded simply as calves which can be sold for a price. . . . The Wakamba have no respect for maidens, and regard a pregnant girl as the most eligible spouse, exactly as if she were a cow in calf."

we saw women wearing the small bead apron which is common in parts of South Africa, though here apparently it is only worn by unmarried girls.

Just round the corner of another ridge we came upon another village and a small native market, and saw the Mission Church about 1¼ mile away amongst more boulders to the west. We reached it at a little after eleven o'clock, and were welcomed by the Père Superieur and a colleague, whom we had advised of our intended visit by a runner in advance. After a cup of tea and an invitation to supper, we retired to find a place to pitch our tents and to get some lunch. But it is a dangerous thing to leave anything to chance with natives, or not to provide for all likely emergencies, and we found that, for once, lunch was not such a simple matter as it seemed. Our boys, opining that we should lunch at the Mission, had not only got nothing ready for us, but had, with really extraordinary ingenuity, absolutely surpassed all records in the completeness with which they had provided for our discomfort. The two lunch-baskets, which had kept up with us with the most exceptional and praiseworthy pertinacity for nearly 20 miles, were found to be empty of everything except a couple of lumps of rancid beef—no bread, biscuits, butter, tea, kettle, cheese, clean plates or anything. Even their legitimate contents had nearly all been carefully transferred to and packed away in other loads, which, of course, were miles behind. One of the boys' explanation of this eccentric appreciation of the uses of a lunch-basket is worthy of a special place in the annals of native logic. "Their fittings had been left out because there were two of them!" The cook and another boy were despatched to find some loads containing food, and we eventually stayed the pangs of hunger with a cold collation of potted sausages and oaten biscuits about 2 P.M.—nine hours after a scanty breakfast. After pitching our tents in a sheltered valley amongst the boulders, we paid another visit to the Mission, and, escorted by the Père Superieur, went over the church and buildings —the latter are constructed in the Arab (*tembo*) architectural style with flat mudded roofs, and the whole is enclosed in a spacious quadrangle of outbuildings, similarly roofed, the outer wall of which, unpierced by any openings except the entrance door, forms a screen between the settlement and the native village without. The wall is some 9 or 10 feet in height and hides everything but the gabled roof and tower of the church from all points except the higher ground to the north.

The church was the finest piece of sun-dried brick architecture that we had seen. Gracefully designed and admirably constructed, the high-pitched roof of heavy thatch was supported by timber couples resting upon the outer walls and the round pillars of the nave. The pillars were connected by stout lintels of timber in place of the usual arches, which are practically impossible of construction in sun-dried brick.

As striking as the building itself were the beautifully wrought and polished pieces of furniture and woodwork which it contained, and which comprised an altar, a half-life-sized crucifix, sedilia, and a set of picture-frames whose simple beauty contrasted painfully with the crude and gaudy lithographs that they held. All were of the same local timber, called *mukula*, that we had seen being sawn at the saw-pits near Tabora, and were the handiwork of one of the Fathers. Later in the afternoon, when taking photographs round our camp, we found the rocks swarming with rock conies squatting and basking in the sun. We were anxious to get one or two specimens for our natural history collection, and so sent for a rook rifle, but, owing to the inaccessibility of the rocks and crannies into which most of our victims rolled, we had to shoot five or six before we succeeded in securing a couple. At seven o'clock we went down again to the Mission and supped with the three Fathers of whom the staff consists. The meal was their usual kind of simple but well-cooked repast—soup, stewed duck, with boiled rice and tomatoes, potatoes and salad; the vegetables, according to their custom, being eaten after instead of with the meat or game, and some very palatable wafer-like biscuits made of the local sorghum flour. The water-supply was not much better than we had been finding it along the road. Our hosts held up a glass of water that looked as if it was diluted with 10 per cent of milk and told us it was exceptionally good for that part of the country. They also told us that the neighbourhood was poor for the raising of vegetables, and that though it carried large herds of cattle, of which they themselves owned a good herd, they obtained but a poor supply of milk and little or no butter. The Wanyamwezi, of whom there are some 3000 within a radius of 3½ miles, never kill their cattle, though they sell for slaughter, keeping them mainly for the sake of the butter, of which they make a fair quantity, but only for anointing themselves or for the manufacture of soap, and not for food. A rupee's worth that, anticipating an unusual treat, we had bought a few days earlier at a wayside market was sufficiently convincing of the truth of this.

The name Wanyamwezi was that given to the tribes of this locality by the people of the coast, which they are constantly visiting, and which they maintain that every male must visit at least once before he can call himself a man. Its meaning is "the people of the moon," and is applied to the tribes of the west as being the quarter in which the new moon is first seen.

Whether they maintain any further connection with the moon than this we did not hear, but the very next day we had proof of their curious predilection for travelling by moonlight.

On arriving at our camping ground a little before ten o'clock (having for various reasons made a late start and a short trek) we found it already occupied by some 40 to 50 carriers from Mwanza, resting with their loads at their side. On asking whether they were not going on, we received the reply that they had finished their day's journey. Till about three o'clock their numbers went on increasing, and finally we had to share the camp with about 200 of them. Up to midnight they had not caused us the slightest inconvenience, but then, the waning moon having had time to get well above the horizon, they proceeded to "get busy." It took them about an hour to get really off, and the last ten minutes, as the main body of them pulled out blowing cow-horn bugles and beating a devil's tattoo on their boxes with knob-kerries and sticks, it was simply pandemonium let loose. Curses were not of the slightest effect, and though we thought seriously of coming out and firing a few shots into the air by way of intimidation, we were much too sleepy to do it, and lay tight until the din should die away and let us slumber again. Hardly had we turned over when a fresh development interrupted the night's rest. Our boys, deceived by the obtrusive energy of the Wanyamwezi and quite ignoring the fact that the moon showed it to be only about one o'clock, brought us our early tea! Resisting with difficulty the temptation to throw it in their faces, we warned them not to come near us again till dawn, and once more turned our faces to the wall, heartily blessing those "children of the moon."

The Mbala plain, of which we had heard both at Tabora and Ngaya as being an exceptionally good shooting ground, we reached after about an hour's travelling the following day. In the morning haze its breadth from east to west looked in places anything between 5 and 8 miles. Its length was about 10. Covered with unburnt grass up to $3\frac{1}{2}$ feet high and with no cover of any sort except stumpy ant-hills only occasionally tall enough to show over the top, it did not look promising, and was very rough going. Our path fortunately did not lead through the whole of it, but, after traversing a corner for a mile or two, turned off into the thick bush, and, after 5 or 6 miles more emerged again into the northern end. On the first section we saw no life except a few ostriches at about 600 yards. In the second we found—and missed—a roan, and ten minutes later spied what we thought were vultures circling over a spot some 500 yards away to our right. In the hope of a possible lion over a kill—a hope which was encouraged by Chumamaboko—we bore down upon it armed to the teeth; but on getting closer found that the vultures were marabout, and there was neither game nor lion anywhere. An excited follower tried to convince us that a herd of cattle that was grazing a quarter of a mile away was one of the things we were looking for, but we disagreed with him.

It was on the following day that we came on the only settlers on our route through German East Africa, a Hanoverian and a Bavarian, who, we had already heard at Ngaya, were establishing a ground-nut oil factory at Salabwe, on the Tabora-Mwanza road. As their settlement was at a convenient halting-place, we were preparing to find a spot to camp in the neighbourhood of the only stream, but as soon as our arrival was noticed we were cordially welcomed, and persuaded to camp in their compound. After seeing to the pitching of our tents, we repaired to the house, a small three-roomed building of mud with an iron roof, where our host, who knew a fair amount of English, assisted by his partner in such perfect silence that for some three hours we blandly believed him to be totally ignorant of the English language, proceeded to dispense his hospitality. It consisted briefly of a couple of liqueur glasses of whisky followed by a gallon and a half of "Gold Bock" lager beer each, which seemed to do us about as much harm as an equal quantity of water.

There was a pause in our potations a little before sundown, and we went round and looked at his machinery. It was not yet complete, but what had already arrived had, he told us, cost him over £100 in transport, and when set up it was apparently going to be quite an up-to-date and effective plant consisting of a hydraulic press, shelling and cleaning machines, &c., equal to the whole process of extracting ground-nut oil. He declared himself certain of making a big success of it, and showed us some samples, which he maintained were really superior to olive oil. We had already learnt that the oil is sold as ground-nut oil in Germany, where their Colonies still have the fascination of a new toy, and commands a ready sale; while in Great Britain, where colonial produce is still regarded with some suspicion, it has to be labelled "Olive Oil" or used in the adulteration of it to find a market. The area of his land grant seemed to be limited solely by his requirements, and he also told me that he was obtaining a concession over a valuable natural salt deposit that was brought down by the rains from some hills to the east. He showed us two lumps of what seemed to be simply pure white salt—picked up, he said, haphazard by the natives. If it was true, as he said, that a load which cost him 4 rupees, including transport, fetched 10 rupees in Tabora, and that he could sell as much as 200 loads in a day, it was a profitable proposition. In the matter of a handful of mineral specimens, including amethyst, garnet, copper and gold, which had come from the hills to the west, although this locality is officially marked in the maps as highly mineralised, and though our host had spent some years prospecting, he was a little less convincing. Dinner, which was washed down with German champagne and vanilla-flavoured Buchanan as a liqueur, afforded us a most entertaining symposium. Herr Wattjen, the partner, proved not only to have a quite useful acquaintance with the English language, but to be a keen and intelligent student of British and German political problems. Our host's most notable contribution was a statement that the Duke of Cumberland had given up his claim to the English throne in favour of Queen Victoria, preferring that of Hanover, to which he adhered quite as obstinately as to another to the effect that there was no such person as Herr Siegel, Distrikts Kommissar, at Tabora. Both were in agreement in their criticisms of the new civil administration introduced by Herr Dernburg, which, they said, was "far worser" than the old military régime. Their illustration was a naïve disclosure of biassed individualism. Formerly, they said, if a native was lacking in what any kind of white man considered the proper respect due to him, the white man had but to report it, and the offender was severely punished. *Nowadays the plaintiff had to produce evidence.* Comment is superfluous.

We bade our hosts farewell on retiring at 9.15, and pulled out before dawn, not a little impressed by the warm and genial welcome that we had enjoyed at Salabwe. With lager beer at about eighteenpence a bottle and champagne at goodness knows what, the extension of this unstinted hospitality to two Britishers travelling through German territory by a couple of settlers who still had their way to make was a thing to remember.

On our next day's stage of 21 miles along a trek that was chiefly like frozen plough and quite unrideable, we saw a good deal of game, including topi, reedbuck, and roan, besides a troop of huge baboons, in chasing which the dogs nearly succeeded in losing themselves in the bush. This was the third time we had come across these beasts, right on our road, since leaving Tabora. We bagged none, but saw them fairly close, and noticed that they were darker in colour and rather shorter in the body, though no shorter in the leg, than those of North-Eastern Rhodesia. In that country they are not uncommonly mistaken for lions at a first glimpse of them stalking through thick bush, and one of our gun-bearers on this occasion fell into the same error. The biggest of them stand every bit as high, and their colour is often almost identical. They showed very little fear of the dogs, and once routed them in hasty retreat to the road by merely turning back to have a closer look at what was chasing them. We also saw some wild ostriches here, and after careful stalking succeeded in getting to within 70 yards and obtaining some good photographs of them.

We killed a couple of topi for the sake of the meat, but the carriers, who would have got nearly all of it, were suffering from one of those occasional fits of "previousness" that so often attack the African, and consequently nearly all of them had to do without. It was only two or three miles from camp that the game had been shot, so those of them that were not fetching firewood were sent back to carry in the meat. On their return we found to our disgust that not only had they ignored our instructions to bring in one of the heads intact, for the sake of the head skin, and had flayed nearly every inch of both of them to make themselves sandals, but had also taken the liberty of helping themselves to a tasty bit, and of cooking and eating it before they brought the meat in. Needless to say, the tasty bits were all they got. Their embryo sandals were cremated, and the spare meat was given to the *Jumbe*, or local headman, whose courtesy and pains to make us comfortable in a spot where there was hardly enough water to go round, and firewood was only visible on the horizon, deserved some special recognition.

Twenty-eight miles short of Mwanza in the great plains, that but for the close-cropped grass and patches of cultivation in place of the scrub reminded one vividly of the Karoo, we encountered some entirely novel methods of husbandry. In between the tiny villages, whose euphorbia hedges were the only trees in sight, the smooth level ground, like patches of English common, was dotted with groups of natives threshing, winnowing, and stacking their corn. The threshing was effected by means of a kind of flail, or carpet-beater, with a handle, 10 to 12 feet long, finished with a padded palm, or in some cases a three-pronged fork. The operators, who were male, worked quite naked (until the approach of the camera), and the tedious effort of wielding the clumsy implement suggested a considerable waste of labour, though it was undoubtedly picturesque. Close by a group of women were engaged in winnowing. Their method was the simple one of holding up a basket full of grain at arms'-length and spilling it slowly to the ground, allowing the chaff to be carried away by the breeze. They also worked with as little clothing as possible, being naked to the waist, with the body, face, and arms well smeared with white clay, which had the effect, we were told, of preventing irritation from the chaff. A little farther on we came across a quantity of the unthreshed sorghum ready stocked in well-bound bundles, the form and the neatness of which were as unusual to us as the native methods of treating it.

The heat in the plains was as trying as we had found it anywhere in the territory, but one good result was that we did not suffer much inconvenience except in the matter of cooking and bread-baking from the fact that the only fuel that could be obtained at our camp was in the form of pieces of split euphorbia at three for a heller. We were by this time beginning to wonder whether we should soon be asked to buy our water, but the natives assured us that things did not go quite so far as that.

On the following day, the 23rd of September, the equinox, after a tremendous sprint to the top of a small rise so as to set our watches right for once as the sun appeared above the horizon, we caught our first glimpse of Mwanza gulf, one of the southern arms of the Victoria Nyanza, some 3000 or 4000 yards in width and extending some 35 miles in length from the main lake.

Almost directly after leaving Misungwi the rocky ridges and kopjes had begun to close in, and the open plains gave place to little valleys and hollows of increasing beauty and charm.

The road for nearly 25 miles into Mwanza was broad, banked up, partially metalled and well drained, with an avenue of *mitawa* and other trees planted on either side, that after a few years should form, as they meet overhead, a complete and welcome shelter from the sun's rays.

The scenery grew strangely like that of Dartmoor at times. The glistening gulf on the left with its cliffs, here green, there gleaming white, and studded with granite islets—the counterpart of the kopjes on the land—of all of which we caught ever fresh glimpses through each little dip and valley that we crossed, gave an added beauty to a landscape that in itself was fair. It were difficult to imagine anything more fine than this approach to the township of Mwanza, and it was quite the best bit of water scenery we had seen in Africa, and, though lacking the breadth and immensity of the main lakes, had a charming picturesqueness of its own.

At times the road wound through weird tangled masses

of granite rocks, and from the foot of one of these was bubbling a clear cold spring for all the world just like an artificial well. Nearer Mwanza itself it led quite close to the shore, which was low and thickly clothed with shrubs and tangled undergrowth, and skirted the edge of a belt of wide-spreading and shady trees. We reached the German port at about 9 A.M. on September 25th.

During the last two days, besides overtaking some hundreds of natives going in for loads, we had met a constant stream of carriers on their way into the interior with bales and cases of goods that had come from Mombasa by the Uganda railway and the lake route; the last day we must have met between 1500 and 2000—the climax to the continuous demonstration of the fallacy of the German Official view.

VII

MWANZA AND THE ADMINISTRATION OF GERMAN EAST AFRICA

Description of Mwanza—Perambulations and perplexities—Protracted negotiations with the Customs department—General impressions of German East Africa—The country, natives, markets and small coinage, climate—An examination of the old régime and the new.

THE township of Mwanza, situated at the end of a narrow level valley debouching on a semicircular bay near the head of the Mwanza gulf, has the makings of quite a beautiful little place.

Some of its best buildings are scattered along or near the foreshore, and some, *e.g.* the fort and residence of the Commandant, are perched in the hills overlooking the bay from the north-east. Near the centre of the town is a fine open square with a magnificent old tree in the centre of it, the Boma, gaol and office buildings on the lake side and the native market on another. The latter is in the same style as those at Tabora, but larger and consisting of a single building. The Boma fort and most of the residences are built in the same substantial granite as we had seen at Tabora, with red iron roofs. To the left of the square, and separated from it by a few scattered buildings, is a broad common bounded on its further side by a huge outcrop of granite rocks which merge in an irregular ridge, hiding from view the waters of the gulf arm before it turns the corner into the bay. In the middle of this was a large square building in process of construction, which we learnt later was the beginning of the wireless telegraphy station for communication with Bukoba. Running south-east from the market square is a broad street with smaller ones branching from it, forming the Indian and native quarter; for Mwanza has

A BALANCED ROCK AT MWANZA.

VIEW FROM OUR CAMP AT MWANZA.

quite a considerable Indian and Arab trading population.

In the town itself there are not many trees, but the rocky hills on either side, especially to the east, begin to be well covered, and in some places the lake shore shows refreshing signs of the energy and foresight of the early planter. East of the Boma the water's edge is fringed for some little distance by a huge clump of palms, the streets are mostly provided with rapidly growing avenues of *mitawa*, while the gardens in front of one house, at the extreme west corner of the town, are shaded by a grove of magnificent old mangoes, guavas, limes, bananas, *mitawa*, and many another tropical tree, stretching right down to the lake shore, that suggested an older occupation than the rest of the town. To the left as one looks out towards the lake the foreground is dotted with a huge granite boulder or two rising out of the water, some grotesquely balanced on the top of their fellows, the remains of the rocky ridge that once doubtless stretched right across the bay.

After a few minutes' rest under the shade of the market-square tree, we got the sentry at the Boma gates to show us the Offices of the " Distrikts Kommissar," which we found were just round a corner and on the other side of the same building. Speaking English without much difficulty he gave us a pleasant and cordial welcome, and after a short conversation, yet long enough to show us that he was another example of the new type of official who takes an interest and a pleasure in his work amongst the natives, pointed out the direction of the wharf, at which he told us we could settle all our Customs and steamer transport business. He then sent a boy along to show us the best place to camp, which he said we could do wherever we liked. After finding the spot, which was well out of the town just short of the gardens mentioned above (in the shady arbour formed by two or three magnificent trees), right on the edge of the lake but screened from it and the breeze by a mass of rocks with a simple but rather impressive memorial to Bismarck at their base, and which was, in fact, about as perfect a spot for a camp as could be imagined, we proceeded to look for the steamer and Customs Offices. With the steamer people we wanted to fix up fares and freight, and with the Customs to obtain the refund of import duty paid at Bismarckburg on the kit we were taking with us. This, we knew, wanted a little engineering, though to save expense we did not intend taking more with us than we were obliged. A pier jutting out into the lake seemed to indicate the spot, so, though it was not exactly where the Distrikts Kommissar had pointed, thither we wended. only to find, however, a busy yard, backed by a large shed which was thinly populated by Indian clerks. As this did not look promising, we decided to try the direction indicated to us at the Boma, and passing what appeared to be the Post Office, though disguised under a totally different title to the same institution at Tabora, we worked round to the other side of the Boma block. By this time the sentry was beginning to know us, but success still eluded our efforts: the way simply led past a shop, which appeared to be a local Lockhart's, to the lake-side, where, under the shade of the palms which clothed it, extensive laundry operations were in progress. Undaunted, we decided to try the Post Office in the hope that it was not one, but were disappointed: it was. The Postmaster, however, spoke a little English, and on hearing our quest directed us to the Steamer Offices—the other end of the town. We should find it, he said, after passing the engine-house, and should see the name "D.O.A. Nyanza—something or other—Gesellschaft" over the door. The scattered nature of Mwanza town may appear to have pleased us at first from an artistic point of view and at a distance, and we are not prepared to say that it did not, but with a house-to-house visiting job such as we seemed to have got in hand by this time picturesqueness and spaciousness were rapidly losing their charm, and we were beginning to wonder why the devil they couldn't have either grouped all their buildings round the square, and put them back to back in a nice solid block like a

A MEMORIAL TO BISMARCK NEAR OUR CAMP.

respectable British slum. However, we had business that nobody whom we had met was painfully anxious to do for us, so we girded up our loins, wiped several beads of perspiration from our brows, and made a start.

After walking eastwards along a regular street for something over a mile, we seemed really to have got there. The polysyllabic signboard was there, so was the engine-house. Turning in and passing the latter, which seemed to contain an up-to-date plant for cleaning rice, which natives were sorting on bucksails in the yard outside, we walked about a furlong up a broad path to an office. Making ourselves understood without very much difficulty by a stout and preoccupied gentleman in the invariable white duck, who first began by mystifying us with facts or fancy anent some German boats of whose existence we had never heard (possibly freight barges or Arab dhows) and seemed in a deuce of a hurry to say good-bye when he had gathered what we wanted, we learnt that we had once more come to entirely the wrong place.

With somewhat impaired tempers, and a feeling that if we met an Englishman he would have the time of his life in Mwanza, we turned sadly away. At quite a short distance on the way back we came on a gateway with a brass plate bearing the legend "Wm. O'Swald & Co.," and thinking that here we might be going to find the animal we longed for, we walked another furlong up another path and besieged another office at the top of it.

There was no Englishman, but there was a very nice little man who spoke very fair English, grasped the situation with a lucidity that we had feared was in some way impossible in the Mwanza climate, and told us everything we wanted to know. The steamer came in on Monday, he said, and left again in a day or two. The office was next to the Post Office and the Boma; it contained a Goanese clerk who spoke English, but if we could not excavate it, Hansing & Co., who were the last house at the other end of the town, and acted as the Uganda Railway Agents, would be able to give us any information we required.

A little encouraged, but wondering what kind of mental aberration it was that was afflicting the Postmaster, we started off again. This time, however, we did know where we were going, for it was the very shed into which we had looked some hours before, but had been discouraged by the appearance of doubtless that very Goanese clerk. However, our perplexities were shortly ended. Without further delay we explained our troubles to the said pundit, and his grasp of the situation and his excellent English so charmed us, that, in spite of his ingenuous attempt to make us believe that the next steamer left on October 10—whereas it was really due on the 26th September, and would leave on the 28th—we felt warmed towards him and his race in general. Steamer fares, &c., would be fixed up on board the vessel when she had arrived, and we arranged to return at 4 P.M. to fix up the Customs business. Our friendly babu was a Uganda Railway employé, but he introduced us to a colleague in the Customs Department, an equally inoffensive specimen with an equally efficient knowledge of our tongue. As the German in charge was quite ignorant of it, the existence of these clerks was decidedly cheering.

These exhausting perambulations satisfactorily ended, it occurred to us that an airy little caravanserai which we had passed as we entered the Boma square, and on the verandah of which we had seen a genial German airing himself, might possibly be Hansing's, or, if it were not, that it had certainly suggested lager beer and such-like refreshment which the situation distinctly indicated.

He was not Hansing, but he was charmed to serve and join us in the matter of a Munchner or two, and for ten minutes we conversed with him in a mixture of English and Ki-Swahili—his knowledge of the former being about equal to our acquaintance with the latter.

After purchasing some tinned fruits, hors d'œuvres, pickled cucumbers, polony sausages and Dimitrino cigarettes from his spotless and well-ordered store, we proceeded to Hansing's to see if they would change our German money into British. We found the firm without difficulty, hidden in the gardens referred to above, just beyond our camp, which was a surprise, as we had thought we were pitched beyond the limits of the township. They could not do any exchange for us, being at the time out of English rupees, but no less than two of the firm spoke excellent English and showed a refreshing willingness to oblige and serve us.

After lunch and a rest in camp we reverted to the Customs Office, taking with us the trophies that we wished to forward to England, and on which there was export duty to pay, hoping to get the whole business through before closing-time. But it was not to be. The airy denial given us at Bismarckburg that any details would be required in order to secure our refund was as much beside the mark as was the clerk's assurance in the morning that nothing was necessary beyond the production of papers. All the goods we were taking out of the country had to be produced in order to see, he said, that the diminution of the same was as we stated, and that their valuation was correct. It was in vain that we pointed out that their valuation, correct or otherwise, was quite immaterial, as, whether we had paid too much or too little, in either case the valuation was Lieutenant Wach's at Bismarckburg, and the idea was that we were going to get it back. Our morning's estimate of the babu's intelligence and eagerness to oblige was evidently a mistaken one. He was quite unable or unwilling to see our point, and further seemed—unless it was merely lack of *savoir faire*—to consider it his duty to place as many obstacles as the law provided in the way of getting through our business with facility and despatch.

It was Saturday, and the property we were taking had to be produced—and produced on Monday on its way to the steamer; Tuesday they would be too busy; they could not send any one to our camp to do the inspection, and the fact that we should consequently have to spend Monday night in the streets with neither tents nor beds left them quite unmoved. The occasional visit of a white clerk or two to the consultation did nothing to relieve the situation.

During an armistice in the matter of deposit refunds, we turned to the subject of the export of horns and skins; this, at any rate, must be a simple matter. We had again, however, underrated the ingenuity of the department. We had intended to pay the export duty on the trophies, take them back to our camp, and there pack them up for despatch to Europe; but no, we must leave them there once they had been checked; we could not take them out again. But, the babu said, they could be packed up for us there. Distrust, however, was growing mutual and we didn't jump at it, especially as he seemed unable to explain how, when, where, why, by whom or what for the packing would be done.

Eventually both of us having all but reached the limit of our patience and chafing not a little at the absence of even a chair—making it necessary to risk our trousers on the top of packing-cases bristling with nails and scrap iron—after the group had been joined by a second German who spoke a little English, and by yet another Goanese who spoke German too, after the German had helped the situation by scattering our horns with his dainty foot into some special pattern of his own, and telling us that a reed-buck was something else and that a jackal did not exist, after these and others had come and gone with a look and a shrug some three or four separate times before they had even succeeded in getting a list of our trophies on to paper, we made the proposal that we be allowed to take the trophies away and pack them, after which they could unpack them again if they suspected us of smuggling, or not as they pleased, and that the rest of our exports should come through on Monday provided that we were able to go on board the steamer that day, a compromise which was actually accepted, with our opinion of the Customs department now thoroughly rearranged, and with a hint we could not resist giving to our friend the railway clerk that if his *confrères* knew what really respectable people we were after all they might be less disposed to suspect our *bonâ-fides* and to tangle us up with red tape, we left the scene of our struggles. We then succeeded in getting some notes changed into rupees at Messrs. Hansing, though it was really past closing-time, and proceeded to pay off our carriers. None made any attempt to move off that day, nor appeared in the least put out at having been paid too late to enable them to do so. In fact, they accepted it, as they really had accepted everything all the way, with perfect good nature.

Sunday was a day of comparative inaction, being devoted chiefly to rest, to the packing of our heads and skins, and a short stroll in the evening to see what we could make of the wireless telegraphy construction, which was not much.

On Monday morning we took our packages for Europe to Hansings in the hope of getting them off our hands, but found that we were bound to take them to the Customs in person. Bracing ourselves for a further effort, we went along, but this time, in spite of their warning that Tuesday would be impossible, they said, "Come to-morrow; plenty of time to-morrow. Declaration has to be made out, and it's nearly closing-time." Analysis of our feelings was becoming too complicated a process by this time, and we returned to camp feeling almost philosophical. At 5 P.M. the arrival of the steamer put rather a different complexion on things, and, though in consequence of the postponement of clearing operations, her arrival before Tuesday was not now a matter of vital importance, it cheered us considerably to pay her a visit and make the acquaintance of her officers, who gave us permission to come aboard the following day.

After our last night on German East Africa soil we were up early, but the Customs department were even earlier, for while we were dressing it sent a message to say it was ready for us, and at about ten o'clock we had packed our kit and, with the help of a couple of trolleys from Messrs. Hansing, managed to convey it to the Customs shed. We were taking but little with us besides personal clothing, tents, bedding and camp kit; the few provisions that were left over we had, in the absence of purchasers, either presented to our carriers or thrown into the lake.

The Customs department were more than ready for us—they must have been awaiting us eagerly since dawn; they met us with the injunction to come again at three o'clock. Thoroughly resigned, we consoled ourselves with lunch on board the s.s. *Sibyl*, and then prepared to obey. Whether it was our probably obtrusive attitude of humility that did it, or whether things had merely arrived at that stage when after all they do sometimes get done, it was soon obvious that there was quite a chance of our various objects being finally achieved. The business of passing our kit was accomplished with quite unexpected despatch, our declaration was accepted almost *in toto*, and scarcely a package was opened for examination.

The business of calculating what was due to us and what was due from us took the particular Goanese who attended to us a most unconscionable time, but, after one or two false starts, he got through it and we really did get back quite as much as we had expected.

Export duty on trophies cost us Rs.24.90. Import duty refund amounted to Rs.137, leaving a balance to us of Rs.112.10.

There remained the business of conveying our property on board. This in our elation we had almost overlooked, but eventually accomplished with the valuable assistance of yet another clerk, of the impressive name of Vasco de Gama, an employé of Messrs. Hansing, who placed a gang of savages at our disposal. With our last load and our Rhodesian staff safely on board at five o'clock, our anxieties were at an end. In conclusion it is but fair to say that this was the only case in which we experienced the slightest difficulty with any department of the German administration, that it was unaccompanied by a trace of intentional incivility or any deliberate attempt to embarrass us with obstacles or red tape, and that it was probably largely due to our total ignorance of the German language.

We thought at one time that we should have some difficulty in exchanging the balance of our German money for English, but found a convenient solution of the problem in the acceptance of a cheque from the firm of Alidina

Visram on his branch at Entebbe, at a discount of 3 per cent. This left us, as a matter of fact, with a net gain of $10\frac{1}{2}$ per cent. on the gold we had changed at Bismarckburg.

A residence of but six weeks in a foreign protectorate does not seem, on the face of it, to provide a very adequate equipment for critic and historian, but the fact that German East Africa is a next-door neighbour to us in Northern Rhodesia, the close similarity of the local conditions to those with which we have been familiar for some years and the frank welcome and open discussion that we everywhere enjoyed, encourages us to offer our commentary without apology or misgiving.

The common impression that we should not find much to learn from the German administration of East Africa is founded on a superficial or out-of-date knowledge of the facts, and recalls a passage in Sir Charles Eliot's work on the East Africa Protectorate dealing with the German colony :—

"I would not, however," he says, "have us lay any flattering unction to our souls, and congratulate ourselves, as we are wont to do, on managing everything better than all other nations."

Naturally enough we judged the German system by our own, and in some ways found it wanting: as a nation we have had far greater experience in ruling tropical dependencies, and we were quick to notice what we considered the weak points in the German administration; but at the same time we saw much to admire, and the general verdict must, we think, be one of congratulation to our neighbours. It should be noted that our experiences and criticism refer to but little beyond the region actually visited ; this was one of the poorest stretches in the territory, and, being so far from the coast, one of the least developed. Our remarks are probably entirely inapplicable, for instance, to the country round Kilimanjaro, the plantation area, and the coast line, and must not be taken to refer to those parts.

As to the nature of the country through which we passed

taken all round there can be no doubt that this section of the German protectorate is poor. It is difficult to see that it can ever come to much in itself, though it may prove useful enough in connection with the whole, and, being fairly well populated, will afford a source of labour for the more fertile and promising districts. The whole country is poorly and most of it badly watered, which is in itself a great handicap. The neighbourhood of Mwazye, known as Lyangalile, was the only part that had perennial streams, and although they were good, they were not very numerous, and the water in them compares unfavourably with that of the streams in the Southern Tanganyika plateau. The rest of the country draws its water-supply from water-holes, poor in quality and generally deficient in quantity. The timber supply is poor; there is a little in Lyangalile, and a small though good belt of forest near Kalula's, and we heard of some near Ngaya, though we did not actually see it. The northern part of the territory visited is reputed to be highly mineralised. One of the most noticeable features was the live stock; the first part, to and inclusive of Rukwa, was stocked with large numbers of sheep and goats and a few cattle; the section from Rungwa to the neighbourhood of Tabora had practically none of either; Tabora has a very large supply of cattle in its immediate vicinity, and from thence to the plains round the Mwanza gulf there are enormous herds of cattle everywhere, but there is no getting away from the fact that most of these cattle live in a dense "fly" belt, and that some at any rate of the fly is infected, so that the prospect is not very bright.

The natives are of a good type, and the main divisions, the Fipa stock and the Wanyamwezi, are both of good physique and quite up to the average in intelligence.

The native chiefs, headmen and population generally we everywhere found courteous and obliging, and also contented and happy. The beginning of the semi-civilised Swahili element not unnaturally jarred a little upon us, though we recognised how infinitely superior it was as a civilising and educating influence to the

"Kitchen Kaffir" element of South Africa that is encroaching on Northern Rhodesia, and nowhere did we meet anything to resent in its attitude. Scarcely a group of natives or a batch of carriers would pass without the greeting of " *Yambo, bwana* " or " *Yambo, Bwana Mkubwa.*"

We were interested to notice during the last two days before reaching Mwanza that the villagers seemed of a distinctly less sophisticated and of a different facial type, many recalling the Mashukulumbwe type though without the hair cones and dental disfiguration. Our carriers gave us no trouble, and though a little slow to realise their duties in the way of gathering firewood, &c., and at first inclined to complain that we wanted to travel by too long stages, we found them willing and cheerful, and able to do considerably more than the local estimate of ten miles a day. On the whole we preferred the southern (Wa-fipa) group, probably because they more closely resembled those to whom we are accustomed. We passed through a good many types, which are largely distinguished from one another by their houses and village systems and by their food. At first the ordinary village of the Nyasaland and Northern Rhodesian type with some 30 to 50 huts, circular in shape, built with poles and mud-plastered walls and thatched roofs, with millet as the staple crop. In Rukwa the villages were of a similar type, but the huts were built of split wood, and millet was replaced largely by maize. North of Rukwa the *tembo* system of building, which we have described at length in an earlier chapter, was in vogue, and the people still relied on maize for most of their food supply. At and after Tabora we came to the group system of village, each one consisting of a family in three or four huts, dotted about on the fertile plains, with the "camp" known by the name of the locality, and not by that of any particular village. These people grow kaffir corn (sorghum). It was in this section that we found the *sokoni* (more correctly *soko*) first properly established. This useful institution is almost a necessity for carriers in a country where the village group system exists, for a big gang that had to forage amongst isolated huts scattered over such a large area could not buy food as it could in a large concentrated village. The village *sokoni* is simply a shed at the camp, whither natives from the surrounding groups of huts come and sit with food for sale—porridge, grain, flour, beans, ground nuts, bananas, milk, beer, butter, meat, and, where it is scarce, firewood. The carriers, who are continually passing in large numbers, can buy all that they require at the *sokoni*. The vendors have small tins (generally old cigarette tins) and sell at a regular rate of 1, 2, or 3 heller per tin (100 heller = 1 rupee). Flour had been a bit scarce the year we passed, though it was not half so dear as it often is in Northern Rhodesia, while ground nuts and beans were remarkably cheap. Meat was obtainable almost everywhere at about 1d. per lb. The prices are officially fixed at each *sokoni*; there is no haggling, nor is there any difficulty whatever about feeding the carriers.

This market system, no doubt originally due to Arab initiation and example, can only be possible amongst natives whose commercial instincts have reached a certain stage of development, and this instinct is fostered doubtless by the existence of the small copper coinage.

The difficulty experienced, for instance, in Northern Rhodesia in inducing the individual native either to present for sale enough food to represent the sum of sixpence or to accept a copper or two for a smaller quantity is overcome. No amount of food, beer, snuff, &c., can really be too small to be worth half a heller, the 200th part of a rupee, and though it was difficult to convince our Rhodesian natives of the fact, the price of food at the *sokonis* averaged rather less than in Northern Rhodesia, *e.g.* 1 or 2 heller for a handful of ground nuts struck them as exorbitant, though 50 or 100 handfuls were probably more than they could usually buy in their own homes for 1s. 4d. Fowls and eggs, though fairly plentiful off the main route, were very scarce along the main roads. Near and at Tabora and Mwanza eggs can be occasionally

MWANZA—GERMAN EAST AFRICA

bought from Indian hawkers and natives at two or three hellers apiece. Milk was very often obtainable, at the reasonable price of about a pint and a half for six or seven hellers, but the raw native, unless specially warned, is liable to bring that of the day before, thinking it as good as fresh. Butter is sold at many of the markets, but is, as a rule, uneatable, being made mostly as an ingredient of soap or for toilet purposes.

The climate of the highlands of German East Africa, certainly as far north as Tabora, presented but little difference from that prevailing in the greater part of Northeastern Rhodesia. The Rukwa Valley may be compared to that of the Luangwa, both in temperature and, to a certain extent, in its vegetation, though the heat was not quite so trying.

From Tabora to Mwanza it grew perceptibly warmer, and we found it quite worth while, especially for treks of twenty miles or thereabouts, to start before daybreak. The open nature of the country and masses of rock probably have the effect of accentuating the heat.

The dryness doubtless accounts for the absence of mosquitoes, of which we noticed barely half a dozen from end to end of the whole territory, and, in fact, with the exception of a plague of tiny flies at two of our camps, and of course the tsetse fly that infested a large part of our route, the ordinary pests were almost non-existent.

Our natives suffered very little from sickness, while we ourselves enjoyed perfect health until we reached Mwanza, where our slight indisposition was probably merely due to the reaction after so many days' hard travelling.

On the whole it was not a good shooting country. The Rukwa Plains and the Kavu River were good, though the variety of species was limited. The Ugalla River had both quality and variety, but it is a comparatively small and secluded area, and the rest was poor. We saw but few traces of elephant, none of buffalo or rhino, a lot of giraffe spoor, a few ostriches, eland and sable, a good many waterbuck, hartebeeste, roan, mpala, reedbuck, and warthog, and huge herds of topi.

With regard to the administration of the country, it must be understood that it is still in a state of transition, being partly military and partly civil, the former of which is gradually disappearing. At Bismarckburg the military régime is still in force, and we were not favourably impressed by it. From what we learnt from the officer in charge, as well as from what we gathered from other residents and from personal observation, it is obvious that the system, of some of the features of which we have already given an account in our second chapter, is a bad one.

Those really in power are the native police, the *wali* or Government headman, and the tribal chiefs. As no native can appeal to the white man except through the *wali*, who only takes up a plaintiff's case when it suits him, and is always open to bribery, the disadvantages of the system are too obvious to insist upon. The collection of the poll-tax (4 rupees per annum) is left to the chief, who receives 5 per cent. of the amount collected. No census is taken, and the tax is assessed very roughly per village, so that the chief is able to make up the total without calling upon his friends, exacting any shortage from those who are outside his circle of intimates. Needless to say, the amount is considerably smaller than it would be if every one were censused and obliged to pay. If the sum produced falls below the estimate, police are sent to fetch in the people and their flocks, and once again it is not the chief nor his friends that suffer. He also exacts in some parts very high tribute in cash, clothes, labour, live-stock, and food from his people, who thus pay a double tax, as well as heavy toll on natives passing through his territory, especially on labourers returning from the railway work and from the plantations. An aggrieved party has the usual difficulty in bringing a complaint to the proper quarter, as the *wali* through whom it must go is easily squared. The liberty allowed to the native police also often amounts to licence, and as a *wali* never dreams of reporting any policeman, it remains unchecked. If there were a regular system of district travelling many of these abuses would be bound to come to light, but, as noted elsewhere, the military officer very rarely travels, and, when he does, he has a large escort of military or police. He does not go into the villages and investigate things for himself, nor try to check cases of irregularities in the collection of the poll-tax; as it is all left in the hands of the chiefs, *walis*, or headmen, he only hears what the local *wali* chooses to tell him, and knows little or nothing of what is going on.

After this example of a military province the civil government which we found established at Tabora, the direct result of Herr Dernburg's visit, and only a year old, was a pleasant surprise. Prior to the change all except one of the officers were military men. Now, besides two officers and two sergeants in charge of 200 soldiers and police, there is an entirely separate civil administration. It consists of two or three holding magisterial rank with European clerks, a postmaster with one assistant, and the District Commissioner.

With the first department we had little to do, but it appeared to be in the hands of capable men doing their work in an effective and unostentatious manner, and fond of their life and of travelling.

The postmaster was civility itself, and transacted our postal telegraphic business expeditiously and without fuss.

The District Commissioner's department, though we have already touched upon it, deserves to be specially dealt with as presenting such a complete contrast to the old military system of administration.

It consists of the District Commissioner himself, with one European and one native clerk. His work is purely native, and, as he has a population of over 200,000 to deal with, it is obvious that his office is at present very much understaffed. In spite of the unwieldy size of his district, he had studied the customs and the languages of his people, takes an interest in them, and knows them well. When travelling he takes but two police with him, one to carry his rifle, the other to "boss up" his loads. His method of dealing direct with the natives, and their opportunities of free access to him, prevent the abuses that must arise in the system outlined earlier in this chapter. He had a genial but quiet and dignified way with the natives, which much impressed us. When meeting a group of them in the streets of Tabora he would exchange a friendly greeting with them in their own language—not in Ki-Swahili—and receive a courteous greeting in reply. A military officer, had we asked him some question about the local tribes, would probably have answered "Oh! they are just *Shenzis!*" and surprise would have been shown at our evincing any interest in them; whereas the District Commissioner knew, as soon as he saw them, to which tribe they belonged, and spoke to them as their chief and their friend. Being, as we had opportunities of learning, just, firm, and keen on his work, it follows that he is liked and respected by those over whom he rules; but almost singlehanded as he is, with a population of nearly a quarter of a million, he is naturally so overworked that he never has time to get to the ends of his district. This inadequate staffing will doubtless be remedied before the civil administration is much older. As it is, he is known to the natives as the *Shauri Bwana*, because so much of his time is taken up at Tabora in the hearing of the native cases.

The Tabora régime is not, probably, unique. The civil system has already been established elsewhere. At Mwanza, for instance, though we had not the same opportunities for judging, it would appear that the Germans are working there on the same sound lines, and carrying on an efficient administration in a manner that is at the same time fair to the natives and good for the country.

A feature which probably first impresses most Englishmen in German territory, just as its reverse impresses the German visitor to British African protectorates, is the inevitable fort, seen at every Government station, and which is conspicuous by its absence in places like Zomba, Livingstone, Fort Jameson, Entebbe and Nairobi, to say nothing of the smaller and more isolated stations.

This, and the practice of the majority of German officials of never travelling without a big armed escort, are proofs of their fear of native rebellion, to show which is bad for their prestige.

The most outstanding feature of the German administration is without doubt the thorough way in which they investigate and experiment on the possibilities of the territory. The way in which they have fostered and organised trade up country deserves every praise. The roads that have been made are excellent, and the manner in which they are pushing on railway construction calls for a good deal of admiration. Thoroughly and systematically conducted, it presents a rather marked contrast to the usual haphazard British methods. The somewhat rigid systems and unbreakable rules in force at their stations may strike an Englishman as a trifle pointless, but nevertheless in an administration of a country discipline and system are of the greatest importance, and probably some mean between the German rigidity and our own casual elasticity would produce the best results. We should study each other's methods, and choose which can be adopted with profit and which discarded. The Germans are openly and admittedly learning from us with our greater colonial experience. We, on the other hand, need not think that we have nothing to learn from them.

Taken all round the country was rather poorer, and the administration control over and relations with the natives more satisfactory, than we had anticipated. There is room for a good deal of improvement yet, as there is in all our own dependencies, but on the whole, considering how new colonial work is to the German nation, they have every reason to be proud of what they are doing in their East African Protectorate. When the forts are less prominent,[1] and more officials mix freely with the natives they govern, get to know them and understand

---

[1] "et errat longe, mea quidem sententia,
Qui imperium credat esse gravius, aut stabilius,
Vi quod fit, quam illud, quod amicitia adjungitur."
—TERENCE, *Adelphi*, i. 40.

them, their administration should prove a real success, but to achieve this they must abolish the military rule, take away from military officers only temporarily in the country and lacking all interests in it, all powers of governance, and leave it in the hands of men who like the country and intend to devote their lives to a colonial career.

We cannot close this chapter without expressing a hope that none of the officials of German East Africa will take offence, should they read these pages, at any of our comments and criticisms. Everywhere we received nothing but kindness at their hands, coupled with all the help that they could give us, and to them we owe much of the success and enjoyment of our journey through their territory.

VIII

THE VICTORIA NYANZA AND THE UGANDA RAILWAY

The S.S. *Sybil*—Our fellow-passengers—Bukoba—Baganda canoes—Bukakata—Entebbe—The raising of the game licence—Definite choice of itinerary—An impression of the beauties of Entebbe—The police sports—Kind reception and hospitality—The ill-fated bicycle—The Ripon Falls—Meeting with Dr. Milne—Port Florence—Scenery on the railway.

THE S.S. *Sybil*, which was our home for the next eight days, is the smaller of the passenger boats, which with one large cargo boat form the fleet, belonging to the Uganda Railway, that plies upon Lake Victoria Nyanza. The *Sybil*, her sister ship the *Winifred*, and the cargo boat *Nyanza* (about 800 tons), travel round the lake at fortnightly intervals, starting from Kisumu (or Port Florence), the head of the railway, and occupying about ten days in the journey. The *Sybil* and *Winifred* take it in turns to start in the southerly and westerly directions. The *Nyanza* travels round as required. All these call at all the German and British ports on the way. The *Clement Hill* leaves Kisumu in connection with the mail train, and travels direct to Entebbe, calling also on its return at the two northern ports of Kampala and Jinja.

The *Sybil*, like the rest of the fleet, is a smart, well-built, and well-appointed boat, just like an ocean liner *en miniature*, and fitted with every comfort and convenience for tropical travelling. She is run by a couple of white officers (Capt. Turnbull and his "chief," Mr. Vereker) and three European engineers, with a trained crew of British East African natives. We had been rather alarmed to learn from Messrs. Hansing before her arrival that every berth had been already booked, and that the whole ship was occupied by a party of professors and students, some seventeen in number, from German universities, who had arrived from Mombasa by the Uganda Railway and were doing a tour round the lake. However, the skipper made no objection to our proposal to camp on the deck, and comforted us by saying that there would be plenty of food, though he didn't know when we should get it.

Our fellow-passengers, a few of whom spoke English, were most amiable and interesting people, who were evidently determined to make the most of their brief visit to Africa. Some were entomologists, some botanists, some biologists, most of them photographers, and all keen observers of everything there was to be seen. Every visit to a port of call was made the opportunity for a collection of such specimens of the flora and fauna and local curios as the neighbourhood provided. At Mwanza these comprised two large basketfuls of crocodile's eggs, a bleached skull of the same reptile, armfuls of papyrus and other botanical treasures, and a fine bag of rock rabbits. The blowing of the first-named provided some of the party with an innocent occupation for the next few days, the pressing and preservation of the second kept others of them busy till Bukoba, while the energy of the sportsman responsible for the last was more than repaid by the appearance, on our first day out, of broiled hyrax upon the *carte du jour*. They had not yet learnt by experience that a conventional khaki kit, with gaiters, puttees, or top boots, is neither the most suitable nor the most comfortable garb for a pleasure trip on a lake steamer in the tropics, and we thought that they must have wished at times that they had adopted the ordinary type of clothing suited for European summer wear.

We had been allotted about half the promenade deck on the port side, and with our camp beds up against the engine room hatch, and our baggage stocked round us we felt no regret at being crowded out of the cabins. On waking after our first beautifully cool and refreshing night, we heartily congratulated ourselves on the opportunity of sleeping in the open air. Before sailing, two more " deck

At Bukoba, Victoria Nyanza, the "Sybil" and Baganda canoes.

Red, green-edged roads.

VICTORIA NYANZA—UGANDA RAILWAY

passengers" had joined the ship, and we left Mwanza numbering twenty-two. Anchor was weighed at a little after two o'clock on Wednesday afternoon, and steaming about nine knots we headed for Bukoba, the next German port on the west shore of the lake. Owing to a misadventure that had recently befallen another of the boats, they had given up travelling by night, and, five hours later, without altogether losing sight of land, we anchored in about thirty-two fathoms of water and in a perfect calm.

A very fine gramophone, the property of one of the passengers, afforded us a pleasant entertainment for an hour or two after dinner.

The ship started again at four o'clock next morning, and though we managed to sleep again after being wakened by the engines, we were eventually obliged to get out of bed a trifle earlier than we had had any intention of doing by the arrival of a deck-swabbing gang.

The glorious sunrise, however, which we were in consequence able to witness, went a long way towards compensating us for our broken slumbers.

After about six hours' steaming, sometimes completely out of sight of land, sometimes passing groups of extraordinarily green and fertile islands, we reached Bukoba. This, the last station before reaching the Uganda frontier, lies for the most part along the shore of a small semicircular bay perhaps three miles long. From the lake side it is distinctly picturesque, backed by cliffs of white rock picked out with vivid green that gave the landscape quite an English touch. The direction of the strata in the face of the cliffs had a curiously terracing effect in places. The more gradual slopes were clothed with rich vegetation, and with fine trees occasionally rising from between bare boulders. The grass was as green as in an English meadow, the consequence of a rainfall much more constant than in the southern parts of the territory.

We went ashore in the afternoon in the captain's gig, and on landing we found the streets and lower slopes thickly planted with avenues and copses of eucalyptus, cotton trees, and other tropical timber, all grown to a fine maturity. What surprised us as much as anything was the short, thick, green grass which, right down to the water's edge, confirmed the impression formed from a distance. Walking through one of the avenues we struck inland, passed through some fertile native and European gardens (where we came across a damsel wearing a good example of the short grass skirt which is the fashion among the Baziba natives of this locality), over a broad and full stream the existence of which we had not suspected, then by a road skirting the native village, where, in the elaborate compound of the chief's hut (locally known as the "Sultan's palace"), we heard and saw a somewhat advanced type of native band consisting largely of cow-horns, which was suggestive of a colossal hurdy-gurdy running "amok"; and so round and back through the market place to the wireless telegraphy station on the beach, which we found in a much more advanced state of construction than that at Mwanza. Then back along the front to the wharf, passing the "boma" square, at the top of which the Commandant was entertaining the German travellers, and the fort, which was less aggressively and more roughly and rustically built than any we had seen. After taking a few photographs in the waning light, we returned to the ship, passing, by the way, some exceptionally fine examples of the Baganda canoes, which are built of strips of bark sewn together and furnished with a false prow for breaking the force of the waves.

Our next stop was across the Uganda frontier, at Bukakata, formerly a Government station. This had been abandoned owing to the presence of Sleeping Sickness and *Glossina palpalis*, and a new post established twenty miles inland. The site is now only marked by a few storage sheds and a small landing-pier, but the place is still retained as a port for the embarkation of goods from the interior. We took on a quantity of cotton[1] for transmission to Kampala, where it was to be ginned, besides a

[1] This cotton was entirely native grown, the seed (Egyptian) having been imported and distributed gratis by the Uganda Government, when under the governorship of Mr. (now Sir) Hesketh Bell.

large number of bales of hides and skins. A considerable amount of ground nuts, rice, and hides had been taken on at Mwanza and Bukoba, and at first it looked as if the latter part of the Bukakata cargo would have to be left behind. Our camping space was a good deal restricted in consequence, but we gathered that we were rather fortunate to have any left at all, as on some of her voyages the *Sybil* at this point had her decks piled up to the awnings.

Anchoring once more on the way, we eventually reached Entebbe in the cool of the early hours of Saturday, October 1, after an exciting race with the s.s. *Nyanza*, arriving from the opposite direction, for the best berth alongside the pier.

Entebbe, the seat[1] of the Government of the Uganda Protectorate, is charmingly situated on a small promontory in the north-west corner of the lake, some twenty miles west of Mengo or Kampala, the ancient capital of the Baganda kings, and now the residence of Daudi, the youthful holder of the title.

Seen first from one side and then the other as we rounded the point of the headland on which it stands, it struck us as one of the most beautiful places we had seen.

We obtained some glorious views from the deck of the steamer of its houses, half hidden in park-like scenery, mingling all the colour of its tropical vegetation with the bright refreshing green of its lawns and avenues; the warm red of its roofs and of its winding roads in complete harmony with the colour scheme, giving promise of rare beauty, which on a closer view was more than justified. We went on shore at nine o'clock, and chartering a convenient rickshaw drove up to the town, which lies half a mile or so from the pier, calling first at the post-office to get our mails, which had been accumulating there for three months. Having secured our letters, and having arranged for the transfer of the bulkier articles to the steamer, we proceeded to the Government Offices to call upon the

---

[1] This is literally the meaning of the word *Entebbe* (or *Ntebe*), which is the Luganda for seat or chair.

Acting Chief Secretary, Mr. Alison Russell, whom one of us could claim as a school-fellow, and who was expecting us.

Up to this point we had been undecided as to the further stages of our itinerary. The news that we had received at Mwanza of the increase of the £50 sportsman's licence by an additional £30 for permission to shoot two elephants (£10 for the first, £20 for the second, the latter sum being recoverable in case of only one elephant being killed) had made us consider whether we would modify our original idea of going right through to Egypt *via* Gondokoro, and proceed instead by the Uganda Railway to Mombasa. It was with the greatest reluctance that we had considered the possible necessity of abandoning the north trip, and it was with considerable relief that we found, after talking with Mr. Russell, Mr. A. C. Knollys his assistant, and Colonel Wyndham the Governor's A.D.C., that we had, while still unconscious of having made up our minds, committed ourselves to going through. We had been looking forward to the elephant-hunting as one of the attractions of a trip through Uganda, but it was hardly going to be worth while taking out two licences at the exorbitant sum of £80 apiece, unless there was a fair prospect of securing exceptionally big tuskers. It was naturally at Entebbe that we made our first inquiries, and when we learnt not only that we might expect, with luck, to get perhaps an average of two eighty-pounders each, but also that, if we wished to give ourselves the best chance, we should try in the northern parts, on reaching which we should already be well on our way to Gondokoro, we came to the conclusion that, after all, there was no reason why we should depart from our original plans. We were soon engaged in fixing up details. This was a comparatively easy business, helped, as we were, by every official with whom we came in contact.

A few days would, of course, be required to make arrangements for the trip through Uganda, and we decided to employ the interval in seeing as much as we could of the East African Protectorate. We each of us had two or three old friends whom we hoped we might run across, and in any case a journey of two or three days on the Uganda Railway, with a stay of a few days here and there, afforded an opportunity of seeing the country which was not to be missed. We decided to go straight on to Kisumu by the *Sybil*, travel down the line as far as Nairobi, possibly breaking our journey for a short visit or two on the way, and come back by the train that would land us in Uganda again seventeen days later.

In an almost incredibly short time we had arranged to take most of our kit off the *Sybil* and stock it in the Customs shed, leave all but two of our Rhodesian natives at Entebbe under the protection of the District Commissioner, and to engage one of the Government motor waggons to take us and all our equipment as far as Mubendi on our return to Entebbe.

These points settled, we went back to the steamer to advise our staff as to our plans, and then returned for the second time to the town to lunch with Mr. Russell at his house. Driving in a rickshaw up the red, green-edged roads, we admired at every turn the beauties of the place, but the climax was reached when we arrived at our host's residence.

The house stands on a little cape with the blue and silver waters of the lake on three sides of the grounds, which, starting with a fine terrace in front of the broad verandah, consist of grassy lawns bright with many-coloured shrubs and gay flower beds, and shaded by magnificent trees. The approach lies through the two finest drives we have seen in Africa, one on either side, which but for their wealth of colour might have been in an old English park; and the porchway of the house and a large part of the roof is wreathed in the green and magenta of a superb bougainvillea. The position would make a poor place into a paradise, but the combination of this glorious garden and the unique situation form a sight that can never be forgotten. Whether the bright African sun is bringing out to the full the rich colours in the grounds, or whether the fitful gleams of the rising moon upon the silver waters of the lake are seen through the trees, it seems like a veritable fairyland. After lunching on the cool verandah with such a view around us, we felt a keen sense of regret at having to return to the boat to excavate our baggage, though it was modified by an invitation not only to return to dinner, but to make it our home on our return from Nairobi.

A couple of strenuous hours saw our superfluous kit and servants disposed of, and we returned once more to the town to witness the Police Sports, which were taking place in the presence of his Excellency the Acting Governor and Mrs. Tomkins, and of practically every man, woman, and child in Entebbe.

The show was excellently managed, and presented a gay and animated spectacle; the whole breathing a typically English atmosphere that was refreshing to us after several weeks in a protectorate which, though friendly, had been indisputably foreign. After an adjournment to the hospitable Club, and then another descent to the steamer to wash and dress, we returned yet again to the Chief Secretary's house, where an excellent dinner, followed by music, ended what will always be remembered by both of us as one of the most enjoyable, as it was one of the most strenuous days of our lives. It was just after midnight when we found ourselves once more on the deck of the *Sybil*, and turned in for a good night's rest. Sonorous murmurs from the lower deck told that our German friends had already yielded to the exhaustion of a day of systematic sight-seeing on shore.

If ever travellers had their paths made smooth for them we had—and we owe a debt of gratitude not easily expressed in words to every one at Entebbe who helped us. All that could be done in the capital itself and everything it was possible to arrange by telephone and letter—the motor journey, carriers at the end of it, guides, hunters, information as to elephants and food supplies, &c.—was done voluntarily, and with a readiness to help that could not be excelled.

The one discordant note in the harmony was sounded

by the ill-fated bicycle that had gone wrong near Abercorn. The new internal mechanism that had then been cabled for had arrived, but, although the number and specification of the bicycle had been quoted in the cable, the mechanism sent was of a different model, and would not fit the machine. The third engineer in the *Sybil* did what he could, but he had not the apparatus necessary for tackling case-hardened steel, and we were obliged to take the cycle and the parts to Nairobi in the hope of getting it fixed up there.

At five o'clock the following morning we steamed out of Entebbe Harbour and reached Kampala Port, which is connected by mono-rail with Kampala, at 8 A.M., but made only a very short halt. Our course lay through a beautiful part of the lake, studded with gorgeous and fertile little islands, and it is easy to imagine the chagrin of the inhabitants when the ravages of Sleeping Sickness necessitated their removal to inland spots free from *Glossina palpalis*. Threading our way through these ill-fated beauty-spots we reached Jinja in the afternoon, and went on shore at once to visit the Ripon Falls. It is at this point that the Nile leaves the Victoria Nyanza, and the cataracts (for they are little more) are one of the finest sights on the lake. To any one who expects to see real falls, such as the Victoria Falls in the Zambezi, or the Murchison Falls lower down the Nile, they would be, of course, a disappointment, but the sight of the great river pouring out of the lake cannot but impress even the least impressionable visitor; and we, who were about to follow the Nile to its mouth, lingered long at its birthplace, where some of the local residents were busy with rod and line catching a fish resembling a chub, which runs on an average to 5 or 6 lbs. and gives good sport. Walking back in the lurid light of a stormy sunset, a bush fire began to show up, winding its snaky path of flame along the face of the hills across the bay, and as darkness fell the flickering fire, lightening the outer darkness and reflected in the water below, added yet one more to the surfeit of spectacles that was becoming almost bewildering.

At Jinja, which is the starting-point of the Jinja-Kakindu Railway, the latest link in the Cape-to-Cairo line of communications, we took on board one or two passengers. One of these, Dr. Milne, the Principal Medical Officer of British East Africa, was destined to prove, thanks to his kindness and hospitality, which must be unequalled even in tropical Africa, one of the most notable factors in the success and enjoyment of our visit to the Protectorate. The morning on which we left Jinja we met him, as he shared the privilege allowed us by the chief officer of shaving in his cabin, and after breakfast we were soon engrossed in conversation with him about Sleeping Sickness, malaria, spirillum, and other tropical diseases, which were of interest to us as well as to him; and the fact that he knew several friends of ours in East Africa helped us to forget that we had met for the first time that day. We were sorry to learn that one of these friends, whom we had hoped to visit at Eldama Ravine, reputed to be the most beautiful station in the East Africa Protectorate, had been moved to a more northerly station near Lake Rudolph; but, as things turned out, it was perhaps all for the best, as in the limited time that our fast-ebbing leave allowed us, it is doubtful if our stay in this flourishing dependency could have been arranged in a more pleasant and instructive manner than that in which we spent it. Moreover, these sudden changes in our plans, and the readiness with which we adopted the kaleidoscopic alterations in our itinerary, added a peculiar charm to the journey that would have been entirely lacking had everything been cut and dried and in accordance with pre-conceived arrangements. It is not only advisable but necessary to map out a journey such as ours beforehand, but it is really no less important to be able to depart from one's plans at a moment's notice, as otherwise one loses half the charm of travel, and frets about the dislocation of the schedule.

Nightfall found us at Homa Bay and firmly aground in the muddy bottom of the lake. It was quite an hour before we got off, but it did not worry us in the least; we

RIPON FALLS.

VICTORIA NYANZA—UGANDA RAILWAY

had another sunset on which to feast our eyes, and there was no train to catch at Port Florence, for the boat was so late that the ordinary train had been missed quite comfortably, and, with such a full tale of passengers, a "special" was a foregone conclusion. At half-past two on the following afternoon our skipper brought us up in a masterly manner at the wharf of the terminus of the Uganda Railway, and we began to realise what a stroke of fortune it was for us to have met Dr. Milne. He promptly secured us a reserved compartment adjoining that engaged for himself and another member of the medical staff, and then took us for a stroll to the market-place, which affords one of the most striking contrasts between civilised and savage Africa that can be imagined. On the one side the well-built township, the railway station with its well-appointed trains, the wharf and jetties, alongside of which are berthed the fine lake steamers, and on the other, at a distance of only a few minutes' stroll, this market-place, where the unspoilt Wa-Kavirondo in a state of entire nudity sell and buy the necessities of life—for a people to whom clothes in any form are anathema needs but few luxuries. The two Rhodesian natives who were with us were more impressed by the unashamed nakedness of these people than by anything that they had seen up till then. At the end of our stroll we wended our way to the house of the Provincial Commissioner—to whom the doctor had introduced us—for tea, and spent an interesting hour with him discussing the conditions of service and of life prevalent in his country and in ours, after which we had a second tea with Captain Turnbull of the *Sybil* and his wife. A halt for billiards at the Club preceded a final dinner on the boat, immediately after which we boarded the train, and, sharing Dr. Milne's roomy compartment till ten o'clock, we returned to our own quarters and turned in, regretting that we had to miss some of the finest scenery on the line during the dark hours of night.

We awoke while passing through fine agricultural highlands, and at 6.30 passed the magnificent estate belonging to Lord Delamere, on which we saw wheat, maize, and black wattle, all flourishing in the fertile soil and fostered by the abundant rainfall and sunshine ; as well as many herds of half-bred cattle and sheep. The wild fauna were also conspicuous, the graceful Thompson's gazelle (" Tommies ") being the most numerous, though there were also plenty of zebra, Coke's hartebeeste, Grant's gazelle and ostrich, and once or twice we saw some jackals slinking across the plains. An excellent breakfast (at Rs. 1.50 a head) was served at Nakuru Station Hotel, and we got a good view of this pretty mountain lake, the utility of which is marred by the brackishness of its water. Between this point and Naivasha, where we lunched (at Rs.2 each), there was a good deal of similarity in the landscape, but it was all good to look upon, only unfortunately Lake Naivasha itself was largely obscured by clouds, which while adding considerable charm to the landscape, prevented us from getting a good view of the picturesque panorama.

After lunch the scenery changed as we passed through the great Rift Valley and on to Escarpment Station on the far side. We here encountered for the first time natives of the Kikuyu, Nandi, and Masai tribes, and were much struck by their graceful bearing and cheerful appearance. The former especially appeared to us the most accomplished loafers we had met, an impression that was fully confirmed latter on. On rising out of the Rift Valley we obtained but a poor view of this remarkable depression, but even when wreathed in mist and swept by rain-storms it has a grandeur that is all its own, and we could well realise that there are many who never tire of looking at this wonderful landmark on the world's surface, that changes with every phase of storm and sunshine. On these slopes, where the railway meanders along in a way that is a triumph of modern engineering, no gradient now being more than 1 in 50, there are magnificent juniper forests, which are, unfortunately, being rapidly destroyed for railway purposes, as coal is not employed on the line, as well as being cut for timber ; and no effort whatever is made

PORT FLORENCE CIVILIZATION. THE QUAY.

Photo by S. T. Lydford, Nairobi

THE UGANDA RAILWAY.
(Note the curve that the train has just passed.)

to replant them—a policy the folly of which will be realised when it is, perhaps, too late.

Twilight found us rattling along at a good pace as we descended towards the Athi Plains, and soon after darkness had overtaken us—the train was not lighted, but luckily Dr. Milne had two lanterns—we saw what we took to be a bush fire in the east. It was, however, no bush fire, but the glow in the sky caused by the electric lights that are such a prominent feature of that mushroom city of the plains—Nairobi.

IX

BRITISH EAST AFRICA

Nairobi—The derelict bicycle is repaired—Visits to dentist, photographer, and other business—Journey to Punda Milia by motor—View of Mount Kenia—Attack of fever—A sisal farm—Sport—Return to Nairobi—Hospitality of the residents—The race-meeting—Lottery night at the Club—Meeting with Wawemba soldiers—Return to Port Florence—Impressions of the country and of the natives—Prospects for intending settlers.

WHEN passing through the suburbs the extent of Nairobi by electric light seemed simply appalling, but this was owing to its straggling nature and not to its actual size—for the European population is but 800—and we were not surprised to learn that it boasts of no less than 42 miles of electrically lighted streets. At eight o'clock the train drew up at the platform, and we were glad that we had wired to the Norfolk Hotel to announce our arrival, as otherwise, being a special train, no conveyances could have been expected. Leaving our baggage in the hands of the hotel porter, we proceeded to walk up to the Norfolk, where we soon settled down, having secured accommodation for ourselves, our servants, and our dogs.

Nairobi is a settlement that has barely a decade behind it, and is placed on the edge of a bare, treeless flat, but relieved from what would have been the deadly monotony of the site, like its greater sister Johannesburg, by the eucalyptus trees that the first settlers fortunately introduced, and which have since been steadily added to. It has grown out of what was originally a railway depôt, and the choice of site was due to the fact that it was the last level stretch up the line, and therefore eminently suitable for concentration of railway stock; though why it should have been chosen as the capital of the country

NAIROBI STATION.

GOVERNMENT HOUSE. FRONT VIEW.

when more suitable and attractive sites are abundant at quite a short distance along the railway no one seems to know.

The railway at this point roughly bisects the town, at the south end of which lies the railway station and workshops from which Nairobi may be said to have sprung. East of the line lies all the commercial quarter, the Indian bazaar, and most of the Government offices, and also the picturesque native hospital, a little beyond which lies the Norfolk Hotel. The road in which these buildings stand is called Government Road, from the fact that it contains in it the offices in which the Provincial Commissioner, District Commissioner, and other important officials work. At first we refused to believe that the row of ancient tin hutches which composed these offices provides accommodation for any Government officials in a town that could show amongst others such fine stone buildings as the Treasury, Post Office, and Government House. Starting as one of the principal streets of the town, this road becomes a fine avenue at the point where these Government offices decorate it, and ends up as the Thika Road, in which form it is the principal artery of the fast-growing suburb of Parklands.

Between it and the railway, to which it is more or less parallel, lie the Episcopal, Catholic, and then incompleted Presbyterian churches, and the Post Office and Treasury, all of which show what can be achieved in the way of architecture with the local limestone. In the extreme south-east lies the race-course.

On the west of the line is the suburb known as The Hill. Here is Government House, an imposing building which is probably very comfortable though it is not in keeping with the rest of the town, the Club, the European hospital, and most of the officials' residences, as well as the Governor's office and the Secretariat. At the top of the hill lie the polo and cricket grounds, golf-links and tennis-courts, and near to them the barracks of two battalions of the King's African Rifles.

Among the residents of Nairobi were two friends whom we had been hoping to meet, Dr. Ross, the Government

Bacteriologist, a cousin of one of us (Cholmeley), and Mr. Montgomery, the veterinary pathologist, who had worked for some time in North-Eastern Rhodesia and was known to both of us. Thanks to them and to Dr. Milne we made the acquaintance of many of the officials and other residents in the town, and spent some pleasant and instructive hours in their company. To the last-named we owe, too, the rectification of the error of the cycle company which had sent out a mechanism that did not fit the disabled bicycle.

On his introduction, Mr. Gallagher, engineer in charge of the Uganda Railway workshops, not only showed us over the whole of his works, but allowed his staff to undertake the task of fixing up the machine. It took a day and a half to achieve, and at one time certainly was occupying no less than three separate lathes, so we had reason to be thankful that we were able to command the services of probably one of the most advanced workshops in Africa. It was equipped with plant for the manufacture of practically the whole rolling stock of the system, and was, at the time of our visit, engaged in the building of some passenger coaches of a new type.

Our two native servants, who were allowed to go over the works one afternoon, looked as if they were going to be permanently open-mouthed with wonder at the white man's magic, and one of them, Kasonde, who eventually travelled through to England, bore off a prize in the shape of a fragment of $\frac{3}{8}$-inch steel plate, which had been especially cut and punched for him, which he will probably treasure to the end of his days, unless he spends it on the purchase of a new wife.

Amongst other attractions of which Nairobi boasted was, we were told, an efficient dentist. Both of us were in need of this kind of torturer—one generally is after four or five years in Central Africa—and, though rather doubting the rumour, took the first opportunity of putting it to the test. It is only fair to say that our scepticism was not justified, and that our troubles were dealt with in a manner which afforded us considerable relief.

Suburban houses on "The Hill."

Nairobi Races. The Grand Stand.

The development of the photographs which we had been taking consistently since leaving Rhodesia was another bit of business that had to be attended to. Photography was not the main object of our journey, and, after thinking over the matter, we had decided at the beginning of it not to develop our photographs *en route*. As we only wanted the pictures as a record of what we saw, and remembering the fact that our camp would hardly ever be two nights in the same place, and that the quantity and temperature of the water would often render development a difficult process, we refrained from attempting it. We had exposed over two hundred films and about fifty plates, and were glad to seize the opportunity afforded by a visit to civilisation to get them developed. This was most satisfactorily done by the local photographer, who took a keen interest in the work, and handled our materials with the greatest care.

It was abundantly evident that time was not going to hang heavy on our hands at Nairobi. We had a little shopping to do and, as for the leisure we had left ourselves, people seemed laying themselves out to give us a good time. In no place in the world, perhaps, does a man find his kindred spirits so quickly, or meet with such a cheering welcome, as in the capitals and centres of our oversea dependencies, and it was a great delight to meet, not only with such a hospitable welcome, but with a willingness to answer our catechisms which was as great as our thirst for knowledge.

It was very tempting under the circumstances to remain at Nairobi, but with over a fortnight to fill in, we felt we must try and get an opportunity of seeing something of the country outside, and possibly of securing some of the common varieties of game that were new to us, such as Thompson's and Grant's gazelle, Jackson's and Coke's hartebeeste.

Hardly had we begun to think of ways and means when, by a stroke of luck, the thing arranged itself. Mr. A. B. Percival, the acting game ranger, had informed us that if, as was possible, we could obtain permission to shoot in one of the estates in the neighbourhood, the possession of a £1 licence would entitle us to hunt practically anything, except elephant and ostrich, for a period of one month.

We had hardly had time thoroughly to digest his information when we met Mr. Rutherfoord, of Swift and Rutherfoord, the owners of a sisal farm some 47 miles from Nairobi. He and his partner would be delighted, he said, if we would come out and spend a few days at the farm and shoot whatever we wanted. As it was but 6 miles from the main road to Fort Hall, to which place a regular motor-van service was running, the matter of transport presented no great difficulties. The return journey had to be arranged for, as the next visit of the van would be too late for us, but the engagement of a few carriers to take our baggage from the motor road to the farm was arranged by telegraph with the District Commissioner, Fort Hall, and the same gang would be able to carry it back to Nairobi at the end of our visit, while we ourselves came in on bicycles. Our beds we had left at Port Florence, the rest of our outfit and our weapons at Entebbe, but Dr. Milne once more came to our rescue and provided us with everything we wanted, in the way of a tent, beds, and camp and kitchen equipment, a rifle and some ammunition, for a few days in the bush. A second rifle and a couple of native hunters were obtained without difficulty from the Boma Trading Company, the same firm that was responsible for the Fort Hall motor service.

Everything so far had been going so smoothly, that we were not altogether surprised when at the last moment the whole programme was nearly wrecked by a fiasco. The van was to start at six o'clock on Sunday morning, 9th October; it was arranged that it should call for us at the Norfolk Hotel on its way out, and as we were given to understand that we were to be the only occupants, we got our baggage, bicycles, and boys ready, and proceeded to await it without anxiety.

It was with something approaching a shock, therefore,

that, a few minutes past six, we saw the thing thunder by like an inspired Juggernaut, only giving us time to notice that it seemed to be full to the brim of baggage and densely populated with passengers to boot. The hotel management realised the situation quicker than we did ; a nigger on a bicycle shot out of the front gate like a torpedo, and gave such effective chase that he succeeded in catching the elusive vehicle just as it was slowing up on a curve not more than half a mile away. It couldn't turn round, we heard (and wouldn't, doubtless, if it could), so we piled our baggage on to a couple of rickshaws and lost no time in picking up its spoor. When we came up with it, we found that our passing impressions had been more or less correct. There were two other European passengers on the front seat with the driver, and there were ten natives and Indians on the top of a pile of baggage that looked the absolute limit. It was not encouraging, but it was absurd to give it up.

The task of piling Pelion on Ossa was once more tackled, and, impossible as it seemed, baggage, boys, and bicycles were eventually stacked more or less precariously on the top, while we squeezed our dogs and ourselves in front, and with a jolt and a buzz we were on our way. The road went up and down, but was mostly quite good, our worst enemy being occasional patches of sand. We sometimes reached a speed of eighteen or twenty miles an hour, and, with a cargo of which the foundation was six 800-lb. casks of tar, we were weighing between seven and eight tons. On the whole it was more comfortable than it looked ; the extra weight, over powerful springs, made it fairly smooth going, and we glided over many a little gutter or bump as if it had not been there.

We crossed numerous small streams on well-built timber bridges, of which a few were in process of being replaced by stone structures. Some looked a bit flimsy and some were definitely labelled under repair, but all proved equal to us. The way in which we rattled over the latter in spite of notices bearing the legend " THIS BRIDGE IS CLOSED FOR REPAIRS," or " THIS BRIDGE IS DANGEROUS," the warning red flag being either ignored or calmly removed by a native who had dismounted for the purpose, was an undeniably stimulating experience.

After going 30 miles we reached the Thika River at about midday, and lunched at the Blue Post Hotel. This consists of one semi-open oblong house, containing dining-room and bar, and a few round bedroom huts, all very neatly built of grass and reeds. The camp stands between two fine streams, the Thika and the Chamia, which meet a few hundred yards behind it, and on each side of which is quite a notable waterfall, the two being hardly a quarter of a mile apart.

One of our fellow-passengers was a settler of some years' standing, who, besides owning an estate some way up the line, which he had successfully farmed for some years, had recently invested in a large area near Mile 35 on the Fort Hall Road, which he was devoting to the cultivation of wheat. He was optimistic and even enthusiastic about the prospects of British East Africa as a wheat-growing country, and already had a large acreage under the plough, which he was going to sow at the beginning of the next rains. He had an additional interest in the country in the shape of an ox transport service which was growing rapidly. His oxen, fortunately, were all immune from the comparatively new cattle disease of gastro-enteritis, which had been causing much anxiety and expense to both the settlers and the administration.

At a quarter to four, shortly after dropping him at his farm, the car drew up by some grass sheds, and we dismounted, leaving all our kit except our blankets and rifles in the care of the natives in charge, and cycled on by a fairly good waggon track to Punda Milia, a distance of 6 miles; passing the estate of Sisal Limited *en route* and getting a glimpse of Mount Kenia in the distance. One of us (Cholmeley) was suffering from an attack of fever which had been growing more acute as the day advanced, and which confined him to bed throughout our stay on the farm, so that the account of what was done there has to be in the first person singular. We were warmly welcomed by Messrs. Swift and Rutherfoord, and the latter kindly gave up his room and his bed to Cholmeley, who turned in immediately on our arrival. After dinner we chatted for an hour or two about the prospects in British East Africa and Rhodesia, the problems of native labour, and kindred matters, and went to bed at ten o'clock.

Cholmeley passed a fair night, but was not fit to leave his bed in the morning, so I went out alone for a shoot. The country was quite open, consisting of bare plains and hills, and the game was extraordinarily wild. The moment I appeared on the hillside every animal within sight began to bolt. After a little manœuvring I succeeded in approaching to within 200 yards of a *Kongoni* bull (Coke's hartebeeste), and my first shot found his heart. This was a promising beginning, and I hoped I might secure one or two good trophies, for I saw plenty of hartebeeste, zebra, and "Tommies" about, besides one herd of eland, and a solitary roan. Of these the only beasts that appealed to me were hartebeeste and "Tommies" as I had shot plenty of the others elsewhere. However, I had no luck, for I failed to get within shooting distance of a single "Tommy." I had a couple more shots at hartebeeste, but missed each time, and returned to the farm at about three o'clock. My tent was pitched by this time, and I moved into it.

Dr. Pritchard of Fort Hall, who was *en route* for Nairobi, arrived at sundown. We hoped that it would be possible to ride as far as the Thika River the next day to catch the motor-car there, but in the morning Cholmeley was still unable to travel, and Mr. Swift, who was cycling in to Nairobi, promised to have a mule cart sent to the Thererika Bridge to meet us on the following day in case he should be strong enough to cycle that far. I walked out to inspect the sisal crops, and was much impressed by the large area devoted to it, and by the splendid way the farm—which is the oldest sisal farm in the Protectorate—was managed. Sisal is grown for its fibre, and resembles a large pineapple plant. It is propagated by suckers and "bulbils," and the first leaves can be cut about the third year, and cutting continues for three more, after which it "poles," like the aloe to which it is akin, and then dies. A good deal of machinery is required for decorticating the fibre, but at the present price (about £28 per ton) it appears to be a profitable undertaking. When first planted, beans are grown between the plants as a catchcrop. The beans are issued to natives living on the farm, who plant them and sell the produce to the farmer at a fixed rate. The natives have the advantage of using ground already ploughed and prepared, while the farmer not only gets a good profit on the beans, which he exports, but their cultivation keeps the sisal ground free from weeds.

At three o'clock I went out to have another try for a "Tommy," but though I saw many, and spent three hours carefully stalking them, I failed to get within range. On my return I found Cholmeley's temperature had not dropped appreciably, and began to doubt if we should be able to leave the next day, but nevertheless I got up at half-past five, packed up the tent and my belongings, and then went round to look at him. I found his temperature had dropped to below normal, and he was very weak. However, he declared himself able to travel, and rose at seven o'clock. Accompanied by a young pupil from the farm who rode my bicycle, while Cholmeley rode a mule lent by our hosts, who from start to finish had been kindness personified, I mounted his bicycle, and we kept together, so that he could change to the machine when tired of the mule. It was a trying journey for a sick man, and though he rode the machine down hill and on the flat, and the mule up hill, he was utterly exhausted by the time we reached the "Blue Post." After a short halt there he felt strong enough to continue the ride to the Thererika Bridge, which we reached at three o'clock, though I doubt if he could have ridden any farther. Here we not only found the Cape cart and four mules awaiting us, but luckily Mr. Ward, the foreman in charge of the repair work, proved to be a true Samaritan, and though

BREAKING UP THE LAND ON AN EAST AFRICAN FARM.

TWO-YEAR SISAL AT PUNDA MILIA.

too busy to look after us in person, invited us to rest in his tent, where his boys brought us tea, whisky, food, cigars, and everything that they could think of, and, moreover, lent me a warm overcoat for Cholmeley, and a flask of whisky, in case Cholmeley should feel the cold when darkness fell. At four o'clock our two boys, who had followed on foot from the farm, turned up, and we started off in the cart for Nairobi. It was shockingly bumpy, and the road, which had seemed so good from the seat of a heavy motor van, appeared in a far less favourable light to travellers in a Cape cart in which the springs were worse than none. The mules, too, shied at all the white posts that marked the causeways through the papyrus swamps, but in spite of it all we reached Ali Khan's mews in three hours and forty minutes, a fairly creditable rate for 23 miles considering the conditions.

At the mews we found a telephone message informing us that we were to go straight to Dr. Milne's and not to the hotel, so transferring our weary bodies to a waggonette, we drove up to the Hill, where the Doctor made us very welcome, though I soon realised that he had had nothing to do with the invitation! However, he insisted on my staying and sharing his room, all his others being full, and Cholmeley went on to Dr. Ross's house. Not only did I get a bed, but I was provided with everything else, from a particularly welcome bath to some dress clothes, and taken out to dinner, finally returning to rest at midnight, very tired after 46 miles trying travelling, and being on the go for over nineteen hours. I rose fairly refreshed at seven, but in spite of repeated telephone messages failed to get any clothes up from the hotel till 8.45, and as those in which I had returned from Punda Milia were caked with the red dust of the road, owing to a sudden descent I had made over the mule's head, I had to remain undressed till nine o'clock, when I went over to see Cholmeley, who was none the worse for his exertions, and quite convalescent.

Having paid off our carriers, who arrived at ten, and having had our baggage removed from the hotel to Dr.

Milne's and Dr. Ross's respectively, we lunched at the latter's house, and then went down with him in his motor to the races.

Race meetings, of which there are three or four in the year, form a notable feature of life in East Africa, for as the meetings of various associations are frequently arranged to coincide, they afford a good opportunity for the settlers and others from outlying parts to meet; and, besides forming an agreeable interlude in their lives, enable them to discuss amongst themselves, and with the residents at the capital, the different problems that mutually concern them. These race meetings are held on Thursday and Saturday, the preceding nights being devoted to lotteries, while a fancy dress ball or other entertainment often follows on the Monday or Tuesday of the following week. On the course we found a fair number of people, including Sir Percy Girouard, the Governor, who had just returned from *safari*.[1] The King's African Rifles, whose band played a selection of popular airs between the races, had a refreshment tent and dispensed tea and drinks. Here we met E. S. Grogan,—a contemporary of Cholmeley's at Cambridge,—who has a big stake in the country, and were interested in talking to him not only about the prospects for settlers in the Protectorate, but also about such parts of our route as coincided with his own traverse of the continent in 1898.

Heavy rain fell just after the last event on the card, so we sheltered in the hospitable tent of the King's African Rifles till the storm subsided, when we motored back to the Club, prior to dining at Dr. Ross's.

The Club, which is the centre of Nairobi life, is a fairly good, though, for Nairobi, rather an old building; it contains reading and card-rooms, besides a fine billiard-room —with two tables—round the walls of which are several splendid shooting trophies, notably one of the few existing specimens of the rare bongo.

The following morning was chiefly occupied with

---

[1] The word is here used to signify "a journey." It is also used to denote the caravan, and everything pertaining to it.

shopping. Our train for Port Florence was to leave on Saturday at noon, and the last twenty-four hours in Nairobi were brimful of entertainment that was as variegated as it was amusing.

We began with a sumptuous lunch, with about a score of fellow-guests, on the airy verandah of the Norfolk Hotel. It had originally been Dr. Milne's lunch, but by the time we arrived the "hostship" had, by some mysterious process, got changed, and we found ourselves the guests of Dr. Chevalier, another member of the medical staff of the country.

Business of various kinds occupied the afternoon till four o'clock, when we drove up in Dr. Ross's car to pay our respects at Government House. We then enjoyed a short spin along the roads by the King's African Rifles Camp and the western suburbs of the town, during which we got a glimpse of the lower slopes of Kilimanjaro—90 miles away—and though the car achieved a puncture, we got back just before dark.

The evening at the Club which followed vividly reminded us that it was race-week, which means, *ipso facto*, that Nairobi is very much *en fête*. A sumptuous dinner at which, with a score of others, we were the guests of M. Argyropoulos, was followed by the serious and protracted business of selling by auction the sweepstake tickets for the next day's races.

This satisfactorily completed, a short interval for rest and refreshment was succeeded by a little wholesome exercise in the shape of billiard fives and billiard hockey. If any of our readers happens not to be acquainted with either of these pastimes, and is finding that the orthodox methods of using a billiard table begin to pall upon him, we recommend him to try billiard fives and billiard hockey, but preferably on some one else's table, and not at all if he suffers from tender hands.

If there were not actually several of our fellow-players wearing their hands in slings and their ribs in plaster of Paris next day, we wager that there were a few who wished they had been.

Supper shortly followed, a meal at which there were some three times as many guests as had sat down to dinner, and at which, we noted with admiration, the only beverage served was lager beer. Supper and a few complimentary speeches and replies disposed of, at about midnight the company adjourned to the card-room, which was also the music-room, and had been cleared for action, and enlivened the next hour or two with a variety, choral, and terpsichorean entertainment. Some of the items were premeditated, some were not. Amongst the former the most notable were the topical songs, written for the occasion, which dealt in a spirit of playful badinage with the political problems as well as the characteristics and achievements of the local celebrities.

Among the latter were the Cake-walks and Apache dancing, and a completely novel equestrian turn. Ordinary methods of applause were quite inadequate to express the enthusiastic appreciation of the dancers' efforts, and the audience were obliged to have recourse to beating a vigorous tattoo with their heels upon the doors, which resulted in the latter being rather short of panels at the end of the performance.

In the circus act, which was the last item on the card, the venue changed from the concert to the billiard-room. A horse, that had been found patiently awaiting his owner at the Club gates, was skilfully ridden by two of the company twice round the tables and up to the bar, at which it was prevailed upon to partake of a little much-needed refreshment in the shape of a small bottle of lager beer.

After a *consommé de partir* in the shape of a round of prairie oysters, we dispersed to our homes at 2.30 A.M., and had to be content with about three and a half hours' sleep, for we had an interesting engagement before breakfast.

One of the companies of the 2nd Battalion of the King's African Rifles (the so-called Yao Battalion) was, we found, entirely composed of Wawemba recruited from Northern Rhodesia. Three or four of them had learnt of our arrival and had already called upon us, and we had promised to pay their barracks a visit with the object of seeing them all on early parade. It was something of an effort, but we had to be up early in any case, to be sure of getting through various little jobs in time to catch our train, and we did not want to disappoint them or ourselves, with Kasonde and Kakakota, who, of course, had found numerous "brothers" and "fathers" amongst them. We reached the parade ground just in time to see them before they were marched off to fatigue duty at the race-course, and, after a few minutes' chat also visited their lines, where we were entrusted with numerous messages to their kindred in Rhodesia from their wives and families. They seemed without exception to be thoroughly enjoying their life and duties, and had nothing to complain of except that they had been left behind at headquarters while some of their comrades were out north on "active service" of sorts. The population of British East Africa, they said, was getting too tame, and there wasn't enough war to go round.

The rest of the morning was occupied in repacking, executing a few final commissions in the town, and conveying ourselves and our baggage to the station. Owing to the eccentric interpretation of his orders by a coolie employé of the local job-master, we as nearly as possible finished up by missing our train, but eventually, with the assistance of a heaven-sent rickshaw, just succeeded in catching it by the skin of our teeth. The station was crowded with travellers of all sorts and colours, who, like ourselves, seemed to be afflicted with the bustle and confusion of having left everything to the last minute, and but for the timely assistance of Drs. Milne and Ross, who had come to see us off, we—who by this time were probably more out of our element on a railway station than any of our fellow-passengers—should almost certainly have been left behind.

We had a few minutes awful anxiety at Naivasha. One of our two boys, who had left the train and trekked into the interior to buy food at a store somewhere near the horizon, was nowhere to be seen when we were on the point of moving off. The engine driver gave us a minute's grace and an extra long blast on his whistle, and to our relief the boy turned up in the nick of time, just when we were seriously debating whether it would be better simply to leave him behind or for one of us to stop behind too. He had not, unfortunately, realised that anything that we were travelling in, even if it were a train, did not necessarily belong to us, or was not entirely under our control.

The rest of the journey was uneventful, and we reached Port Florence at eight o'clock on the following morning. What we had seen of the Protectorate had far from disappointed us. Having heard, as one mostly does, of the principal feature of the country being its huge open plains, the valleys and escarpments and the tropical wealth of vegetation in the highlands came as a magnificent surprise. The highlands generally, though much greener and fresher, owing to the greater rainfall, are vividly reminiscent of the high veld of South Africa. The scenery through which the train passes before descending into the Rift Valley, with its glimpses of Nakuru and Naivasha Lakes, and the majestic profile of the extinct volcano and its sister peaks throwing their purple shadows across the plains below us, far surpassed anything we had seen in Africa, not excluding the Hex River mountain pass in the Cape Colony. That of the Mau escarpment, on the first stage after leaving the lake, is held to be quite as fine, though we unfortunately passed through it at night-time.

The plains, though dotted with game as far as the eye could see, and evidently magnificent both for stock-raising and agriculture, did not at first impress us much more than any other practically treeless country, but it was not long before we began to realise that, though presenting a marked contrast to the woodlands of Northern Rhodesia, it was a type of landscape that would, in a very short time, grow upon one more, perhaps, than a less open landscape ever can.

In considering the prospects of the territory it must be borne in mind that it falls into two parts that are quite distinct from each other; the low-lying tropical coast-belt, including the fertile province of Juba-land, which is mainly devoted to plantations, consisting of Ceara rubber, cocoanuts, and sea-island cotton with many catchcrops such as maize, sim-sim,[1] and ground nuts ; and the more temperate highlands, chiefly occupied by agricultural farmers and ranchers.

Our observations were confined to the latter, as we were unable to find time to travel farther than Nairobi, East of which point the plantation area begins. The highland farming community must, moreover, be divided into three groups, those who confine themselves entirely to agriculture, those combining agriculture with stock-raising, and finally those whose energies are restricted to the latter.

The principal crops cultivated by the first-named are sisal, wheat, and black wattle, the first of which we have already described. Wheat-growing has taken its place more recently as one of the principal industries of the Protectorate, and the view taken of its possibilities by those who have invested their money in it can only be described as enthusiastic. Such diseases as have so far attacked the crops have been mastered, and with a fertile soil and climatic conditions that permit of two crops a year, and an average yield of about 20 bushels per acre, the outlook is certainly most promising. We were informed that the area under wheat is increasing by leaps and bounds, and that on some estates as much as 700 acres can be seen in an unbroken block, so that its cultivation is already well beyond the experimental stage.

The cultivation of black wattle is also carried on on a large scale, and is reputed to be very profitable. The tree can be stripped of its bark in the sixth year, and catchcrops, especially maize, can be grown during the first three years. There is apparently some difficulty about drying it by natural means owing to the climate, which adds considerably to the cost of production, but this need not deter the farmer, as wattle has many uses besides its tanning bark—which is worth about £5 a ton on the farm.

[1] A plant which is grown for its oil.

The land along the railway and near the Nairobi–Fort Hall Road, where a branch line is in course of construction, is all taken up, but fresh tracts are continually being opened as the demand increases; the Uasin Gishu, Nandi Gishu, and part of the Kenia District are being rapidly occupied, and when these areas are taken up more will be opened for settlement. It is in these less accessible areas that stock-raising appeals to the settler, since livestock can go on its own legs to the railway instead of having to be carried. It must not be inferred, however, that there are no cattle ranches or sheep, pig, and ostrich runs on the line, as some of the most important stock farms—as, for instance, Lord Delamere's estates in the Njoro District, which are mixed, and E. S. Grogan's sheep runs at Naivasha—are right on the line. Owing to the different nature of the grazing required, cattle and sheep are not to be found in close proximity. Ostrich farming forms a not inconsiderable branch of stock-raising, and with careful selection is proving a profitable industry. Lucerne, which is useful for ostriches as for pigs (which also thrive on bananas), grows well, and can be cut four times a year.

We gathered that for a young man coming out to farm a capital of about £1200 is considered advisable, and that the wisest course is for him to start as a pupil on an established farm, taking up meanwhile a tract of land for which he pays, but on which he need not immediately fulfil the development conditions. Labour is fairly cheap, natives being obtainable at Rs.3 to Rs.5 a month, but the necessity for some kind of Labour Bureau seems to be beginning to be felt, as competition between the farmers, and more especially between the planters and the farmers, is driving up the rate of wages.

The Uganda Railway has at the present more exports than imports, and the former are increasing steadily, especially from Uganda and the lake, which results in a steady fall in the rates, even now quite moderate for most of the main crops. The German railway will probably hit the import trade hard, as we have pointed out elsewhere, but it will hardly touch the export traffic. There seems to be no doubt that the country has a bright future in store. Farms of 1000 acres purchased six to ten years ago for £66 (Rs.500) are now worth £1000, and land is steadily increasing in value, the usual price in a newly-opened district being now Rs.2 per acre. The class of settler is distinctly above the average, and the Protectorate seems to offer more to men of the public school type than Canada or Australia, where mere manual labour is principally in demand. No one afraid of work should go to British East Africa, but what is wanted most is essentially the man that can make a good overseer and manager: one who, while working himself, can manage and direct others, especially natives; and this is the very type that our public schools, whatever their faults may be, produce.

It is a well-favoured country, and amply justifies the construction of the great railway from the coast to the lake. With its plantation area near the coast, its enormous tracts in the highlands suitable for farming and ranching, and with Uganda producing cotton, cocoa, coffee, and rubber in the interior, the railway should within a reasonable time pay interest on its capital as well as paying its way. It has simply created the country as it now is, and has lifted it from savagery and slavery into a fairly well-populated agricultural dependency.

The natives were some of them the most interesting we had come across, and we should much have liked to know more of them. The Wa-Kavirondo we saw at Port Florence and Kibos, the next station to the Port, at which were a dozen or so of both sexes in their "national costume" of nothing at all, were principally striking for their lack of shyness or false modesty. Of the Masai we saw but few, but were impressed by their graceful carriage and independent air.

Of the Wakikuyu we saw most, in and round Nairobi itself. Their costume consists of a single blanket or skin hung from one shoulder across the body, and little else, except red paint and ornaments. One of the things that delighted us was the manner in which they stroll about

Nairobi without the slightest ambition to affect a more elaborate attire, and the fact that the Government has not attempted to coerce them. Their ear ornaments are remarkable, often five or six to each ear, and their red paint gives them quite an artistic appearance. As workers they are obviously a failure at present. The glimpse of their efforts as displayed at the Thererika Bridge only confirmed the impression made by each and every one of them as he strolled through the streets of the town. They are elegant and artistic loafers. Their women are an exception; they seem to do more carrying than the men; they carry their loads in the small of the back, supported by means of a skin band passed round the forehead, instead of balancing them on their heads. Occasionally a child is seen straddling its mother's back, and perched on the top of the load, and not infrequently the Wakikuyu women are seen at a run.

The towns also contain a large trading population of Indians, and coast natives of Arab extraction. They seemed to be a decent and law-abiding, if not particularly attractive community.

The country to which the Protectorate most invites comparison is undoubtedly Southern Rhodesia, which being also a mixed agricultural and ranching territory, and not many years older, has many points in common. Both offer sound prospects of success to much the same type of man, and, apart from differences in crops, such as the predominance of maize and tobacco in Southern Rhodesia and of wheat and sisal in East Africa, there is so much resemblance that the intending settler may well find it difficult to decide to which of the two countries he will entrust his fortune. The point that struck us most was that, whereas East Africa is perhaps more favoured by nature, Southern Rhodesia has a tremendous pull in having a large and ever-increasing market at its doors in the Union of South Africa, apart from the demands created by its own mining community.

The climate of the East Africa highlands is good, but perhaps a little more treacherous than that of its southern rival—a fact which is attributed not only to its proximity to the equator but also to its altitude, which has a trying effect on residents who stay too long without an occasional visit to a temperate zone.

We were exceedingly glad that we had had this brief glimpse of British East Africa, especially as the people whom we met in Uganda were rather inclined to speak disparagingly of it, and we might, had we not gone, have carried away with us a false impression, imagining, from the proximity of the source from which our information had come, that it was a correct one. This delightful fortnight showed us a great country in the making, a country where an enormous amount has been done in the brief space of ten years—*i.e.* since the railway rendered development possible—and as fine a monument to the colonising genius of the British race as one could wish to see. Under the guidance of its present Governor, Sir Percy Girouard, who appears to have made an equally favourable impression as a sound and able administrator on the non-official population as he has on the members of his administration, the steady progress of the territory, at any rate during the next few years, seems sufficiently assured.

X

RETURN TO ENTEBBE AND BY MOTOR TO MUBENDI

Across the lake on the s.s. *Clement Hill*—The Entebbe Customs—Botanical Gardens—Preparations for journey north—The golf-links—Further impressions of Entebbe—Departure by motor-waggon—Rain at Kampala—Wonders of the motor road—Its maintenance—"Mosquito Camp"—Our fellow-passengers and the prospects for settlers—Mishap to the car and other incidents—Mubendi—Meeting with the Acting Governor.

AT a little past eight we left the train and embarked on the s.s. *Clement Hill*, which was berthed alongside the quay, and found to our relief that breakfast was awaiting us. The *Clement Hill* is the newest and largest of the lake fleet, and corresponds more or less in size with the *Nyanza*. It is even better appointed than the *Sybil*, which we had found comfortable enough, though overcrowded. Our fellow-passengers this time consisted of a young engineer taking up an appointment in the Public Works Department of the Uganda Government; two intending planters; a couple of subalterns of the King's African Rifles stationed at Bombo, who were returning after a spirited effort to lift a cup at Nairobi with two reputed Somali ponies that had been disqualified as being nothing of the kind, and who were pretty cheerful considering the unfortunate and rather expensive fiasco that had awaited them; and, lastly, Mr. and Mrs. Akeley of America. This enterprising and interesting couple had already seen a good deal of Uganda and British East Africa, and on a previous visit had succeeded in securing specimens of most of the game in the two Protectorates, and were looking for more. Their object was the collection of specimens for a museum, and their intention to spend three or four months on a round trip in Uganda. Mrs. Akeley had just succeeded in bagging two lions under exceptionally trying circumstances and a big elephant near Mount Kenia, while her husband had had about as near an escape as he wanted from being annihilated by another one, which, he explained, had strongly objected to what must have appeared to be an attempt to extract its tusks while it was still alive.

In the early afternoon we had our attention called to an extraordinary phenomenon, which is, however, quite common on the lake. The chief engineer, on coming down late to lunch, told us that he had seen a waterspout quite close. As we had finished our meal we hurried up on deck to obtain a glimpse of it, and saw near the southern horizon a grey smoke-like column arising from the surface of the lake and expanding into what looked a cloud above. Thinking that this must be the engineer's waterspout we approached Captain Gray and Mr. Akeley, who were also intently observing it, and asked them if we were right in our conjecture.

"Waterspout!" said the skipper without a smile—"Flies."

"Flies?" we repeated, and thinking our legs were being pulled, turned to Mr. Akeley in the hope of eliciting a more sympathetic explanation.

"Quite true," he said. "Flies. Haven't you seen the lake fly before?"

"No," we retorted, "we haven't; we didn't know it flew."

Assuring us that neither he nor the skipper had any intention of deceiving us, he explained that he was really referring to the insect known as the "lake fly,"[1] and not to any spasmodic frivolity on the part of the waters of Victoria Nyanza. The apparent waterspout was nothing more or less than a huge cloud of myriads of tiny flies, which rise from the surface of the lake in such dense columns as sometimes to obscure the light of the sun like a pillar of smoke.

We anchored for the night in the open lake, and were

---

[1] Also found on Lake Nyasa and possibly on Tanganyika. Vide *George Grenfell and the Congo*, footnote to vol. i. p. 233.

not a little disturbed by the ship's mosquitoes. In the innocent remembrance of our cool untroubled nights on the deck of the *Sybil* we had forgotten to suspect their existence, and thought mosquito curtains a superfluity. We reached Entebbe shortly after noon on Monday the 17th of October, and after lunching on board proceeded to the business of rescuing our baggage from the sheds and passing it through the Customs. Owing to the lack of transport we were unable to remove the property we had left stored, but, after four hours, succeeded in getting nearly all the baggage we had with us through the office, which was at the end of the pier, and up to the town to Mr. Russell's house. To our surprise and relief the Goanese clerk whom we found in possession informed us that *nothing* was dutiable, and only guns and ammunition required permits of importation. As a matter of fact our joy was short-lived; *all* our property except personal clothing was, as we had indeed believed, subject to an import duty of 10 per cent. *ad valorem*. The babu's mistake was due to his failure to realise that we had come from anywhere else than the East Africa Protectorate. But by means of a roundabout communication from Mombasa on the subject of a revolver that we had had with us, and had left at Kisumu on proceeding to Nairobi, the Customs Department had been apprised of our existence, and on meeting the Customs officer later in the day we learnt the bitter truth.

A stroll in the Botanical Gardens and a short visit to the Club brought us to dinner-time, after which, as tired as if we had been doing a busy day's shopping, we retired early to bed.

The Botanical Gardens gave us a hint of the tremendous fertility of the Uganda Protectorate, of which we were to see such ample proof later on. The beds and groves of cultivated flowers and trees are interspersed with clumps and arbours of forest giants and patches of creeper-tangled jungle which, in their original unspoilt luxuriance, lend a convincing air of naturalness to the whole. Coffee, cocoa, rubber trees of various kinds, including the Funtumia which is indigenous to Uganda, are flourishing in their separate plantations, while beds and shelters are devoted to the nursing of cuttings and the propagation of seedlings or rare orchids and local floral treasures.

Partly for experiment, and partly with the double purpose of keeping down the vegetation and discouraging the *Glossina palpalis*, whose presence on the shores has so largely restricted the enjoyment of the lake at Entebbe, a large area has been planted with lemon grass, of which the tufts already measured some two feet by five or six in circumference.

We left by one of the main approaches to the Gardens, which was bordered by a double row of firs that were beautiful even for Entebbe, after passing a lawn that might have been lying in front of an old English home, well rolled for three hundred years.

Not much remained to complete our arrangements before starting north, but we had none too much time to spare.

The motor van that was taking us as far as Mubendi, about 130 miles, was to start at dawn on Thursday. Wednesday, they told us at one time, which would have meant an uncomfortable dislocation of plans, but it proved to be a false alarm.

Licences and permits had to be procured, a few more purchases made, photographs to be rescued from the local expert, Alidina Visram's cheque cashed, and arrangements if possible made by which we could cash up-country any others of the kind that might come our way in exchange for our ivory.

The second and third presented no great difficulties, the first revealed to us rather an amusing anomaly in the laws of the country, and the last-named nearly resulted in a painful fiasco.

The anomalous feature of the licence negotiations consisted in the necessity of paying the exorbitant sum of Rs.5 for a licence to kill birds, when for a trifle of £80 one had secured permission to kill two elephants and every other quadruped in the country except eland and a few other fauna that probably do not exist. We were able to appreciate the feelings of the sportsman who, having been similarly bled, returned to the office and humbly asked if any other payment would be required for permission to kill mosquitoes.

Alidina had scored off us—or rather we had allowed him to score off us by inadvertently accepting his draft on three days' sight. As the document was written in a combination of Ki-Swahili, Hindustani, and other unknown tongues there may have been some excuse for us, but at all events the net result was that the Entebbe branch obstinately refused to convert it into cash—except at 5 per cent. discount, which seemed rather irrelevant—until two days after we had left Entebbe. Argument with a pock-marked and oily Hindu who was not even manager at the local emporium was obviously futile, so with a few expressions of pained surprise, and of wonder that under the circumstances it would advance any worthy cause for him to gaze for three days at a dirty piece of paper ornamented with his Mwanza colleague's favourite hieroglyphics, we tried the National Bank of India, and were much relieved to find that the manager was willing to cash it without any elaborate delays. The arrangements for cash up-country seemed unlikely to result in any difficulty, and we felt solvent once more.

There still remained the task of excavating our baggage from the Customs sheds: but it was eventually accomplished with the assistance and co-operation of the Customs Officer, who added to his kindness by giving us the opportunity of judging the prosperity and progress of the country by an examination of the Customs returns for the past few years. One of our assorted packages of equipment, by the way, had been adopted by a honeymoon couple of rats during its sojourn in the shed, and the discovery was signalised by the funeral of fourteen promising youngsters.

After these exertions the situation indicated some form of recreation, and the evening was spent in a short but pleasant game of golf on a turf links, that seemed to us ridiculously good for Central Africa, but which we were assured were not nearly as good as those at Kampala.

Mr. Alison Russell and his Bougainvillea-covered porch.

The Uganda Government motor car on the road.

The latter had been laid out on a patch of land that, as little as four years ago, had been a mass of elephant grass (of which more anon), and now, after being first cleared, then lying under a sweet potato crop for a year, and then sown with grass, constituted a course that would not have been discreditable to a South England watering-place.

Our opponent was Mr. J. F. Cunningham, of the Secretariat, who had been one of the first comers to the country as a member of Sir Harry Johnston's staff. He also evinced a great interest in the ethnographical notes collected on our journey, as would be expected in one who has himself published a work on the customs and the history of the natives of Uganda. Wednesday was devoted to re-sorting and re-packing a few boxes, confirming motor-transport arrangements, a view of the Treasurer's strong-room full of elephant tusks, amongst which was a pair of over 150 lbs. weight each, lunching, golfing and leave-taking at the Club.

Our stay in Entebbe had been an interlude which we shall remember with as much pleasure as any section of our journey from its beginning to its end. Assistance and advice had been given as soon as asked with a readiness that it would be difficult to over-appreciate, and every one with whom we had come in contact, from our host downwards, had welcomed us with a cordiality that made us feel as if we were amongst old friends.

The gaiety of Nairobi in race-week, though entirely enjoyable, had been a trifle too exuberant to be taken in more than homœopathic doses, and it was with no small regret—except that we knew we wanted to be trekking again—that we had to tear ourselves away from the tranquil and recuperative atmosphere of Entebbe society and its Club.

The Government motor-lorry did not call for us till about nine o'clock after all, and it was nearly an hour more before we had stowed away ourselves and our baggage and were ready to make a start. Though we had it almost to ourselves, it was a considerably smaller vehicle than the Nairobi vans, weighing $1\frac{1}{2}$ tons empty, and capable of carrying 25 cwt. of baggage, besides four passengers and the driver.

Our impedimenta must have come to about 3000 lbs.; for a part of the journey there were two other passengers with a little baggage, and there were four or five native servants. However, it was all packed in and piled on somehow, though the top layers, mostly chairs, tents, tables, and buckets, which depended chiefly on a few stray ropes for their security, were to cause us a good deal of anxiety and tribulation before we had got very far. Our own staff still consisted of the two Rhodesian boys we had taken with us into British East Africa; those who had been left at Entebbe had been forwarded, as we had requested, by road, to await us at Mubendi.

The car only boasted engines of sixteen horse-power, but we had been making very fair headway along the excellent road between Entebbe and Kampala, when it suddenly dawned upon us that *all* our property had not been piled on; we had left our bicycles behind! Fortunately there is telephonic communication between Entebbe and Kampala, and though we were not going to pass through the latter place, a boy could probably be found on the outskirts who could be sent in with a message, and there was a good chance that either at Entebbe or Kampala a couple of natives could be found sufficiently accomplished to ride our machines out to Mubendi.

At two miles from the native capital an intelligent native was encountered who was willing to take a note in to the transport manager, and just at that moment the rain came down. It was the genuine tropical downpour, and though it lasted less than an hour, it was soon obvious, even before we had lost sight of the charred ruins of Namulembe Cathedral (destroyed by lightning three weeks before), that we should not, as we had hoped, be able to make the half-way resthouse to Mubendi that day.

The road all the way from Entebbe was really a remarkable bit of work. Broad enough nearly its whole length for two motor vans to pass abreast, it was edged by a wide margin, cleared of vegetation, which had been taken advantage of by the natives for the cultivation of sweet potatoes and similar crops. The highway itself was metalled, bridged, and culverted all the way. The bridges were of stout railway-sleeper timber on piers of cemented stone, and the culverts which crossed the road every few hundred yards were constructed of lumps of local rock firmly cemented together. Considering the number and substantial nature of these bridges and culverts, and the fact that it was metalled throughout, it is not surprising that a road for heavy motor traffic now carved through the densest of tropical jungles, now raised on solid causeways through spongy and yielding papyrus swamps, and often cut out of hillsides with a slope of forty-five degrees or more, was constructed at an initial cost of something like £150 per mile, and had recently been repaired at nearly a third of that sum.

The existence of this artery, and the fact that the traffic upon it is already remunerative, is in itself a proof of the country's natural resources and the enterprise with which they are being exploited.

The efficient maintenance of such a road is attended with difficulties which exist in but few other countries. It passes over a variety of soils and a variety of gradients, while the rapid growth of the rank vegetation, and the heavy rains which fall twice in the year, are factors that no amount of surface metalling or the most thorough drainage system will permanently withstand. Small grounds for wonder, then, that after the recent rains the soft clay soil on some of the jungle gradients should have absorbed the top dressing and proved almost more than our van, with its exceptionally heavy load and its rather inadequate power, was able to manage.

We had not, as a matter of fact, covered more than 44 miles when our driver warned us that we ought to camp where we were by the roadside if we wanted to get our tents pitched before dark. Recognising the soundness of his advice, we got to work with as little delay as possible.

It was hardly an ideal spot for camping under any circumstances, and in the absence of the usual gang of carriers to clear the undergrowth, pitch the tents, fetch firewood and water, and do a hundred other irksome but necessary little duties, we had about as tough a job as we could wish for.

Some forty yards from the road we found a spot which, if it had nothing else to recommend it, was clear of trees and comparatively level. With but one hoe there was no time to do more than just scuffle a couple of patches for our tents, while the rest of the grass, which was waist high and sopping wet, had to be brushed aside or trodden down as we came to it. The water supply was close at hand, for we were almost on the edge of a swamp, but firewood presented a real difficulty. Incredible as it may seem to those who know Rhodesia and such countries in Central and South Africa, where the drier atmosphere and the regular bush fires, not to mention the natives' tree-looping methods of cultivation, provide the traveller with an ample supply of fuel on every side, there simply was not a dead tree or stick anywhere to be found. The prospect was not brilliant, but with a few pieces of packing cases, a few logs of green wood, and some candle-ends we eventually managed a fire which, while it did not succeed in adding materially to the cheerfulness of the scene, proved just equal to the simple culinary operations that the occasion demanded. Our fellow-passengers, two brothers named Outram, had naturally been expecting to reach their destination, which was only about ten miles farther on, without halting *en route*, and were unprovided with tents or camping equipment. Fortunately they were able to make themselves fairly comfortable with our second tent, and our spare fly on which to lay their bedding, though, without a mosquito curtain, their night's rest could hardly have been described as undisturbed, nor indeed could ours : if this was a sample of an average night in Uganda, we did not feel very enthusiastic about it. As a matter of fact, though fortunately they were of the *culex* and not the *anopheles* family, the continuous, combined, and ferocious attacks of those mosquitoes from sunset till sunrise were unequalled by anything we had experienced before, or have suffered since, excepting perhaps in some of the Bangweulu swamps, and at Lado on New Year's Eve. To us the place will always be known as "mosquito camp"; and the fact that we were occasionally able to raise a mouthful from our plates to our lips without interruption was probably only due to the fact that we plentifully anointed ourselves from time to time from a bottle of lavender and citronella oil.

This is one of the most effective anti-mosquito mixtures that is made, and we recommend any one who is exposed to the attacks of the insects never to be without it. It is cheaper than pure lavender oil, which is itself very effective, and lasts quite as long. We constantly dabbed faces, hands, and ankles with it when seated or camped in insect-ridden spots, and a small four-ounce bottle, purchased in October, lasted us right through the remainder of our trip.

Though the afternoon's shower had soaked everything and sunset was followed by a drenching dew, we fortunately had no more rain during the night, and woke up feeling comparatively dry. It took some little time striking camp and re-loading our baggage, which had been removed from the van for the accommodation of the driver and his bed, and it was just eight o'clock before we got going again.

Our first halt was about ten miles on, at a turning up to a plantation belonging to Mr. Speke, a relative of the famous explorer, where we dropped the Messrs. Outram.

Our fellow-passengers were visiting the country with the object of finding some suitable land for planting purposes. They were much impressed by the vegetation and appearance of the Uganda soil: they were men who had done a variety of work in a variety of lands, including Canada, Australia, New Zealand, and Ceylon, and they maintained that the fertility of the last-named was not nearly so great as that of the country they had been passing through. The plan they were thinking of adopting, supposing suitable planting land in Uganda to

K

be available, was to take up a second plot in the highlands of the East Africa Protectorate, which they would also cultivate, and to which they could resort in turn as they needed a change. The idea seemed to be a good one. There must be plenty of suitable land in British East Africa within comparatively easy reach of the central parts of Uganda, by means of rail, lake, and motor, and experience shows that, though eminently suitable for the growing of valuable crops, the greater part of the latter country has a climate which does not admit of long-continued residence for Europeans.

The acquisition of land in Uganda proper (*i.e.* in the Buganda province of Uganda) is, however, a difficult matter. To begin with, there is extremely little land available, as the Government owns hardly any and the land held by the Baganda cannot be alienated. Of the small tracts which are available for plantations the Government has a few plots which it is prepared to lease to suitable settlers, but freehold is not granted, the best terms that a planter can obtain being a 99-year lease. Under these circumstances it is hardly to be wondered at that very few settlers have hitherto taken up land in this province.

Near Mitiana we passed close to the north end of the beautiful little Lake Isolt, which, though insignificant when compared with the Great Lakes, is quite a gem; and at mile 44 from Kampala, 66 from Entebbe, we had to stop again: this time to await the same erratic youngster who had delayed the train at Naivasha, and who had skipped off the back of the car to buy some bananas as we were crawling up a hill. By the time he had completed his purchase the incline was in our favour again, and we had been going at ten miles an hour for something over ten minutes before we discovered his loss. The invective with which he was naturally greeted seemed to have hurt his feelings, for in the evening he electrified us by asking for his pay and permission to return home. It had not occurred to him that about three tons of van and baggage could elude him so quickly, and was quite confident that he would have caught us up again in the evening—thirty-four miles farther on. Needless to say, he did not get his pay or his *congé*, though it took a little argument to convince him that the middle of Uganda was not the best place to try and score off us by sending in his resignation.

Five or six miles from our destination, a slight mishap—the only one that occurred during the journey—looked for a time as if it was going to prevent us reaching the second rest-house that night.

In avoiding an open culvert which was in course of construction or repair, we had to leave the metalled surface of the road and take to the soft ground at the side. After the recent rain there was naturally a risk that our heavily laden car would not get round without some difficulty, and, sure enough, we stuck when we had got just half-way. The engine made a noble effort, but the revolutions of the wheels made matters rather worse than better, as they only succeeded in digging themselves a deeper grave without in any way altering the position of the car. The mud was up to the axle-trees on the off-side, and we were beginning to think that it was going to be a case at any rate of unloading or perhaps of outspanning for the night. Eventually, however, after the chain had come off twice and had been as often replaced, after the chauffeur's admirable and habitual *sang-froid* had been entirely destroyed by his wallowing and burrowing operations under the car, when the road gang had been furiously digging and pulling for half-an-hour, we threw ourselves on to the rope and pulled her out. The dog Jock, as we discovered afterwards from the photograph, rendered valuable assistance by fixing his teeth in the loin-cloth of the end man on the rope. No further delays occurred, and we reached Chakakusenga bungalow at half-past three.

The bungalow consisted of a small two-roomed wood and iron building standing on piles some four and a half feet above the ground. Doors and windows were mosquito-proofed throughout, and it was furnished with a bed, blankets, tables, and chairs, a complete set of crockery and kitchen utensils, and—a visitors' book! There were kitchen and boys' huts at the back, and a resident native caretaker. For the use of the house and everything in it, a charge of Rs.2 per diem was made. Periodical inspections were made by officers of the Public Works Department. An embryo vegetable garden provided us with cabbages and tomatoes, eggs and milk were obtainable close at hand without any difficulty, and the night spent in these comfortable quarters was in pleasing contrast to that passed at " mosquito camp."

Starting again at eight o'clock next morning, our third and last day's stage was free from rain or long delays, but not without incident. The road was dry again and fairly firm; greater speed was generally possible, and we negotiated nearly all the hills and rises at the first attempt. But it was not long before we realised that this was no unmixed blessing. The driving was skilful, but the road, though wonderful, was not a Brooklands track, and as we swayed and jolted round bends and over switchbacks no known device could have kept our top layer of impedimenta permanently in its place or prevented the cargo from shifting forward and back.

The first thing to go was a camp-table, and as this had been poised on the top of the hood, its detachment had only been a matter of time. Fortunately the boys, who were wedged in some marvellous way between the roof and the cargo, noticed its flight, and it was rescued—the damage only two loose screws. Next, half a tent shot off from behind—why a boy didn't go off with it was a mystery—and then a bundle of bedding, but the staff were on the *qui vive* and nothing escaped unnoticed. In fact by this time they had more or less detected the weak spots in the structure, and were doing their best to keep it together by hanging on to the packages that looked most like sliding off. The packages were occasionally too much for them, but a warning shout from behind now and again reached us in time to stop the car and readjust the balance.

The last thing to elude them was a new bucket. As

we were taking a fresh kick-off to get up an unusually steep incline, it contrived to slip out sideways through a loose spot in the hood and fell in front of the back wheel. As it was no longer a bucket when it emerged, and we had no use for a coal scoop, we left it behind as a souvenir of our passage.

But the work of salvaging the gear that was falling off behind was a mere bagatelle beside the perilous situation of ourselves and our live stock in front. We were well below the upper strata, not sitting on it. The car was admirably impartial in both the direction and force of its kicks and jolts, and we soon learnt that whenever something happened astern it would be quickly followed by trouble forrard. But we had taken the precaution of stacking the larger and less erratic articles at our immediate backs, and though their displacement looked occasionally menacing, a push here and a pull there, when we stopped to find out the damage, seemed to be all that was required. Deluded we! Lulled into a false sense of security by a longish stretch of smooth road, and by lunch, one of us had lain at full length on the bench behind the driver, while the other sat comfortably smoking in the seat at his side; consoling ourselves with the reflection that things had settled down, and there would probably be no more eruptions. But a strange thing had apparently been taking place in the contents of that resourceful car. Instead of settling to the bottom, as is expected of all orthodox masses of objects of various sizes, the more mobile articles had in some mysterious way been gradually coming to the top. First a camera descended suddenly on to the nape of some one's neck, then a cartridge-magazine shot into the small of his back, and the climax seemed to have been reached when the larger of our two luncheon baskets violently deposited itself on to the waistband of the post-prandial sleeper. But it had not. Five minutes later, when we were all once more awake to the possibilities of the situation, though feeling philosophically resigned to our inability to anticipate them, a volcanic concussion and a sensation that the world was staggering to disruption over our heads, was followed by the piercing yells of one of the dogs from underneath the front seat. There had been a combined effort on the part of the cargo: everything had shifted about a foot, and the seat carried away from its bearings, and, with fourteen stone of living weight and half a hundredweight of camp equipment on the top of it, had settled down on the top of the unfortunate Jock, and was apparently flattening him on a small box on to which he had crawled to avoid the vibration that he and Nyunshi so heartily detested. As his howls died away into a pathetic whimper before we could extricate him, it looked as if he was done for; but five minutes later our strenuous exertions were rewarded with success, and he emerged, frightened, but not a whit the worse.

No further catastrophes occurred, and in less than an hour our suspense was at an end as we pulled up at the foot of Mubendi hill at half-past one on October the 22nd.

The last few miles had been up a tortuous incline, through a strikingly beautiful forest, affording an example of perhaps the finest bit of engineering on the whole of this remarkable road.

There was a suitable spot for our camp right where we halted. The four members of the staff, Chumamaboko the hunter, Saidi, Bakali, and Nkamba, had already arrived from Entebbe, and with them, curiously enough, two Northern Rhodesia boys, named Kamata and Yamba-yamba, who said they had been brought all the way up from the " Star of the Congo " near Elisabethville by two Europeans of sorts, and then incontinently abandoned at Entebbe, about a month before, on their employers leaving Uganda *via* Victoria Nyanza. We took them on as kitchen helps and bicycle runners—a chance of earning their repatriation which the poor beggars had hardly expected, and seemed to appreciate.

The District Commissioner was away, but a telephone message from Entebbe through the Provincial Commissioner, Kampala, had come through, and the Indian clerk had already secured about half the gang of carriers we needed. We pitched our camp right where we had drawn up, on a grass patch at the corner of the Toro road and the ascent to the Boma hill; the spacious porch of a cotton store of Hansing's just across the road afforded shelter for ourselves and our loads from the heavy rain which fell before our tents were up.

In the afternoon we learnt that the Acting Governor, Mr. Stanley Tomkins, with Mrs. Tomkins, who were on their way to Toro, were at the Boma, and heard from Dr. Owen, who was in attendance, that a message had arrived from Kampala to the effect that our bicycles were on the way. They arrived next morning more or less intact, ridden by two exhausted native youths from Kampala. As it was quite inconceivable that they could have travelled safely with the rest of our kit on the motor-van, things had turned out rather satisfactorily.

The motor-van left again for Kampala early the following morning partially loaded with bales of raw cotton purchased by Hansing's agent from the local natives, whom we had seen bringing a few bundles in for sale during the afternoon.

Sunday morning was devoted to the bringing of our accounts up to date and to the writing of our diaries, which we had been keeping day by day since we started.

The afternoon till five o'clock was spent at the Boma, whither Mr. Tomkins, in reply to a suggestion that we might come and pay our respects, had invited us to lunch. The simplicity and heartiness of our welcome by our host and hostess, as well as the opportunity of enjoying discussion and exchange of views on the problems and prospects of this country and our own, made the day one of the pleasantest we spent in a country where every one was pleasant.

The District Commissioner's house is substantially built, on a plan well suited to the climate, and in a magnificent position. Placed on the very summit of one of a group of more or less isolated hills it affords a glorious view of the country on all sides, particularly in the northerly and westerly directions and towards

Ruwenzori. From the point of view of convenience its position is not perhaps so ideal. We ascended to it by a bridle-path cut more or less directly in the face of the hill. The distance from the foot was a mile and a half, and took us forty-five minutes. The descent—on bicycles which we had had pushed up by boys—by the carriage-road of two miles and a half took us twelve minutes, with both brakes hard on all the way.

The following morning nearly our full tale of porters had been procured, but as we did not want to start at all short-handed, we decided to give the balance another day and ourselves an opportunity of completing preparations.

A few punctures had to be mended, and a nearly worn-out tyre replaced; our loads had mostly been re-sorted the day before, but could do with a little more readjustment, and the remainder of our leisure was devoted to the examination and arrangement of the photographs that we had had printed in Entebbe and Nairobi.

We engaged here an amiable and intelligent-looking Munyoro native named Musa, who had been, in a previous existence, a bricklayer and, subsequently, apparently a rather reliable gun-bearer. As his testimonials from his last employers (who, he declared, had each shot two colossal elephants under his guidance) told how he had stood his ground in a tight corner when their professional hunters had sought safety, we felt rather inclined to give him a trial. And, as a matter of fact, he did, later, behave in exactly the same way with us in precisely identical circumstances.

Before nightfall our gang of carriers was complete and everything was ready for a start next morning. The local *Mwami* or chief, who had produced them, carefully expounded to them the period and terms of their engagement with us, and the deference with which they listened to his explanation was a striking proof of the standing of the chiefs among their people in Uganda. Those who were going with us were mostly Baganda, and the

THE FINEST BIT OF ENGINEERING ON THE ROAD.

MRS. TOMKINS.   DR. OWEN.
MR. STANLEY TOMKINS, AG. GOVERNOR OF UGANDA.

conditions were that they should accompany us for a couple of months, more or less, while shooting, and eventually get paid off wherever we happened to have got to—probably Butiaba. The extent to which they adhered to the bargain will be seen later.

The boy Kasonde had an unpleasant experience in the evening, which might have had serious consequences. While pounding some lumps of calcium carbide for an acetylene lamp, a small piece of it flew into his eye. He started rolling about on the ground, evidently in acute pain. Considering its properties it was rather a problem as to how to deal with it. Chumamaboko, though of course ignorant of the exact situation, showed great resource and presence of mind, and probably did the best thing possible by promptly seizing him and sucking the affected optic. Probably only a speck had reached it, for in about half-an-hour, after the insertion of a few drops of sweet oil, the victim had completely recovered.

XI

MUBENDI TO HOIMA

Our new carriers—A chief's house and garden—The civilisation of the Baganda—System of feeding carriers—Rate of pay—Agricultural development—The cotton industry—A native market—Bukumi mission—Elephant grass—Our camp—Crossing a swamp—Hoima—Ivory poaching in the Congo—A Nubian wedding at the military camp—Marriage laws of the Banyoro—Land settlement and communications in the Bunyoro province—Missions at Hoima—Start for Bugoma.

AN early rise, our last breakfast at Mubendi, and we settled down to the work of allotting our loads to our new carriers. Our incursion into civilisation, the division of our kit necessitated by it, and the purchase of new stores had disorganised matters a little, and it was a quarter past ten before we moved out on the trail again, though our new carriers were very orderly and amenable, and everything went as smoothly as possible. We started on this stage with a caravan of sixty-four porters, counting the two Wawemba waifs who were written on as bicycle boys, and two more for carrying chairs, besides the newly engaged Musa and our own Rhodesian staff of six, making a total of seventy-one.

Our route to begin with lay down the Kampala road, along which we cycled, side by side for the first time since our ride from Abercorn to Kawimbe. After a couple of miles we turned off sharp to the north on an excellent carriers' track some ten to twelve feet broad, which had a good surface for cycling and was particularly well embanked in the swamps. The road was hilly and often made it necessary to dismount, but these intervals of walking were not too frequent, and only provided a welcome change of exercise. The soil on either side was very

MUBENDI TO HOIMA

fertile and the vegetation rank and dense; fresh buffalo spoor attracted our attention a mile or two out, but a country more hopeless for this particular branch of hunting it would be hard to find, and we went on without investigating its possibilities.

After a couple of hours we came to a group of villages under the local district chief, Yekula. His own dwelling was a fine two-storied building placed in well-arranged gardens containing cotton, coffee, and other tropical products, all in a flourishing condition and surrounded by an elaborate fence of plaited reeds. Everything was well laid out, and looked more like the abode of a European than of an African native, though, as we were to see in the course of our wanderings, it was nothing out of the way for a Muganda chief. The camping-ground was a little farther on, and hard by some of the local Baganda were engaged in a fierce argument as to the measurements of a bean-field, an incident that amused and interested us, accustomed as we were to none but the most haphazard allotment of gardens.

Even at this early stage we were much impressed by the Baganda, who show an advanced stage of development remarkable in a Bantu people ; and we continually met fresh examples confirming the impression. They earn large sums of money by the cultivation and sale of cotton, coffee, and other crops, and appear not only to know the value of everything, but to realise, as few African natives do, that an article is worth more when it has been transported for some distance than it is at the place of origin. The feeding of carriers is simplicity itself. Each man receives an allowance of two cents (roughly a third of a penny) a day; and, on arrival at a camp, the traveller sends a message to the local chief informing him how many men he has to feed, in response to which the chief collects the requisite number of bundles of food, and brings them round at about sunset. These bundles contain bananas—which form the staple food of the country—sweet potatoes or beans, attached to which are smaller packets containing herbs, which serve as a side-dish.

Unless the order has been given too late, the food is generally brought ready cooked, which saves the carriers from being embarrassed with additional weight in the shape of cook-pots. The average bundles are worth one cent (a sixth of a penny) each, and as one usually contains sufficient food for one day, the carriers can often save half of their food allowance.

The rate of pay in Uganda is reckoned everywhere at Rs.3.60 (4s. 8½d.) a month, inclusive of the food allowance (60 cents). This is as low as anywhere else in Africa; similar work in North-Eastern Rhodesia, where labour is also cheap, costs 5s. 2d. a month, of which 1s. 2d. is the food allowance.

At Mubendi it was the local chief's "secretary" who produced our carriers, with a complete list of their names, districts, and chiefs, explaining to us to which of the latter we should complain in each case if one deserted—a good example of the way in which the administrative organisation of the Baganda, beginning with a king, ministry, and parliament, reaches and pervades the lower grades and is felt in daily relations with the people.

Next to the general organisation the most impressive feature is the agricultural development of this tribe, which is far more advanced than that of any natives we encountered in other parts. Nevertheless, a country like Uganda, which is probably equal to any country in the world for the growth of tropical products such as rubber, coffee, cocoa, and sugar, is really largely wasted even with a fairly dense population possessing exceptional energy and intelligence; for though they make much, if not the utmost possible, of such land as they cultivate, there remain large areas eminently suitable for plantations which are at present entirely untouched, and produce nothing but elephant grass and other rank vegetation. No one would wish to hustle a people who, like the Baganda, present a probably unique opportunity for the growth of an African State, but it is a thousand pities that something cannot be done with the large areas that they themselves

Fencing Yekula's garden.

Allotting our loads to carriers at Mubendi.

are unable to develop. The natives, for instance, might be required to show a certain degree of development or improvement within a certain period in the land over which they hold rights, failing which their proprietorship should lapse—a remedy which we gathered had long since been suggested, but for some reason has not been carried into effect. Another point that suggests itself is the possible risk attending the now flourishing cotton industry. The amount of cotton grown in and exported from the Protectorate is increasing annually by leaps and bounds. It is all grown by the natives and sold by them to European and Indian traders. The selling price of the raw cotton is not fixed, as competition has proved this to be impracticable, and so long as prices keep up this will not matter; but unless the Baganda are even more remarkable than they appear to be, a sudden fall in price might deal a serious blow to, if it did not actually destroy, this flourishing industry; for a native who has grown accustomed to a certain high scale is not only apt to be discouraged at a drop of, say, 25 per cent. in his earnings, but is liable to suspect that it is but the prelude to a further one, and, regarding it as no longer worth his while, he may decline to continue growing cotton.

The ordinary laws of supply and demand do not apply to the industry of the Central African native. As a general rule he wants no money—or very little. Among the Baganda chiefs there are certainly many who enjoy a regular income and have got used to spending it, but these derive it from other sources. If such a fall in the market value of the cotton should occur it may prove necessary to guarantee some minimum price in the lean years rather than risk the principal source of wealth in the Protectorate.

After cycling for an hour and forty minutes on the following day we came to a good native market under some shady trees, where we found natives selling bananas, sweet potatoes, kaffir corn, sugar-cane, tobacco, salt, lentils, meat, rope, mats, and bark-cloth. Of the last-named we purchased a large piece—chiefly for re-covering our water-bottles—for 85 cents (1s. 1d.), our only other purchase being a pint of lentils for 8 cents (a trifle over 1d). Just after leaving this wayside market a bad puncture delayed us for a quarter of an hour, but before very long—after two hours twenty-five minutes nett cycling from the start—we reached a place which Musa told us was our camp. This annoyed us somewhat, as, though we had been warned not to expect too much from Uganda carriers, thirteen miles easy going seemed a trifle too short. However, we accepted the situation for once, and decided to stop.

It certainly was a comfortable enough camp, with two open-walled shelters, kitchen hut and boys' quarters, in a large cleared space, in the centre of which stood a roomy and well-built wattle and daub building, which we were informed was the court-house of the local chief, whose name was Eloma. It had a large open doorway in the front, two more at the side, two or three smaller compartments, while the principal chamber was furnished with a daïs for the "judge's" chair.

Eloma paid a call upon us shortly after our arrival, bringing his own chair, on which, after a greeting and a murmured request which seemed to mean, "I will sit down if I may," he took his seat.

He was a most courteous and intelligent old gentleman, and after a few minutes' conversation, in which he told us, in reply to inquiries, that there were elephants two days ahead of us, he rose and took his leave as gracefully as he had introduced himself. The courtesy and friendliness of natives of all classes was rather striking. All whom we encountered or passed on the road greeted us cordially and respectfully, generally bowing and bending the head, and at the same time removing the fez cap that is generally worn. We saw some pine-apples in the native gardens, and passed some wild raspberry bushes, on which, however, the fruit had not yet formed. The country was undulating with granite kopjes in the hillsides and very long grass even on the summits of the hills. The carriers

BUKUMI MISSION.

THE DWELLING-HOUSE, BUKUMI.

had mostly been using an old road which was more direct though much more of a switchback than the new one, while we used the latter for the sake of its easier gradients, which we could generally manage without dismounting.

The next morning, after an hour and ten minutes alternately cycling and walking, we reached Bukumi Mission, a post of the French Fathers, the existence of which was a surprise to us. The buildings, which were erected in 1904, are of sun-dried bricks, with thatched roofs, and excellent of their kind. With additional excuse of a fresh puncture we called upon the Pères, and found ourselves welcomed with great cordiality by the Superior, Père Tomaselli Santo, a missionary of twelve years' residence in Uganda who had been at Bukumi when it was besieged during the rebellion. This post is the centre of a large district with 7000 baptized natives controlled by a staff of four "Fathers." We received welcome assistance in the shape of an itinerary as far as Hoima, and an equally welcome gift in the shape of a supply of cabbages, carrots, turnips, and beetroot. An hour after leaving the mission we found all our carriers settled down for the day at the next camping-place, but we came to the conclusion that it was time to assert ourselves, and informed them in as simple and direct a manner as possible that we were only going to halt for lunch and intended camping at Kauwa, the place indicated on Père Santo's itinerary. They had already unhitched their loads and were making themselves comfortable for the rest of the day, so our announcement was received without much enthusiasm. However, they obeyed, and with but little demur, and in spite of our halt at the mission and again for lunch, we reached camp by three o'clock, and all the loads were in before four: nor were any complaints made at the length of the twenty-one mile trek.

The next day we camped at Akanasi, seventeen miles on. For some two miles before reaching it, the road was plentifully pitted with hyena and lion spoor, some of it quite fresh, and we wondered if we were going to have a chance of bagging anything. As a matter of fact, lions did visit us, and the uneasiness and excitement of the dogs, who were barking and making occasional rushes at the long grass at the side of the camping-ground between nine and ten o'clock, probably meant that they were lurking close at hand. However, they did not reveal themselves, and it was only in the morning that we learnt from the natives that during the night they had been heard grunting somewhere a little way down the road, and that their fresh spoor showed them to have come right into the camp and within a few yards of our tents. Chuma said there had been several of them, but he was probably more impressed by the variety of their tones than by the plentifulness of their tracks. We protested that the boys might have called us when the beasts were obviously pretty close, but Chuma seemed to think that that was the very last thing to have done.

It was at this camp that we first had an example of the ease and rapidity with which our carriers erected grass shelters for themselves, without the aid of any but the slenderest sticks, and sometimes with none at all. With very little timber close at hand they had learnt to do without it, and in many cases made their little huts entirely of grass, framework as well as thatch. The grass so used is, of course, the "elephant grass" which grows to a height of twenty feet and more, and boasts a reed-like stalk on which it is quite possible to bark the shins. In some cases the tall stalks on the outer edge of a thick clump of this grass are simply pulled together and tied at the top, so forming a framework of walls and roof over which the thinner grass is laid to form side-screens and roof. In other cases the stalks are collected and driven into the ground and utilised as before. Those shelters would spring up round the camp in a marvellously short space of time. Our camp itself was usually formed by placing our tents more or less facing each other; one of them was furnished with an extension in the shape of an extra fly which served at times as a dining-room, and in which most of our spare loads were stacked. Chairs and tables would be, as a rule, in the "*banda*"—the reed-and-grass shelter which was an almost invariable feature of the camps and chiefs' compounds in Uganda—while our tents were left as empty as possible of everything except a bed and a small table, boxes containing clothes and immediate necessities, firearms and cameras. Close to the tents and the servants' shelters or huts was erected a small bucksail which served as a kitchen, the heavy rains often making it impossible to get a temporary one built where there was nothing already in existence.

Between our two tents or, if the wind was unfavourable, a little to one side a large fire was lit, and was supposed to be kept burning. If, as occasionally happened, every one went to sleep, it went out, and sometimes, *e.g.* in German East Africa when there was a dearth of firewood, we had to do without it altogether. Each carrier had to contribute his share of fuel, by making one or sometimes two journeys into the bush and returning with a load of sticks or logs. It would sometimes happen that, feeling a little lazy, they would shirk the duty and retire after bringing a dozen logs or so. This was easily remedied by the simple course of waiting till they had settled down for the night, each group with its own fire and a good stock of firewood, and then going round with one or two of the staff and a "munyampala" or so—who thoroughly enjoyed the job—and transferring their whole supply to our pile. We had no need, as a rule, to do it more than once with the same gang of carriers. The camp fire is an item of no small importance. Besides affording quite frequently needed warmth—especially after a day's elephant hunting in the rain—and a useful meed of protection at night, some of the pleasantest hours of the day are those spent lolling in an easy-chair in its comforting blaze either just before dinner or for an hour or so ere turning in for the night.

With our own Rhodesian staff as a nucleus, and the headmen engaged at different times, such as Musa, who was with us at this stage, the carriers very soon fell into the way of arranging things according to our ideas, and did their work in the smooth and automatic way which is so conducive to camp comfort.

The day before reaching Hoima we had to cross a bad swamp early in the morning. It was formed by a tributary of the Kavu River, which at this point takes a sharp bend, and was about a third of a mile across, and much too deep to ford. There were no canoes, but we and our loads were ferried across on rafts made of papyrus stalks. These are slow, heavy, and clumsy craft, but they have the advantage of being comparatively dry and safe, and practically non-capsizable, besides accommodating many more loads than the average canoe. The crossing occupied nearly three hours, but the beauty of the rising sun dispelling the early morning mist, and the cunning with which one of the natives ferried us across, helped to modify the tedium of delay. This unfortunate old gentleman had, besides minor facial mutilations, suffered amputation of both hands at the wrist—presumably a punishment by his chief for some trivial offence in his almost forgotten youth—and the way in which he wielded his punt-pole with his skinny arm stumps, mainly by gripping it in his elbow-joint, was a thing to admire and remember.

We heard hippo grunting somewhere in the swamp, but they remained hidden. The elephants of which Eloma had told us did not come to anything. There had evidently been plenty of them crossing and recrossing the road, sometimes within a few hours of our passing, but as the herd apparently consisted of nothing but cows, calves, and small bulls, we wasted no time in following them. Of smaller game we saw no trace whatever.

Hoima, the administrative centre of the Bunyoro province, we reached at half-past nine on the 30th of October. It is well situated on high ground, with hills on three sides, and on the fourth, to the west, can be seen the mountains of the Belgian Congo, on the far side of the Albert Nyanza, which is not itself visible, as it lies too low. We went up to call on the District Commissioner, Mr. T. Grant, who had been advised of our journey by our

MUBENDI TO HOIMA

friends at Entebbe. He extended a cordial welcome, bade us pitch our tents close to his house, and invited us to take our meals with him during our stay. More than this, he at once set about making inquiries as to elephants, and wrote to the Assistant District Commissioner at Masindi asking him to do the same.

Without a map before them the majority of readers probably do not realise the enormous length of the eastern border of the Belgian Congo.

Beginning as it does on the west of Northern Rhodesia far south of the points from which we had started, it was with something akin to a thrill at its immensity that we found ourselves still travelling alongside of it in the Hoima district of Bunyoro in Central Uganda; even then we had not reached the end of it, as for more than sixty miles farther it is still the neighbour of the Protectorate, and then inclining west lies on the borders of the Lado province of the Soudan for nearly another two hundred miles.

Its mere hugeness may supply a reason, though not an adequate one, for the difficulty of effectively administering the territory from end to end. That considerable portions of it, nominally under control, are still hardly administered at all is a matter of common knowledge, and it now made our mouths water, now filled us with shame to listen to the tales that were told us of the opportunities that lay under our very noses, as it were, for an enterprising elephant hunter untroubled with too scrupulous a sense of the fitness of taking advantage of the weakness or apathy of a neighbouring nation. There seemed, in fact, to be little if any difference between the conditions obtaining in the Congo territory just west of Albert Nyanza and those in the Lado Enclave after the lapse of its tenancy on the death of King Leopold and before its incorporation in Soudanese territory.

It was a happy hunting-ground for all and sundry who cared to try their luck and take their risks. Risks there were, of course; while some had made small fortunes, others had come out with less than what they had taken in. One successful filibuster had within the last twelve months obtained some two and a half tons of valuable ivory. Another who, after securing nearly as good a prize, made the inexcusable mistake of being caught by and compelled to disgorge his ivory and his battery to the Belgian authorities, returned to the British territory, borrowed a cheap rifle, and within three days of his re-entry into the Congo had made good his losses with a bag of seventeen big bull elephants. The victim in this instance must either have shown a lamentable want of tact or been unfortunate in underrating the calibre of the dignitary whom he met, for there seems to be evidence that in other cases a very little well-placed diplomacy has been sufficient to soothe the suspicions of an indignant Belgian official and induce him to turn a blind eye to the depredations of his visitors. Yet others, not content with their opportunities in the rôle of sportsman-poacher, have added to their gains not only by trading with and purchasing ivory from the natives, but even by the more economical if less orthodox method of commandeering ivory and trade goods from the hapless emissaries of some Indian traders on the British side, who, being poachers themselves in a territory where might was right, had no redress.

More recently, it should be said, the conditions have somewhat modified. Prizes are not secured with the ease that formerly marked a trip across the border. But it is difficult to say whether the reason is not merely that the elephants, which are, of course, the chief attraction, have shifted westwards, and that the hunter, in consequence, has to go farther afield.

It sounded tantalising, but, after all, it is not playing the game, and the Uganda Government is naturally doing all in its power to discourage the irresponsible freebooter from ruthlessly exploiting its neighbour's weaknesses.

That it is powerless entirely to check the abuses which, after all, it is somebody else's business to deal with, is sufficiently obvious, and we had sufficient proof of the fact that the trade in smuggled Congo ivory is by no

Resting in a "Banda."

Ferrying our loads across a swamp on papyrus rafts.

means dormant. An important firm of Indian traders at Hoima told us that they were expecting a caravan of tusks amounting to over three thousand pounds' weight in all, and that they were receiving a similar consignment about twice a month. All was coming down the Nile to Butiaba, the port on Lake Albert, and all was frankly admitted to be poached from Congo territory.

The staff at Hoima station at the time of our visit consisted of the District Commissioner, Mr. Thomas Grant, the Medical Officer, Dr. Strathairn, with some subordinate officials, besides two subalterns, Messrs. Trewin and Carew, officers in charge of a detachment of the King's African Rifles. This detachment is a company of the Nubian battalion, and is composed of natives from Soudanese territory, who are entirely distinct in many salient features from the local population. They are exceptionally black, broad-faced and thick-lipped, and the faces of both men and women are somewhat unusually disfigured by gashes rather than tattoo marks. The coiffure of the women is quite different to anything that we had seen farther south. The hair is allowed to grow long at the back and curled up at the ends over the neck. But it was not only because they presented a contrast to the type of native amongst whom we have been travelling that we enjoyed an opportunity of obtaining a glimpse of the Nubian and his family at home.

After dinner with the officers at "Military Hill" on the evening of our second day at Hoima, it was suggested that we walk up to the camp and witness a native dance that was forming a part of a marriage celebration, and was being carried on for several days. We readily accepted the invitation, and were presently seated in small armchairs, the property of the police, in an open space between the huts, with as good a view as it was possible to obtain of a scene that was only lighted by a couple of hurricane-lanthorns and a very small fire. For a time the dance proceeded in much the same style as among the southern tribes; the drums, which beat a constant accompaniment, were placed in the background out of the way of the dancers, who in two opposite rows, one of men, the other of women, swayed and shuffled to and fro, generally without coming into actual contact with one another.

Thus far the performance was poor, and the singing, provided by a batch of little girls sitting in a group round the drums, of a most inferior type.

But presently the programme changed. The women retired from the line, and one by one began to give *pas seuls* in the space between the drums and the row of men, who, now more or less in a line with our chairs, kept up a swaying stamp of uncouth rhythm, accompanying their movements with constant grunts. They struck an incongruous note, the men, with their white shirts and trousers or "kanjus" of white linen, canvas shoes, and, if possible, cigarettes. The women were naturally and gracefully robed in flowing cloths, bound tightly round the breasts below the arm-pits, but loosening ere they reached the ankles. There were some six or eight of them performing now, finely developed girls of perhaps twenty years of age, with a magnificent carriage and averaging rather over than under five feet six inches in height. Less coarsely suggestive than the typical Bantu dance, there was a grace and finish in their performance which it is not easy to describe.

Beginning some fifteen feet from the men, the dancer stood erect, her head thrown back, with her draperies held close to her side with one hand. Then by almost imperceptible shuffling she gradually approached her *vis-à-vis*—the man at whom she had selected to dance—her whole frame rippling with unceasing sinuous movements that must have exercised every muscle in her body. As she drew to within an arm's length the shuffling ceased; the back was gradually more and more hollowed and the body curved further and further till the head was almost on a level with the buttocks. At this point she made a momentary pause, during which her *vis-à-vis* stepped forward and, with a flourish, touched her lightly on the breast, murmuring, "Allub"—a word of encouragement, compliment, or approval. Thereupon she straightened herself once more, shuffled sinuously on till almost touching her objective, when, suddenly but gracefully, she sank in a mixture of prostration and abandon in a kneeling heap upon the ground. The man she was dancing at then promptly touched her once more—this time as if raising her—upon the breast, saying, "Ashmeer Bilkeer" (apparently meaning something like "You are the girl for me"), and, rising, the girl quietly returned to her place, and her performance was at an end.

We each and all of us were danced at three or four times, and did our best to make the right remark at the right time, for the failure to do so implies a slight upon the efficiency or charms of the dancer.

The marriage customs and morals of these natives present another contrast to those of the tribes of Northern Rhodesia and kindred races. Nubian girls, unlike those of the average Bantu peoples, are not, as a rule, married until they have well passed the age of puberty, and during their earlier years their chastity is jealously guarded.[1] The dowries, moreover, paid by the husbands for their wives are considerable, and sometimes amount to very large sums. We heard of one native non-commissioned officer having given as much as a thousand rupees for his bride, while there was a rumour that in another case the sum had reached fifteen hundred.

In the Baganda and, to a lesser extent, the Banyoro, we have an instance of Bantu tribes pure and simple, who contrast favourably with many of the southern tribes. There is little doubt that their greater intelligence and the higher social organisation already in existence before the establishment of British protectorate has rendered easier to combat the demoralisation that is so likely to occur among undeveloped natives whose affairs are in a state of rather violent transition, but the facts are none the less interesting or instructive. Though not so high as among the Nubians, the marriage price is considerable and regu-

---

[1] In primo juventutis flore labia majora puellarum ligamento consuta nil nisi angustissimum meatum relinquunt; itaque illis in matrimonii mysteria inductis post primam noctem conjux, e thalamo emergens, ut argumentum virginitatis ejus ligamentum sanguinolentum ostendit. Si tamen vir ligamentum ante nuptias disruptum invenit, femina pro incasta statim demissa, aliam conjugem plerumque postulat.

larly paid, and satisfactory proof of the regularity of a marriage contract, whether according to native, Mahommedan, or Christian law, has to be produced before it is recognised as valid for any purpose whatsoever.

One cannot help contrasting this with the practice of the Wawemba and their kin. While the "dowry" seldom amounts to more than a few shillings' worth of goods and ornaments, as often as not so-called marriages are a matter of mutual arrangement between the man and the woman without reference to or even the approval of any one who might consider themselves concerned.

It follows as a matter of course that divorce or separation is a matter of equally easy arrangement, and that "marriage" is liable to degenerate into nothing more than licensed but haphazard concubinage.

This has not, of course, been always so, and it is only fair to these tribes to bear in mind that in former times certain sanctions and conventions were regularly and strictly observed.

The Government generally is, of course, taking steps to discourage and prevent the irregularity that has recently begun to mark connubial relations, but there can be no doubt that this irregularity is, to a very great degree, the indirect result of the substitution of the white man's government for that of the native chiefs and headmen.

The latter have rather naturally been unable to realise that the loss of most of their administrative and judicial powers were not intended to involve the destruction of their authority in social and domestic matters, and the mistake has been made of regarding these matters as being none of the white man's business. Since the cession of their powers to British authority, the chiefs have mostly regarded every detail of their lives and social relations as the white man's business, and if therefore we hesitate to assume the censorship of any part of their conduct which they have given up, the inevitable result is irregularity and demoralisation.

Particularly likely is this to occur in the case of tribes such as the Wawemba, whose chiefs exercised such arbitrary control over the inter-marriage of their subjects. Except in the case of chiefs and their families, a male Muwemba had no choice in the matter of marriage. On reaching the age at which he thought he would like to wed, his only course was to apply to the chief, who, if he approved, would look out for a suitable bride for the applicant amongst his people. The would-be bridegroom did not even go as far as to mention any particular individual as suiting his taste. It is sufficiently obvious that the disappearance of this ultra-paternal power of the chiefs, who have relinquished it without coercion or protest, needs to be followed by a definite and effective system of control, if the prevention of moral laxity and social degeneration is to be secured.[1]

The methods adopted may in time have the desired effect, but it is at least interesting to notice the difference in the conditions prevailing where the old social system has been encouraged and developed and where it has first of all been simply allowed to slide.

While at Hoima we learnt something of the local conditions of land purchase and the prospects for settlers, which impressed us as being far more favourable than these obtaining in Buganda. The former, the Bunyoro province, suffers from the fact that it lies farther from the Victoria Nyanza, which, with its steamers and outlet by the Uganda railway, is easily accessible to the outside world, but the disadvantages under which it labours in this respect are being rapidly reduced. The motor road to Mubendi is already close to its southern borders, and another from Kampala to Hoima is projected, while the Jinja-Kakindu railway is in course of construction. This railway starts at Jinja by the Ripon Falls, and will go to Kakindu at the south end of Lake Chioga, where navigable water is again met with. Steamers already run from this point to Kishilisi (Port Masindi), near the abandoned Maruli

---

[1] So in South Africa also. "The clan system took in hand the regulation of the intercourse of the sexes, and until Europeans broke up the clan system this restraint was wonderfully effective within certain limits"—Dudley Kidd, *Kafir Socialism*. *Cf.* also: "There is need of the utmost caution not to provoke unrest and discontent by rooting up prevailing systems until the native mind is prepared and effective substitutes are in readiness"—Sir Godfrey Lagden.

station, to Palango and Foweira, near which the navigable waters are again interrupted by rapids which culminate in the Murchison Falls. A motor road is being built from Kishilisi to Masindi, and this will be carried on to Hoima, giving an easy outlet to the produce of a large section of the Bunyoro province. It is further hoped to carry on the rail and river connection from a point near Foweira to Fajao or Butiaba, whence steamers already run to Nimule, on the Bahr el Gebel, and thence no doubt a further line will be laid down to connect with the Soudan steamers at Gondokoro. The cost of these connecting railroads is estimated at £4000 per mile.

The undoubted intention of the Government to improve communications in this part removes from the intending planter all fears that he will be unable to export his produce, and the only remaining considerations are the quality of the land, rainfall, labour supply, &c., and the terms on which he can acquire the land. In the course of the two and a half months following our arrival in Bunyoro, we travelled incessantly in the province, and formed a very favourable impression of it. The soil is indisputably fertile, the rainfall adequate, and labour cheap and easily obtained. Cattle appear to thrive, and we saw no tsetse except close to the Victoria Nile opposite Palango. The climate is by no means unhealthy. In all of these respects it compares not unfavourably with the Buganda province ; and in the matter of land purchase it is far superior. Land in Bunyoro is Crown land, and freehold can be granted to planters. Instead of the many difficulties that a planter has to contend with before obtaining a grant in Buganda, and then only obtaining it on a 99-year lease, land can be acquired—first on a lease for three years, for which ten cents per acre per annum is charged ; and then, if the Government is satisfied with the development shown, it will be sold outright at Rs.2 per acre, so that the total cost to the purchaser will be Rs.2.30 (about 3s. 1d.) per acre. Under these circumstances it seems that a planter would do better to buy land in Bunyoro than to rent it in Buganda.

We called one afternoon on the Pères Blancs, whose mission is about a mile and a half from the District Commissioner's house. The buildings are of their usual sun-dried brick, plastered white, resting on a foundation of ironstone. The dwelling-house is a new and well-constructed building, but the church struck us as inferior to those at Ngaya and Bukumi.

The Father Superior was absent, but we were entertained by Père Bidourin, a French Canadian, and chatted with him for half-an-hour, the conversation being mostly upon the usual Hoima topic—ivory poachers. Hearing of our plans, he kindly promised to send a message to his native catechist in Bugoma instructing him to supply us with vegetables while we were in that locality.

The station of the Church Missionary Society, a few miles out of Hoima, we unfortunately had no time to visit.

On November 1st we took up the trail once more, going in a south-westerly direction to the Bugoma forest and the Albert Nyanza, as it appeared from information collected by Mr. Grant that we should have a better chance of big elephants in that locality than elsewhere. We were accompanied by a local hunter, Duawiri, and two friends of his. Our loads left at 8 A.M. for the first camp, twelve miles out, and we ourselves started on our bicycles at ten, being very pleased at the thought of getting in touch with elephants once more—an elation that was more than shared by our hunter, Chumamaboko, who had been wondering if we should ever reach the elephant country of which we had told him. We added a local cook and a personal boy to our staff, so that by working with our Rhodesian servants they could get accustomed to our habits by the time the latter left us for their homes, which was probably going to be on December 9th at Butiaba, on our embarking for Nimule.

XII

ELEPHANT HUNTING NEAR THE ALBERT NYANZA

The "Kabaka" of Bunyoro—Heavy rain—The Bugoma forest—Colobus monkeys—Death of our dogs—After elephant in "elephant grass"—Helplessness of the hunter Duawiri—The Albert Nyanza—Our first elephant—A wet night—Example of native stupidity—An important change in our projected itinerary—More elephants near the lake—A big one wounded and lost—More blank days in difficult country—The forest hog—A herd of elephants bogged in a stream—Return to Hoima.

CYCLING leisurely, and walking up the hills, which were numerous, as the road was a remarkably good imitation of a switchback, we reached our camp, Kikubi, in two and a quarter hours. Luckily there was a good *banda* at the camp in which we could shelter, for we only arrived just before a heavy fall of rain, which lasted most of the afternoon and a part of the night. While sitting in the *banda* after lunch, a native arrived bearing a letter from the representative of the *Kabaka* (king) of Bunyoro—the *Kabaka* himself being absent—stating that the bearer had been sent to accompany us during our wanderings in Bugoma, as he knew the country and people, and would be able to assist us in obtaining information and in the purchase of food for ourselves and our carriers. This was an entirely spontaneous and voluntary act of courtesy on the part of the *Kabaka* which proved of no small benefit to us.

The title "King" is accorded to the *Kabaka* of Bunyoro as it is to his more important neighbour in the south, the *Kabaka* of Buganda. It is not altogether inappropriate, as some distinctive title is necessary to differentiate between the more important rulers and ordinary chiefs. The king of Bunyoro, like the king of Buganda, has a very considerable revenue, part of which (including a percentage of the poll-tax) he receives from the Government, and part from a rent of Rs.2 per hut per annum paid him by all the Banyoro, besides ivory, royalties on salt, and other forms of tribute. He lives in excellently constructed brick and iron buildings, and is an enlightened ruler on a distinctly higher plane than the ordinary tribal chief. He travels about in considerable state, as we ourselves had an opportunity of observing on the occasion of our second visit to Hoima.

We also saw his dancers on our return, weird skin-clad performers who stood on their heads, beating time with their feet, and accompanied by discordant noises blown upon cow horns.

On the third day out we entered the Bugoma forest, after a journey of no particular incident, except that on the second night an exceptionally heavy shower nearly swept away one of our tents. They had been pitched on a slight slope, and trenches had been dug on all sides as a precaution against rain. The higher of the two tents was sufficiently protected, but the double stream of water swept round it with such force that, uniting between it and the lower one, it filled up the next line of ditches and swept over them and into and through the tent in a stream of some four feet wide and two or three inches deep. It was a most complete swamping, and everything that could float was floating, but fortunately there was nothing particularly perishable on the ground.

The Bugoma forest is of the type known as primeval; the densest of jungle, with big trees rising to an immense height to seek the light, a tangle of creepers, and a soft spongy surface of the decomposed vegetation, through which courses many a cool, clear stream, now sparkling in some shaft of light that penetrated the forest gloom, now lurking in deep, dark pools that have the limpid clearness of a rain-pond in some moorland peat-hag, but framed with the dark, dead green of the sunless forest.

When we stood on the edge of it, looking down from the rank grass and scrub into its uncanny darkness, we thought that we might find in this forest the steaming hot-house heat that so often spoils one's march through tropical jungle, but our fears were groundless; for leaving the bright glare of an almost overpowering sun, we stepped directly into a cool, even chilly atmosphere, and a gloom that was so intense and impressive in its dark stillness that unconsciously one spoke in whispers, as does the traveller when, leaving some crowded thoroughfare, with the dazzling white of its pavements and of its dust, he enters the doors of some old cathedral, and, standing with bared head, waits till the eyes have grown accustomed to the sombre light. And indeed the similarity is not unreal, for in both cases the senses are impressed by the change from bright sun and objects of ordinary size to dim light and impressive massiveness—an idea that doubtless inspired the mediæval architects of our great religious buildings which have served for centuries not only as houses of prayer and praise, but as havens for many a tired worker's quiet meditation and refreshing, though momentary, rest from the stress and turmoil of the outside world.

The presence of elephant spoor soon dispelled any sombre feelings that the unaccustomed solemnity of the scene had produced in our minds, but the examination of the bruised blades of grass where the herds had forced their way through the tangled vegetation or slipped down the slimy forest slopes, showed that though the leaves and boughs torn off in their passage were still green and moist, owing to the damp, cool atmosphere, the spoor was far from fresh. We were cheered a few minutes later by the sight of a family of chattering colobus monkeys sitting in the topmost limbs of the lofty trees, and springing with wonderful agility from bough to bough. We had hoped for an opportunity of acquiring one or two of these creatures' beautiful skins, and secured three specimens. After lunching in a lovely glade while Chumamaboko and Musa skinned our victims, we went on our way and reached our camp at Daudi's after five hours' nett travelling. It had been slow walking all the way—for cycling had been quite impracticable—and most of our

LOOKING FOR ELEPHANTS ON THE ALBERT NYANZA.

THE KABAKA'S DANCERS.

carriers took nine hours and a quarter for the fifteen miles, averaging a mile in thirty-eight minutes. No wonder that fifteen miles is considered a long day's trek in Uganda. The day before reaching Kasama, at the commencement of the journey, some Wawemba carriers took but little longer to cover thirty miles.

This march brought us to within four miles of Muhemba's, which we intended to make our headquarters; and sending Chumamaboko, Nkamba, and Musa with Duawiri and his companions to find out anything they could about elephants, we moved on there the next day. Here we received a supply of potatoes and cabbages from the Mission catechist, more potatoes, pine-apples, pawpaws and bananas from Muhemba himself, besides plenty of food for carriers, the chief producing 175 bundles at half a cent and one cent each that night. Sheep, too, were obtainable at Rs.2, so we congratulated ourselves on having found so good a place at which to camp, but our enjoyment of it was not a little marred by the death of both our remaining dogs, "Jock" and "Nyunshi," from tick fever, the latter being put out of her misery when recovery seemed hopeless. They had been good friends to each other, as well as faithful companions to us, and were buried, as they had lived, side by side.

Chumamaboko returned about 8 P.M., and cheered us with a report that he had seen some good elephants to the north. He seemed confident that they were worth finding, so we started at dawn in the following morning, and after a little less than three hours arrived at a small village, in the gardens adjoining which the herd had been feeding the previous night.

We lost no time in taking up the spoor, but had as heartbreaking and blank a day as it had ever been our lot to endure. The country was an endless waste of rank tangled elephant grass, twenty to twenty-five feet in height, and all but impenetrable. Had we come on a herd it would have been impossible to pick out the bulls, much more to see their tusks, for it would have been necessary to approach to within a yard to see anything at all. It was only at rare intervals that even in the elephant paths one could see a man ten yards away; off their tracks one could see nothing at all but the everlasting "grass." There were very few trees from which we could survey the surrounding country, and no ant-hills. This kind of jungle was not altogether unfamiliar to us; we had often come across it when hunting elephant and buffalo in our own country, but there it exists in relatively small patches (known as *chipia* by the natives) dotted about a fairly easy country, but here there was nothing else; it seemed interminable. The sun was oppressively hot, there was not a breath of wind, and after five hours of what would have been hard enough going in any conditions, without coming up with the herd, we had had enough of it, and returned to camp at three o'clock. There we had the doubtful consolation of learning that the elephants had passed behind us some hours earlier, crossing our own tracks, and had moved in the direction of Muhemba's.

Even one day was enough to show us the utter uselessness and incompetence of our new hunter, Duawiri. On the few occasions when he roused himself sufficiently to simulate interest in his work, he would invariably differ with Chumamaboko as to which tracks to follow, but being as invariably wrong, he soon gave up the pretence. When, at a brief halt, Chumamaboko and some local natives went reconnoitring for fresh clues, he crowned his general ineptitude by lying down and going to sleep. As we were satisfied that he was less help than hindrance, we let him sleep.

The next morning while retracing our steps to Muhemba's we met a few villagers, waiting on the path to intercept us, who told us that some elephants had passed through their gardens in the night, and had been seen the same morning in quite short grass. They seemed to know something about elephants and elephant hunting, so, sending our tents and other gear on to Muhemba's, we struck off to the west in the direction from which they had come. Words fail one to describe the tangle through which we toiled at a rate of a mile and a half per hour. For some two hours the going was even worse than on the preceding day. Then, to our intense relief, we emerged into a large open plain clothed with fine grass that was not more than six feet high. Far below us, stretching right across the western horizon, were the beautiful blue waters of the Albert Nyanza, backed by the cloud-strewn purple mountains of the Congo on the far side. Great granite boulders, from which we gained magnificent views of the lake, rose like islands in the sea of grass. But a little later when standing on one of these we discerned that the whole slope below us was dotted with elephants, some standing singly, some in groups, the tops of their backs being visible above the yellow grass. North and west were bunches of cows and calves, the latter playing restlessly, the former occasionally rousing themselves from their midday lethargy to rebuke the exuberance of their offspring, or raising their trunks to call shrilly for a missing youngster.

On a ridge to our left, towards the south, were several bulls bringing up the rear of the herd. Three or four of them seemed fair-sized animals—they were moving drowsily along, each contented with his own society; while two younger bulls were carrying on a playful fight, untroubled by the heat of the day, and between them and the main body were perhaps a dozen others whose size was a matter for conjecture. The whole herd must have stretched over a distance of nearly two miles.

For two hours we watched their every movement through our glasses, moving from one point of vantage to another; unable to decide which, if any, were worth going after, now and again resting our eyes with a look at the unrivalled view of the lake that lay before us. Finally we came to the conclusion that two of the bulls in some thick vegetation to the south were the best—the farthest of all and the fourth from him—and, making our way towards them, approached the nearer of the two that we had selected. Duawiri and all the locals except Musa we left behind. The former expert had actually proposed that we should leave the isolated bulls alone and go after the main herd. As it was obviously composed of cows and small bulls (and was down wind to boot), his object could only have been to get us into a mess which might have resulted in our wounding two or three of them, to be picked up later by the natives. A more barefaced suggestion we had never heard. Though we got quite close to the bull it was some time before we could see his tusks—short thick ones of about 50 lbs. a piece. After a good look at him from the top of a convenient tree, Chumamaboko declared that the more southerly elephant had better ivory, so we moved on, and were lucky in finding a large granite boulder which gave a moderately good view of his ear and shoulder. We had drawn lots to decide who should begin, and the winner (Cholmeley) decided to try the brain shot with his double .360, though our rock was sixty yards from the quarry. The other stood by with his double .450 ready to put in a right and left in the shoulder in case the first shot failed to bring him down. We waited no longer than was necessary for a steady aim, and then the .360 rang out and the elephant toppled over, getting a .450 bullet in the side of his face by the ear as he fell. Not a single step did he move, but we doubted if the first shot had reached the brain direct, as he fell sideways and gave a defiant trumpet-call as he reached the ground. It had got him, as a matter of fact, in the ear-hole, while the other had entered a little further forward and came out at the forehead, and he was quite dead when we got up to him. He measured 10 ft. 4 in. at the shoulder; the tusks measured $66\frac{1}{2}$ in. and $64\frac{1}{2}$ in. total, and 39 in. and 37 in. outside measurement, with a girth of $16\frac{1}{2}$ in., and weighed $46\frac{1}{2}$ lbs. and 46 lbs. He was rather disappointing, but we were glad to have made a beginning, and consoled ourselves by hoping for better luck next time. As it was by this time two o'clock, we sent Musa to fetch our luncheon baskets, which we had left a mile behind us, and to despatch two of our local village guides to

OUR FIRST ELEPHANT.

BARGAINING.

ELEPHANT HUNTING

Muhemba's to bring along our tents and camp gear. Within an hour the luncheon baskets had arrived, but so had all the natives who had remained behind. Wondering who had been sent with our message, we called Musa.

"You have presumably sent off some men to Muhemba's?" we asked.

"No," he replied, "they have not gone."

"Why on earth not? We told you to send a couple of men back to the village to fetch our tents and gear, and you say they have not gone."

"Well," he said, "it was Duawiri who stopped them going. I told them to go."

Somewhat amazed at the latest eccentricity on the part of our erratic expert, we asked him to explain.

"Oh," he replied airily, "when the white man shoots an elephant he goes back to the village where he slept. He does not camp in the bush."

A homicidal impulse all but overpowered us, but we made an effort, succeeded in keeping fairly cool, and, with a big breath,

"Whatever any other white man," we retorted, "who has been unfortunate or imbecile enough to be guided by your counsels may have done or left undone under these or any other circumstances does not interest us in the very least. We thought we had made ourselves clear that we intend to camp where we are, and we shall be grateful if in the future you will refrain from taking upon yourself to improve our programme according to any ideas of your own."

"Oh, well, just as you like, of course, but there is no water nearer than the lake, and none of the men will have any food."

"As to the food," we said, "there is enough of that elephant for a couple of hundred starving hyenas; and as for water, you have not looked, and we will bet you six months' pay to a pinch of salt that you are wrong."

To do him justice, he did not behave as if he expected to acquire sudden wealth, and indeed we did not have to pay. Water was found within five minutes' walk.

He was not, however, in the least upset by our attempts at rebuke; evidently resigning himself to the prospect of following two cantankerous and selfish lunatics about the bush, he retired and consoled himself by gloating over his coming gorge.

The delay was sufficiently annoying, and probably made just the difference in the chance of our tents reaching us before night.

It was now nearly four, and as we had but a slender idea of the distance of Muhemba's and but little confidence in our messengers, we took the precaution of having a grass hut built in case nothing turned up. And it was fortunate that we did; there was never a sign of our carriers, and it rained from midnight till nearly dawn. We were lucky in having some food left over, and with a *consommé* of fresh elephant-tail soup made a very fair meal by the light of our camp fire. We missed our blankets considerably, but wrapped up in our "slip-ons," one with a camera and the other with a cartridge-bag for a pillow, we managed to get a certain amount of sleep in spite of the fact that our roof was leaking in four or five places. We woke somewhat unrefreshed and aching, but, curiously enough, both of us cured of sore throats that had been annoying us considerably the previous day.

Three of our staff who had intended to sleep in the open at the fireside crawled into our shelter when the rain began, and huddled up near the door, for which, though one of them snored immoderately, we were not sorry, as they helped to keep out the draught.

A cup of tea cheered us a little, and at nine we welcomed our carriers and, *ergo*, our breakfast, with real delight. They had left at five and had lost their way, so we could not be more than a couple of hours or so from Muhemba's after all.

A wash and breakfast soon lessened our woes, the discomforts of the night were quickly forgotten, and we spent a quiet day while the elephant was being cut up.

A curious example of native stupidity occurred in con-

ELEPHANT HUNTING

nection with the disposal of the meat. When it had been cut up we divided it into five portions, allotting one to the Kabaka's representative, Muhemba, and the local villagers and guides, another to our Rhodesian staff and the hunters, and the remaining three-fifths to our carriers. Knowing that Baganda do not eat elephant meat, we explained to them that they could use it to purchase food from the local natives to whom it was not taboo, and thus either save their cents or supplement their rations. We were dumbfounded when they curtly and emphatically refused to take any of it. Pressed to give a reason they explained that they would rather have cents than meat, so once more we told them that the meat, being a gift, was supplementary to and not in lieu of cents: that they could have their cents and the meat, or the cents only, but that there was not and never had been any question of their getting meat only. This only elicited the cool suggestion that if we liked we could give the meat to the villagers and instruct them to provide our carriers with extra food, gratis; to which, restraining our irritation with difficulty, we replied that we were not going to do their marketing for them, and that if they left the meat it would be given unconditionally to the local natives. They preferred to leave it, so the local Banyoro profited considerably by their stupidity.

We discovered later, when we knew them better, that the real reason for this remarkable attitude on their part was that they feared we should, in spite of our assertions, use the gift of meat as an excuse for docking their food allowance of two cents a day, as had been done by some other travellers.

During the day we received a note from Mr. Grant containing news which was to make a considerable difference to our journey on to the Soudan. While still at Hoima we had wired to Alidina Visram's agent at Nimule to ask if he could procure carriers there for us on our arrival by steamer from Butiaba, for our next stage to Gondokoro. We had received a reply that it was impossible to obtain any, so Mr. Grant kindly wired to the District Commissioner at Nimule to enlist his help, but in the letter which we received at this elephant camp he wrote:—

"I am not at all sanguine that men can be got at Nimule, in fact I am almost sure that it will not be possible. The natives in the Nile district will not carry loads at any price, and on the rare occasions when they get carriers they only go from village to village."

This made it practically certain that we could not go by steamer from Butiaba to Nimule, as it would be quite useless to arrive at the latter place and be stranded there for lack of carriers, while the conveyance of sufficient men by steamer would be very expensive. The alternative, which we decided to adopt, was to go overland all the way, taking our carriers through. This meant missing the most picturesque part of the river journey, but held out instead a far more entertaining prospect, in the shape of the trip through the little known and unadministered Lango territory south of Nimule, through which we had been informed we could travel if we wished to, though that part of the territory was really closed to travellers. To anticipate a little, after we had left Hoima for Masindi a fortnight later a telegram arrived from the District Commissioner at Nimule stating that he could arrange for thirty carriers if we would bring the balance, but the prospect of travelling through the Lango country had grown more and more alluring as we dwelt upon it, and we decided definitely to give up the idea of the easier river journey.

The abandonment of the steamer journey and the choice of the route made it necessary to calculate how much time remained at our disposal; and we reckoned that travelling direct by the overland route we could arrive at Gondokoro in thirty-two days. This would leave us a margin of eighteen days for shooting and occasional rests. We had not many more days to spare for the Bugoma district if we were to get any sport in the Masindi country; but as the prospects seemed fairly good where we were, and we were getting a plentiful and almost daily supply of pine-apples, cabbages, and potatoes, we decided to give the spot a fair trial before moving on.

Muhemba, who had come to our camp with plenty of food for our carriers, had cheered us by declaring that the neighbourhood of his village was the regular habitat of small groups of big bulls, and suggested sending out scouts early next morning who might get back the same night with news. We accepted his offer, and returned once more to his village to await developments.

By noon the following day news came in of a herd with one big bull about a couple of hours away, but the hour was late, the report not very convincing, and we decided not to move that day.

The following morning we were off at dawn. For about three hours, progress was very dull, tramping and crushing through elephant grass and water, for it had been raining daily for nearly a week. But at about nine o'clock, after being on fresh spoor for half-an-hour or so, when we were quite close to the south end of Lake Albert and within sight of the swampy delta of the Semliki River, we heard the rumbling of a herd of elephants some little way ahead.

The country of this corner of the lake consists of a series of undulating hill-ridges running east and west, the intervening valleys being formed by the watercourses which drain the surrounding country and act as feeders to the lake.

It was some fifteen minutes later that, when topping one of these ridges, we sighted our herd slowly mounting the opposite rise, about 500 yards away. They had brought us still closer to the lake, and we could see the sandy foreshore at the foot of the escarpment.

We let them disappear over the crest, and then, the wind being right, went after them. On topping the rise ourselves, we soon saw a portion of the herd emerging from a "gully" below us, and another a little farther on, apparently cows and calves. While taking a good look at them, the snapping of trees close on our left showed that the tail of the herd was still near by.

Stepping cautiously forward, we were presently rewarded by the sight of a fine big bull moving across our course, and feeding as he went. Others were close by, and as they were probably all bulls, bringing up *more suo* the tail of the herd, we advanced more warily than ever, wishing neither to lose a chance of a good tusker, nor to get into any kind of trouble. A minute or two later, the beast that we had first sighted gave us a better view of himself than ever, and we decided that he was quite good enough.

Taking steady aim for the heart we fired—first the .450, right and left, then a single shot from the .360.

A tremendous commotion followed—the whole countryside seemed alive with elephants. We did not see another worth bagging, so while the herd was scrambling and scattering, goodness knew where, we retired to a clump of boulders close by from which we could see what was happening—not for a moment doubting that the victim was sufficiently disabled to allow us time to look round. The herd, which must have been nearer two hundred than one (we counted a hundred and forty), took a long time to move off, particularly some small cows, which hung about so persistently just on the top of the next small rise, apparently perplexed by what we thought were the dying groans of our beast, that it was about half-an-hour before we descended to investigate. We had had a good view of the whole herd going up the next big rise, and we laughed at a suggestion that the wounded one had been helped off by his pals, quite expecting to find him dead or near it.

Our disappointment and chagrin may be imagined when we discovered not a trace of him anywhere, nor, at first, even a drop of blood. The mystery was further deepened when Chuma, who had gone back to the point from which we had fired to pick up the trail, returned to say that all our three bullets had struck a tree a long way from the ground, and consequently must have missed him.

We went along ourselves, and, when we had taken everything in, were more mystified than ever—the tree had

ELEPHANT HUNTING

certainly been struck, a small branch some nine feet from the ground bearing the three bullet marks, almost in a dead straight line, and less than a foot apart.

We carefully reconstructed the whole while the details were fresh in our memory. The tree was twelve paces beyond the spot on which the elephant had been standing, and here the height at which the bullets must have passed was but seven feet.

As the elephant was at least ten feet eight inches in height, the bullets cannot have passed over him, further proved by the fact that blood was found in four different spots, and it was almost equally impossible to believe either that all three bullets—two .450 and one .360—had passed clean through him, or—considering the distance of thirty-two yards at which we had been standing—that any of our shots had clean missed him: they were much more likely to have passed through and close to the base of his heart.

However it may have happened, we never found a trace of him again. We had already sent back for our tents, &c., before leaving the rocks. After realising our loss we lunched, and then went on for two or three hours more in hopes of finding the wounded beast. We got quite close up to parts of the herd three or four times, but never saw anything worth shooting at; and the heavy rain which fell for the rest of the afternoon destroyed all chances of the blood spoor being any longer visible. The herd had broken up into small groups, none of which appeared to contain large bulls. It was nearly always in the thickest of stuff that we found them, but as they were moving slowly, we generally got a glimpse of everything in the group.

It was with one of these groups that we had what might have been a very unpleasant encounter. We had been for some little time following and watching the movements of a batch of twenty or thirty, which we thought might contain the wounded bull, when suddenly we heard on our right the low rumbling sound that indicated the close proximity of yet another detachment. We had just descended from a point of vantage and were making our way along a dip between two little ridges, the right hand of which was broken up into smaller hills. The sounds seemed to come from beyond these latter, so we worked round the first of them, hoping to obtain a sight of the beasts from the top of the second.

The pass between the two was narrow, steep-sided, thickly overgrown and rough underfoot. We had actually entered it and were looking for a good spot to mount the next incline, when a stick snapped like a pistol-shot, swish went a thick patch of grass less than ten paces in front of us, and a swaying trunk and a pair of huge flapping ears were towering above us at what seemed like a height of twenty feet.

We had met the herd right in our gully, and coming from the opposite direction! We just had time to see that it was a huge cow that was upon us, so we scrambled up the slope to our right without any further delay and awaited developments. Fortunately we had not been seen, and at first they began filing quietly out of the gully suspecting nothing. As they passed within a few paces of us we saw that there were fifteen or sixteen of them—all cows or young bulls, with a calf or two. Some were huge beasts, but none carried tusks of any size. A step or two farther and some of the foremost had reached the spot on which we had a second before been standing. Up went their trunks sniffing the tainted breeze, and as they got clear of the gully six or seven of them wheeled round, stood and stared at us with a suspicious and uneasy air. For nearly half a minute they hesitated, and we were wondering whether they meant trouble after all, when, to our relief, their alarm got the better of their pugnacity, and they turned and stampeded in the opposite direction.

It had been an anxious moment; we were in a fairly good position, and we might or might not have succeeded in stopping a charge, but at the best it would have meant the murder of a cow or an underweight bull, which would have been unfortunate.

After examining yet two more groups that were bring-

ELEPHANT HUNTING

ing up the rear of the scattered herd, and seeing no trace of our wounded bull or any more big tuskers, we came to the conclusion that the old males must have gone off in a different direction, and we decided to give it up. Turning back, we reached the stream at which we had told our carriers to camp, at above five o'clock.

Our instructions had once more been improved upon, however, and after waiting an hour, during which we had another hut built in which to pass the night, we discovered that they had selected a spot a mile or two up stream. We reached it at nightfall, to find the indefatigable and obliging Muhemba awaiting us with a hundred bundles of food.

It had been raining off and on most of the day; we were soaked to the skin, and fairly worn out, and for once were content to make the best of a warm bath and a camp fire without discoursing on the ethics of meticular obedience.

The next day was spent in much the same neighbourhood, but a little farther east, and it proved equally fruitless.

It was about half-past nine when elephants were first heard. The wind was variable, but mainly in our favour, and after moving in their direction for twenty minutes we sighted them on a rise about a mile away, with a hollow and a stream between us. Some were descending the slope, others were in the stream itself, but the grass and vegetation were so high that even their backs were not visible all the time.

For some thirty minutes we could see nothing but young bulls and cows; then a huge bull appeared two or three hundred yards behind the rest, and following slowly in their wake. His tusks were hidden, but his bulk suggested the possibility of a big pair, and we proceeded to try and get up to him. It was going to be a difficult task, and we had hardly decided which direction to take when our attention was attracted by a score of vultures hovering and circling over a spot about a mile to our left. Thinking that it might be our quarry of the day before that had succumbed, we hastened to the spot. Another and a peculiar disappointment! The attraction was the *placenta* of an elephant that had given birth some few hours before.

Returning towards our original objective, we climbed a tall tree that ought to have given us some sort of glimpse of the herd, but only to find that the beasts had got our wind and had all stampeded. Another big herd, however, was sighted to the north, moving south-east, and after a little rest and refreshment we proceeded to try and cut them off.

We had been going less than an hour when we found that there was yet another herd considerably closer on our right. Investigation showed them to be in a dense forest patch near the top of a slight incline, and we started off in their direction. We had but little idea of the difficulties that lay before us.

The grass and vegetation in which we had been working all the morning was tall and thick enough, but it was not "elephant" grass proper, and it presently gave way to a big patch of the latter that surpassed all our previous experiences. This was fifteen to twenty feet high, and so strong and close as to be every bit as impenetrable as a bamboo brake, but closer and denser than any bamboos that ever grew. For fully three-quarters of an hour, during which time we travelled perhaps half a mile, we were painfully and laboriously forcing our way through it. Chumamaboko—an exceptionally powerful six-foot native of just twelve stone—led the way; armed with a stout alpenstock, he threw himself bodily on the tough and matted stems, and forced, pulled, pushed, and tore them aside, and crushed them down by sheer weight and strength. It was quite tiring enough following in the passage that he made, and it was with many a gasp of relief that we finally emerged and found ourselves on the edge of the forest strip in which we had detected the presence of the elephants. We had trees of all sizes and tangled undergrowth to make our way through now, but, except in patches, it was free from tall grass, and we had a fairly clear view in most directions for as much as twenty yards.

We struck fresh spoor almost at once, and had gone but a few steps when a snorting, trumpeting, and crashing to our right warned us that the herd had not gone far. The noise died away again as quickly as it had begun, but they were evidently still there, and giving no indication of the direction of their next move.

Just as we were moving cautiously on, a giant forest hog stepped out in front of us and stood and stared at us for fully six seconds before he cocked up his tail and, with a contemptuous grunt, dived into the undergrowth, where he remained till a clod of earth thrown in his direction caused him to beat a final retreat. He was a fine young male, with no tushes visible, standing about three feet nine inches[1] at the shoulder, and we deeply regretted that our close proximity to elephants lost us a probably unique chance of securing a specimen of one of the rarest of African mammals.

Moving on once more, we were suddenly brought to a standstill by a fresh outburst of snorting, trumpeting, screaming, and splashing just in front of us and closer. The elephants were either crossing a stream or having a bath; they were closer than ever, and sounded as if they were coming our way.

After a brief halt, a little scouting by Chuma resulted in a report that they were stuck in a stream which they were trying to cross. Following him through a dense fringe of reeds and grass, we reached the edge of a stream or swamp some fifteen yards broad, and saw the rear-guard of the herd standing in the water and reeds that fringed the farther side. There were only cows visible, and as they began to show signs of returning our way we retreated a little way back to a spot where we should have more room to move. After one or two more false alarms we sent Chuma up a tall tree to reconnoitre. He

---

[1] In Rowland Ward's *Records of Big Game* the height of the forest hog is put at much less than this, but we carefully noted the height to which this beast reached on a sapling, and then measured it.

descended five minutes later, saying he had seen them all as they were moving off, and that there was not a big bull amongst them. Had the report come from Duawiri we should have climbed that tree ourselves, but we knew we could trust Chuma: he was as keen as either of us on getting a big one, and ready to go through any kind of country.

It was another blank day, and the only thing left to do was to get back to camp, which we had had pitched at a small village near Muhemba's. The walk back was very much like the afternoon's scramble through the elephant grass, only there was much more of it. After we had thought that we had got to camp at least three times on the way, and when we reached a condition in which it really did not seem to matter whether we got there at midnight or dawn or whether we ever got there at all, we eventually found the spot at a little after dark—too tired either to think much of our disappointment or even fully to appreciate the rest and refreshment for which barely an hour before we would have given almost anything we had.

We had had enough of Bugoma ; we had seen hundreds of elephants, at least a score of bulls with tusks of forty to fifty pounds, but only one—the one that we had wounded and lost—with as much as sixty-pounders, and we decided there and then to try the Masindi district without any further delay, and were back in Hoima three days later.

XIII

ELEPHANT HUNTING IN THE MASINDI DISTRICT—I

Sale of our ivory at Hoima—A civet cat—Total eclipse of the moon—Encounter with Captain Tufnell—Masindi—Elephant hunting in a forest belt—Our second elephant—Blank days near Samusoni's and Benjamin's.

ON our arrival for the second time at Hoima we found that Mr. Grant had been called away to other duties, and that Dr. Strathairn, the Medical Officer, was acting in his place pending the arrival of a successor.

Though sorry to have missed our former host, we had nothing to complain of in the change, for besides enjoying the delightful hospitality of Dr. and Mrs. Strathairn, we got every kind of assistance and advice that it occurred to us to ask for.

We also found Messrs. McLure and Bain, Superintendent of Public Works and District Engineer, whom we had previously met at Entebbe. The former had just arrived from there on a motor bicycle, a distance of 150 miles, only sleeping at Kampala, twenty-two miles out, on the way. The following day he started back, and, we heard later, accomplished the return journey in the same time—not an insignificant achievement, considering the effect on the roads of a sudden tropical shower, and the discomforts and inconveniences that would attend a breakdown at, say, half-way between Hoima and Kampala.

Dr. Marshall, another medical officer, had also arrived, and knowing something of the Masindi country, gave us a very useful little sketch-map showing the most likely spots for elephant, as well as some welcome advice. His estimate of our chances of success, as well as the sight of a pair of tusks which he himself recently secured—the larger of which scaled ninety-one pounds—gave us some encouragement.

Duawiri and the local natives who had been of special service to us in Bugoma had to be paid off, but before doing so we sought advice.

We really could not, without protest, pay that amiable muddler what he seemed to think he was worth, nor, to our relief, were we required to.

Five men of Muhemba's, who had really put us on to the herd out of which we bagged our bull, received Rs.5 a piece, and Duawiri Rs.3! As he had been boasting that he was going to get Rs.30 per elephant, it was something of a shock to him, but he had been less than no assistance to us, and it was quite as much as he had earned. Chuma, needless to say, was delighted. He had had no use whatever for poor old Duawiri, and had chaffed him unmercifully round the camp fire, the evening after the death of our elephant. They were cutting up their meat into the usual strips, and hanging them on rude trestles over the fire, and Duawiri was trying in vain to face the running fire of sarcasm that was being poured on him by Chuma and the others. He was indiscreet enough to begin crowing:—

"Ha! we have killed an elephant to-day!"

"We!" shouted Chuma. "We? I say, he thinks he had something to do with it! Here, hand me that knife, and don't pinch my meat."

"Meat!" from Duawiri, with an attempt at buoyancy. "Yes, elephant meat; there is no meat like elephant meat, is there? and there is plenty of it."

"Well, you have earned a lot, haven't you? Oh, well, I suppose even the hyena gets a meal if he hangs on long enough behind the lion. Talk about hunters! Now *I am* an elephant hunter, I am. I have tracked elephants, killed elephants, lived with elephants all my life. If I am not an elephant hunter, who is? Have I not been at the death of all the elephants that the Bwana has killed? Has he ever killed a cow or a small tusker when I have been with him, and has he ever been trampled on or driven away by them?"

"Oh yes," murmured the other, with a shake of the head, "you are a hunter."

"And have I," resumed the modest Chuma, "ever suggested that he leaves the bulls of a herd, and go for the cows and calves?"

Here Duawiri, with a brave effort to keep his end up, replied with a word or two of Chiwemba that he had picked up. It was not tactful, and Chuma turned on him.

"Mulenga strike me! You would imitate me, would you!" On that the vanquished Duawiri relapsed into silence, with a tolerant and easy smile, as if to say, "Well, have it your own way," and Chuma went on with his cooking.

We next approached the local firms, with a view to the sale of our ivory. There were two who were buying—Alidina Visram and the British Trading Company. Sound medium-sized ivory was selling at the moment for Rs.5.50 to Rs.6.50 per pound. We did not expect to get more than Rs.5.50 from Alidina's agent, but we told him that the British Trading Company were offering Rs.6, and he eventually gave the larger price—though protesting, after the manner of his race, that one tusk at least was defective, that the price was excessive, and that he was buying at a loss.

The patched bicycle had been running quite satisfactorily since leaving Mubendi on October 22nd, and we had begun to flatter ourselves that we were going to have no more trouble with it. Our gratification was short-lived. Its evil genius had merely been lying dormant for a time, to wake into activity when we least expected it. During the last mile into Hoima, it suddenly began to run abominably stiff, and we took the first opportunity to strip it and discover the nature of its fresh developments. This time it looked as if the climax had been reached. Another cone had split, probably owing to a faulty ball-carrier, the fragments had got into the two-speed gear mechanism, and the result was an advanced stage of mechanical mincemeat, which it seemed hopeless to attempt to remedy. Cogs were chipped, stripped, and jammed, and the case-hardened rim of the perimetral gear-wheel was cracking and peeling like an egg-shell. Fortunately we had one spare sound cone on the discarded mechanism. It was for the wrong side of the wheel, and it could not remedy much of the damage, but we found that by using the machine on the high gear only, though it was bound to revolve stiffly, the wheel *would* revolve, and we left it at that, wondering whether it would last a week, a day, or even an hour.

The road to Masindi was an excellent one, with well-placed and comfortable camps. It was but a distance of thirty-one miles, but we took it easy, and leaving Hoima on November 16th, got in on the third day at 10 A.M. The journey was comparatively uneventful. We secured an interesting addition to our bag on the first day, in the shape of a civet cat, which though common enough is rarely seen owing to its nocturnal habits. The beast was lying asleep on one of the lower branches of a large tree in the camp compound. All the carriers had passed right under it as they came in, and it was the last arrival of the whole caravan who first detected its presence. At four o'clock the following morning occurred an exceptionally fine total lunar eclipse; the sudden change from the brilliant light of the full moon to the inky blackness of night was enough to impress even the lethargic and apathetic native.

At our second camp we met Captain Tufnell, District Commissioner at Palango, who was proceeding home on leave. Many of his carriers were of the Lango tribe, and though of a distinctly savage type, they impressed us considerably with their athletic carriage and fine physique. Kelobong, one of the most important chiefs of the tribe, was accompanying him as far as Hoima, to be shown a little of the white man's civilisation. Unlike his people, who, at the most, wore a narrow strip of skin, he was attired in a European serge suit, and a felt hat with a white puggaree. On our arrival he came forward, and shook our hands with a grave and easy courtesy of which we were to see a good deal more later in our journey.

We were naturally deeply interested to hear all that Captain Tufnell could tell us about the country through which we were going to travel. Neither the Acholi nor the Lango, he said, would come near us for anything—except perhaps to eat an elephant—and any food that we wanted in the Lango country would have to be procured from the Baganda agents, through whom the Government is beginning to exercise some control over these natives.

It was mainly for this reason that Captain Tufnell emphatically approved the suggestion made to us at Hoima that we should apply for a small escort of police from Palango to Gondokoro.

Masindi station proper is built, like most of the outstations, on a slight rise, and a little removed from the township, native market, and Indian bazaar. The offices are ranged on three sides of a large open square, from the back of which a drive of over a hundred yards leads to the officials' residence. The drive is sheltered by a magnificent avenue, principally of *mutawa* and gum trees; a grassy paddock at one side was enclosed by a tall, leafy fence of growing saplings that had been driven into the ground as stakes, and had subsequently taken root. It was composed of all kinds of local trees, and provided a further testimony to the fertility of the Uganda soil and the forcing powers of the climate.

The Assistant District Commissioner, Mr. Postlethwaite, was away when we arrived, but returned next morning with a pair of seventy-pound tusks that he had secured while travelling in the neighbourhood. He provided us with a cheerful and intelligent-looking young pagan, named Udala, who had been out with him, as Duawiri's successor. He was a hunter in the service of one of the local chiefs, but was more than willing to take service with us as far as Palango on the understanding that his work was chiefly to get information as to the whereabouts of elephants, and his pay to be reckoned at a maximum of Rs.20 for an elephant—supposing he were really of assistance—and at a reduction for two or three. He was despatched at once to order supplies and make inquiries at our next camp.

Our carriers left at about noon, and an hour later, during luncheon, a report came in to the effect that two large bull elephants had been seen that morning in some native gardens within six miles of the station and only a mile or two out of our way.

A couple of bulls by themselves sounded rather promising, so after despatching a messenger to inform the *Mwami* of our coming, and sending our gun-bearers ahead to await us at the turning off the main road, we started at half-past two. At four o'clock we reached the *shamba* from which the report had come, and found the owner and some of his people awaiting us. The herd was said to be still quite close, but it consisted of five, not two only. This was not so encouraging. An underestimate even of three was suspicious. There might be many more after all, and our chances of finding one or two solitary bulls—always more likely to be big tuskers than those running with a large herd—were gone again.

Their morning's spoor was close by, but no fresher traces were found until after an hour's plodding through very thick grass, some seven or eight feet high, they were faintly heard blowing some distance away to our right.

From the upper branches of a tree could be seen a belt of thick jungle half a mile off in the direction from which the sounds had come, and it seemed likely that the herd had found a pool in the shade and were enjoying themselves in it. In a few minutes we found ourselves on the edge of a shallow depression, overgrown with very tall grass, on the farther side of which rose the forest belt that was our objective. The fresh spoor that we had found ten minutes before led down through the grass and into the jungle.

We had had no further indications of their presence nor any of their departure, so, though we could seldom see anything more than fifteen paces away and in some

IN CAMP.

THE D.C's HOUSE AT MASINDI.

directions but three or four, we groped our way cautiously in and hoped for the best.

Every minute we expected to come on some member of the herd. Once or twice we were brought to a standstill, peering and listening, as a snapping stick or a shaking bough close in front of us warned us that we might be getting a little too near. Then a deep cough from a clump of reeds on our left made us feel certain that we were right in the middle of the herd, till we realised that it was only a leopard whose voice had been exaggerated by the tension of the moment. This forest patch proved far harder going than anything we had encountered in Bugoma. Masses of leafy creepers here and there lay across our path that had been brushed aside by the elephants, and yet scarcely gave a passage.

For at least a hundred yards we had to pick our way over and through a slough of mud and water, stepping as best we could from root to root of mighty trees and hanging on to the vines that festooned them; testing every inch of our path before we trusted our weight to it. Sometimes a false step meant a plunge into clinging viscous mud up to the knee or further, sometimes the swamp seemed bottomless to Chumamaboko's probing spear, and a fallen log or hidden root had to be discovered before we dared move on. It was not the best of places in which to surprise a herd of elephant, and there were moments when we wondered how we should feel if round the next corner we were to meet some of them as we had done in Bugoma—coming the opposite way. However, though we could have sworn from a dozen different signs that they were on that forest belt at the same time as ourselves, we saw nothing of them, and when we finally emerged—after turning and twisting, climbing and crawling, dodging and stooping through mud and water—and slithered and stumbled up a grassy bank into the open bush, we found that they had left it some minutes before. Their noiseless exit was not the least remarkable of our afternoon's experiences.

We pressed on for a while and heard them once more

before the setting sun warned us that it was time to give it up if we wanted to avoid the risk of losing our way. Our local guides, however, found us a path back to the village sooner than we expected, and at half-past six we reached the spot where we had left our bicycles and taken up the spoor. Here we found that our new guide from Hoima had sent off to camp to fetch our tents to us, but as there was no question as to which would be the best place to camp, we started off to meet them. After a long and rather difficult tramp through an overgrown path, which we only succeeded in keeping by almost touching the native in front of us, we got to the camping-place on the road at 8.15, meeting the boys about half-way.

The following day we kept to the road, and pushed on twenty-four miles to a camp called Kiliandongo's, as its neighbourhood had been recommended as offering good opportunities, and there was little chance of finding anything in between. The distance was almost too much for our carriers, and after a breakfast at 6.30 we got no lunch till four o'clock.

The same night we had a report of a big herd seen at sundown by local scouts, and next day at noon, while we were waiting for further details, came news of another whose habitat was said to be within two hours' walk.

For three months it had been feeding during the night in their gardens, said the natives who brought the report, moving during the daytime into a path of bush less than a mile away. Sending Chuma and Udala ahead the same evening, we followed at daybreak, and in less than two hours reached the little village in a country called Chilelambachu, from which the report had come. In obedience to a message awaiting us from Chuma we followed him, and in ten minutes were with him on fresh spoor. He had already caught sight of the herd : nothing more than a forty- or fifty-pounder had so far shown itself, but there were others a little way ahead, and the wholesale destruction in the banana groves as well as the stripping and uprooting of several large trees bore witness to the fact that the herd contained some huge beasts. After half-an-hour through tall grass and a small belt of jungle, we came out into a comparatively open country with a few big trees and grass only six or seven feet high, and heard them trumpeting close by. Chuma sighted them from a tree-top, and reported a pair of tusks of the same size as our first victim's. A large tree some forty paces on promised a better view, and thither we made our way. Chuma climbed up it as usual, and the lighter of us followed him.

There were elephants all over the place. Eight or ten that were standing in the shade some 150 yards away to our left front were cows, with perhaps a young bull or two; another group, right in front, was obviously composed of small fry; no more were at first visible, though the shrill trumpetings that broke out at frequent intervals showed that there were other groups hidden by grass and trees close by.

After nearly an hour's waiting and watching, two huge bulls were seen slowly emerging from cover to the right and advancing towards the nearer of the two groups. Their tusks were as yet hidden in the grass. After one of them had raised our hopes by taking a few steps right in our direction, they halted at a distance of a hundred or a hundred and twenty paces, and seemed to go to sleep.

For another hour we watched them, hoping to get a glimpse of some tusks. It was not exactly a comfortable occupation; the tree was of the variety that is studded nearly all over with short thorns, the foothold was an unpleasantly narrow fork, and the view was partially obstructed by foliage. Presently Chuma announced from a higher perch that the nearer of the two bulls had tusks of much the same size as those we had secured in Bugoma, and a minute later the whole herd began to move. One of the smaller groups came within eighty yards of us, and some newly arrived cows looked like advancing right on to us from a belt of trees to our right, but eventually all bent their course away from us, the last to shift being the two bulls, on whom we had pinned our hopes. Sadly we realised that there was nothing really good enough, and decided to return to camp. But we had been working round more or less in a circle, and our way led us right over the spot just vacated by the bulls and in the wake of the herd.

Five minutes later we scaled a small tree to see what might be in front, to find that three or four of them were standing like rocks less than forty yards away. The blankness of the day had begun to tell upon us, and already —the wish being father to the thought—we fancied there might be a big enough one among these after all.

They moved off and we followed. After about fifteen minutes' stalking and scouting, we suddenly came upon eight or ten of them standing drowsily in the shade of some big trees at the farther side of a " donga " ten or twelve feet deep and fifty or sixty yards across. It was a surprising thing to come across so ideal a spot in that country. The bank on which we stood was dotted with big trees, and afforded an almost perfect strategic position.

At first we could only see three or four pairs of quite small tusks, but the beast which, from his size and colour, was evidently the veteran of the bunch, was dozing with his head hidden behind a tree trunk, and we decided to wait till he should move and show his ivory. While waiting, we were treated to a very pretty little exhibition of tree-breaking, and, though it turned out a comparative failure, we secured a snapshot of one of them in the very act. It was a rare situation, and one that made us long for cinematograph apparatus to do it full justice.

Presently one of the beasts, a little more ambitious or vicious than the rest, tried a very big branch of the tree under which he was standing. It must have been over twelve inches thick, and it resisted his efforts. Thrusting a tusk into a fork, and curling his trunk round the offending limb, he shook the whole tree furiously. This aroused the veteran from his lethargy, and he emerged from behind his tree, made a half turn, and stood looking straight at us. We ought to have resisted the temptation when we saw his tusks, but they looked nice and thick at about forty-five yards, and whispering almost simultaneously, " He is good enough," we opened fire with a .450 bullet near the right eye. He staggered and reeled to one side, and for a second looked as if he was going to turn and make off. Then he recovered, and faced us again; a second .450 in the forehead seemed to stimulate rather than discourage him, and, pulling himself together, with ears outspread and trunk uplifted he made straight for the spot on which we stood. At the first report the rest of the group had made incontinently off into the bush—yet not all of them. Another large bull whom we had hardly noticed standing by during his first advance, turned and joined his comrade, and for a few steps they came on side by side, and it looked as if we were going to have a couple of them to reckon with; then, at a third shot at the wounded one from the .360, the second one turned off at an angle and disappeared, and the veteran came on alone. He was within twenty yards when the .360's second barrel missed fire. Regardless of a bullet in the chest from the .350 that Chuma was carrying, he still kept on. There was now just time for the one carrying the .360 to reload and little more—the other with the .450 having turned to descend into the donga so as to attack his flank. We had the advantage of him in our position on the bank, and the next shot took effect. He was within fifteen paces and just beginning to clamber up when a bullet between the eyes toppled him over in his tracks.

It had been a trying moment for the natives apparently. Chuma, of course, had stood his ground, and Nkamba and Musa with spare cartridges were within a foot or two all the while, but the rest, headed by Udala and the luncheon baskets, had lost no time in seeking safety in flight. Once assured that the elephant had succumbed they reappeared —but not without an effort to communicate their fears to us—"Don't go up to it," they cried frantically, "don't go up to it! It is not dead! It is not dead—it will get up again!" Chuma's contempt was for once too much for his customary caution, and with a bound he was on the top of the fallen beast and dancing a tarantella on its ribs. However, it was as good as dead, and after a blink and a sigh they all had to admit it. " By George," we said almost simultaneously, " what a chance for a cinematograph missed." We had been told just after leaving Entebbe that a cinematographer had recently arrived in the country with the express purpose of obtaining a record of the death of an elephant, and there was no doubt, so extraordinary had been the combination of circumstances—position, view, light, and every detail of the scene—that pictures of unique interest might have been secured in comparative safety.

He stood 10 ft. 6 in. at the shoulder. His tusks measured $55\frac{1}{2}$ in. and 55 in., showing 38 in. and 35 in. outside, with a circumference of 18 in. each and weighing 49 lbs. and 46 lbs.

The following day we moved south-east *viâ* Samusoni's, a camp at the junction of the Foweira and Palango roads, to Benjamin's, a few miles south of the latter.

There was plenty of fresh spoor on the road near Samusoni's, and later in the day we heard elephants trumpeting close to our path, but in both cases it was almost certainly the herd out of which we had killed two days before, and we pushed on. Chuma, who had preceded us, went off thinking he had possibly found something in the tracks of a group of three, but came in soon after us, reporting them to be a cow and two young bulls.

Scouts sent out on our arrival returned in the evening reporting nothing, but next morning our hopes were raised by the arrival of a native from a neighbouring *shamba* who declared that his brother had just seen three large elephants feeding close to his gardens. We started off at once, and reached the *shamba* before midday, but we were doomed to be the victims of native inaccuracy, and to the exasperation of another blank day's hunting. We were taken to the spot by the man who said he had seen them, and shown the very tree on which they had been feeding, he declared, but six hours before. He had particularly noticed the tusks of the biggest, he said, and they measured at least four feet outside the head. Half-an-hour's tracking convinced us that he had been drawing

Our second elephant.

"The stripping and uprooting of several large trees."

on his imagination and that the spoor was quite twenty hours old, but a few minutes later we found a spot where they had rested the previous evening and then separated, and we took up and followed the tracks of the biggest. About noon, the spoor being still quite stale, we were startled by a rumble on our left. Mounting a convenient ant-hill, we found ourselves looking at a large bull elephant standing by himself in the shade, broadside on, at about sixty yards. He was partly hidden by the foliage of a small tree, but the grass being short and the wind right, there was nothing to prevent us getting close enough to be sure of his tusks. We eventually got within less than ten paces on one side, and again some twenty on the other, without him being aware of our presence, but only to find that his tusks were smaller than either of our first kills, being probably a good deal under forty pounds.

It was a tempting chance for a photograph, but we did not want to run the risk of having to shoot a beast with thirty-pound ivory, so we turned away and left him. Water was found a little way off, and while we sat and lunched we could still hear him sleepily flapping his ears amongst the leaves and pulling off an occasional branch of the tree under which he was standing.

Reports of nothing more than a few cows and small bulls greeted us on our return to camp, and we decided to move on next day to Kishilisi, on Port Masindi, on the Victoria Nile.

XIV

ELEPHANT HUNTING IN THE MASINDI DISTRICT—II

The Victoria Nile at Kishilisi—Jackson's hartebeeste and steinbok—Back to Kiliandongo's—More blank days after elephants—Risks run by *shamba* dwellers—Our carriers go on strike, but are appeased—Still more blank days—Our third elephant—An evening outing—Crossing the Nile—Palango—Repatriation of our Rhodesian natives—Arrival of Captain Place.

REACHING the Nile in three and a half hours we followed it more or less south and reached camp at noon. The landscape close to the river presents a very different aspect to the country in which we had been travelling for upwards of a month. The river itself is thickly edged with papyrus, the grass on all sides is much shorter, and the trees, which are plentiful, are mainly thorns.

The soil is black and evidently fertile, and large quantities of excellent cotton is grown by the natives, as well as crops of millet, maize, kasava, sim-sim, and sweet potatoes.

The population live in the non-gregarious *shamba* settlements, as in the rest of Bunyoro and Buganda, cultivating the land all round their dwellings. They do not appear to like the actual river bank, and do but little fishing.

Of the natives some were Banyoro, and others, probably Bakedi, from the east side of the river. The latter were the much less clad and less civilised in appearance, but were unquestionably the finer in bearing and physique. Elephants, we were told, came to the neighbourhood during the rains, but none had been seen or heard of for at least a month. Game of other kinds was reported to be found, as a rule, feeding within a mile or two, so we

CHUMAMABOKO STANDING BY A JACKSON'S HARTEBEESTE.

gave ourselves a rest from the more strenuous form of sport and were content with securing a steinbok and three hartebeeste in two short outings. This was, as a matter of fact, the only game besides elephant and the forest hog that we had seen during the forty odd days we had been travelling in Uganda.

The third day after reaching Kishilisi we retraced our steps to Kiliandongo, and heard on our arrival no less than three distinct reports of elephants in the near neighbourhood, probably all of the same herd.

Starting at daybreak for another attempt, we had a fruitless day of ten and a half hours, during nine of which we were on the move. It began with another instance of the astounding inaccuracy of the local natives. One of them, just after we had heard some trumpeting close to the road, led us to a spot where, he declared, he had seen a huge solitary bull feeding that very morning. He had, as a matter of fact, seen nothing of the kind. There had been a bull elephant there without a doubt, but it had not been there that morning, it had not been there alone, and—he had certainly not seen it. This piece of native ineptitude delayed us a little in coming up again with the herd, but it was not a full hour before unmistakable rumblings and trumpetings showed that we were pretty nearly in the middle of it. Then followed a morning which, but for the merest details, was just the same as any other of the long days we had spent among the Uganda elephants.

There was the same eight to twelve foot grass, the same big tree from which we located the various sections of the herd, the same huge bull that looked so promising at about three hundred yards as he emerged from a thick patch into an open space as if coming straight for us, and then did not even come at all, the same batches of calves with their mothers, and of old cows that seemed for an instant as if they had detected us and might be going to make trouble, and the same failure at the end of it all.

After the herd had made their first move, and we had moved after them some little way, our hopes went rather higher than they had been for some time. We found ourselves tracking an isolated group of four or five bulls, whose spoor contained some of the largest footmarks we had seen. A rather breathless chase along their well-beaten but tortuous tracks through the highest grass brought us suddenly upon them having a mud bath in a swampy pool, and only partly hidden by a screen of small trees. But before they moved lazily on we had a good view of their tusks, and there was not a twenty-pounder amongst them.

Poor old Chumamaboko, returning from twenty minutes' scouting, sat down and gradually but freely gave vent to his disappointed feelings.

"Waugh," he said, "what is the good of trying to hunt elephants in this country of grass, of huge herds and no big bulls? There *are* no big bulls. They have gone somewhere else. *Fikungulu* (big tuskers) don't walk about with herds of cows and calves."

"Not in your country, Chuma," we said, "but they do in this. Look at the big tusks you have seen yourself that have been got by the white men in this country. They were found in the big herds."

He snorted frank scepticism, and a local native chipped in.

"There are big ones, and they are with the big herds, but they keep in front and the cows keep all round them so that they cannot be seen."

We had heard this before, and found it rather difficult to believe; but to Chuma, coming from a local romancer, too, it was the last straw.

"You have seen them, have you? You have seen them? *You!* Oh yes! And you have seen bull elephants feeding, you have seen, and measured, their tusks, you have brought us to the place, and—they had not been there since the last sun had set. You *saw* a mighty *chikungulu* this morning, alone; you took us to the spot: ten cows had passed—the night before. You have seen them, have you?—you have seen the cow-guard round the bulls? Then tell me where is their spoor? Do the cows lift them off their feet so that they leave no tracks? And do they lie upon them and cover them so that I see nothing of them when I look down upon them from the tree-tops? Oh yes! you have doubtless seen them; let me see, and perhaps I will believe."

Chuma's feelings were very much our own, but as he was getting discouraged, we did our best to disguise them. If we had any doubts left, the next half-hour effectually dispelled them. Less than half a mile on the herd had stopped again, and first from one tree and then another we got a view of every beast in it while it was slowly moving off, the cows and calves trumpeting and squealing, the bulls nonchalantly uprooting trees and tearing off branches as they glided solemnly in their wake. There were no good tuskers, so we sat down and lunched, and then turned campwards.

The beasts had been within six hundred yards of us while we rested, and were still audible for nearly an hour of the two and a half that it took us to get back.

We passed through several small *shambas* on our way that afforded ample corroboration of the complaints we had heard from the natives that the elephants were invading their *shambas* and destroying their crops and bananas, and occasionally killing the inhabitants.

It is really rather surprising that their huts were not more often annihilated. The *shamba* system, with the huts of the owners scattered over a large area each in the middle of his plantation and gardens, is of course better adapted for watching the marauders than that of the large compact village with its cultivated land necessarily some distance away in the bush. But considering the flimsy construction of most of the *shamba* dwellings and their isolation, it is not to be wondered at that a herd of elephants, intent on a meal, sometimes tramples them and their inhabitants underfoot without noticing where it is going.

The elephant's notorious aversion to the smell of human beings would ensure immunity from such trampling of the inhabitants if they lived in villages—though then they could not guard their crops so efficiently.

We were to have our patience still further tested in the evening. Our carriers presented themselves in a body, and demanded their pay. It was possible that the dearth of small change, from which nearly the whole Protectorate was at that time suffering, had aroused their suspicions as to our solvency, so we met them with a promise that they should be paid up to date on arrival at Palango, adding that our stock of rupees was short, but that a messenger was on the way with a fresh supply (which was a fact). And we further reminded them that the conclusion of a month's work did not necessarily mean the conclusion of their contract, which was that they were to accompany us as long as we wanted them, and we left it at that for the night. Early in the morning, as we were on the point of leaving camp to investigate a fresh report of elephants, we were informed that the porters had struck work. Summoned and asked what more they wanted to say, they replied with no uncertain voice that they had no intention of going to Palango. They would not mind taking us to Butiaba, whither we had told them at Mubendi that we might be going, but nothing would induce them to cross the Nile. It was in vain that we assured them that Palango station was only three miles across the Nile, and only two days' journey from where we were. They had their own notions of Lango amenities and Lango hospitality to strangers—coloured, no doubt, by a story we had heard at Samusoni's from a youth who had just had some cattle looted from him in their country, and who was ready to paint them and their delinquencies in any kind of colour.

Ten of these malcontents were willing to go on with us, but as the rest seemed to have made up their minds, there was nothing to do but to make light of it. Any or all of them, we said, could go home if they liked, and we had no intention of trying to stop them, but—of course they realised that they were running the risk not only of losing their pay but of being imprisoned for breach of contract at Mubendi. "Go at once," we said, "if you are going, and we will get substitutes from the *Mwami*, and—

ELEPHANT HUNTING

thank you for the present of the pay due to you." With the exception of the ten, they jumped to their feet without another word, shouldered their bundles of meat, &c., and started gaily down the road towards Masindi. The ten sat and smiled—and it was not altogether at our expense. We then made inquiries, and learnt that the local supply of men might amount to a dozen, but certainly no more, as all the males were away on telegraph construction work or something of the kind. Asking them to do their best we went off, wondering how on earth we were going to get to Gondokoro in time to catch a steamer on the 28th if the carriers persisted in their bluff, for though we could get to Palango with twenty-two men, it would have to be in reliefs, and would take seven or eight days.

Then came the day's work—yet once more to end in failure. Again the local natives put us on to a hopelessly wrong scent. Declaring that they had seen a herd that morning, they brought us to spoor that was at least twenty-four hours old. When, in response to their entreaties, we eventually came on something fresh, it was not elephant spoor at all, but the tracks and the blood of a buffalo wounded apparently by a native hunter the day before. It made but little difference. As a matter of fact, we found the morning's spoor of the elephants in an hour's time, only to find unmistakable proofs that they were changing their feeding-ground and had been going so steadily since dawn that it would have been quite hopeless to catch them up.

Returning wearily to camp, we found some consolation in the discovery that our carriers' bluff had failed. All, without exception, had returned to work, and would accompany us to Palango. We smiled, but let the matter rest.

Mika, *Mwami* or Chief of Kiliandongo, who had been absent, had meanwhile returned and paid us a visit in the evening. He was obviously a man of position and importance, as testified by the refreshing humility with which our Hoima guide flopped on his knees and remained there while conversing with him. A native of dignified bearing and courteous and easy address, he came with his chair and his court, and, smoking one or two of our cigarettes, sat and discussed the hunting prospects of the neighbourhood for half-an-hour with the cool judgment of an educated European.

Following his advice we moved northwards to Reuben (or Geki). The road had been cut up for some distance by elephants—the herd which we had followed the previous day, and another that on investigation proved to have gone in the same direction, and probably quite as far. There was no object in remaining, so we pushed on the next day eastwards to Chisuna, a spot suggested by Mika as likely to bring us success. Most of the way we were on the Palango road, which we had struck first at Samusoni's. In parts it had been ploughed out of all recognition by elephants that had been disporting themselves upon it and beside it a month or so before.

The old headman whose *shamba* was close to our camp brought us in word that a solitary bull elephant had been feeding for several days in a neighbouring plantation. A stick that was said to represent the length of his footmark measured twenty-two inches, and our hopes accordingly rose higher than they had been for some time. They would bring us word at dawn should he revisit his feeding-ground that night, and a little before sunrise we started off to meet them should they be on their way. But he had not returned, nor was it known in which direction he had moved. Scouts sent in likely directions found nothing but a small herd of insignificant beasts, and our own efforts were equally fruitless.

By midday we had returned to camp feeling more disgusted than ever over the day's failure. It had not been so long or hard a day's work as many others, but after spending day after day with huge herds in which we knew we had but a remote chance of finding a big tusker, it was sufficiently exasperating that—with what was the most promising prospect of the whole trip—the beast should slip through our fingers.

While reflecting that evening on the arduous and

profitless days spent in our efforts to secure something more than an average specimen of the Uganda elephant—to achieve something a little beyond the mere right to boast that we had shot so many elephants, regardless of number, age, sex, or size—we were reminded of some correspondence that appeared in the *Outlook* in January 1909. "The dangers and labour men will undergo to kill big game," wrote the contributor, "bear witness to the absolute truth (*sic*) that taking life is the prime object of the blood sportsman."

The elephant hunter undoubtedly has one eye on his pocket when discriminating between the big and small tusker—'twere pointless to deny it; but this blood-lust indictment—well, unless it be a case of self-inflicted flagellation as a balm to a conscience guilty of past excess, one is tempted to wager that the petulant dogma of the inexperienced platitudinist would not long withstand a first-hand knowledge of the attractions and hardships of the pursuit of big game.

The following morning brought us no further news of our elusive bull or of any other herd, so we moved on again in the direction of Palango, deciding to camp at Gabrieli's, about fifteen miles farther on.

Our time was getting uncomfortably short. Even supposing it to be possible to get carriers at Palango to go with us to Gondokoro—about which we had no particular reason for feeling sanguine—we had but four days to spare, and two more elephants to make up our number.

We were not much encouraged, therefore, when we met the messenger we had sent to Palango a few days before with a note from the clerk at Palango to say that Captain Place, the Assistant District Commissioner, was away from the station. However, he might conceivably come back in time, and at the worst we should only have to spend another month in the country, and catch the January boat at Gondokoro.

Our messenger told us that a herd of elephant had crossed the road a little farther on the same morning, and half-way between Samusoni's (the same camp at which we had previously spent a night) and Gabrieli's we came upon Chuma and others examining the spoor—not at all optimistically; optimism was not in the air. The spoor was that of two or three bulls with no cows, and gave us hope. But they were going the wrong way, *i.e.* their tracks led south towards the only plantations within some miles, and must have been made before they went to feed. After feeding they may have gone left in the opposite direction, still farther south. However, some natives going west told us that a herd had crossed the road and were going north, and that they had just heard them trumpeting. Chuma would not express an opinion—he was frankly tired—and we decided to send on the loads to Gabrieli's and go and investigate.

After following a mixed trail for a short distance we found ourselves on the spoor of a single bull, and within an hour of leaving the road we killed. This had been quite easy work; we had been close to him for some time, but even though we climbed trees within a hundred yards of him, the undergrowth and foliage were too dense to give us a view. Finally from the top of a low ant-hill we caught sight of a branch that he was shaking, some fifty paces away, and within a couple of minutes he obliged us by emerging from his hiding-place and coming straight towards us. He had evidently faintly smelt something of which he disapproved, and which he wished to investigate. At thirty yards he showed his tusks, and though not the eighty- or ninety-pounder we had been dreaming of, he was plainly as big as those we had shot, and we drew a bead.

We had a good strategic position on the ant-hill, and though we planted a few in his ribs as he reeled and staggered and sat down with a squealing trumpet-blare, the first two in the forehead would doubtless have been enough. His measurements were: height at shoulder, 10 ft. 9 in.; forefoot diameter 21 in., circumference 62 in.; tusks, length outside lip, 42 in. and 39 in., greatest girth, $18\frac{3}{4}$ and $18\frac{1}{2}$ in.; weight and length, 53 lbs. and 51 lbs. and 69 in. and 66 in. respectively.

We reached camp at four, and soon after had a visit

ELEPHANT HUNTING

from the *Mwami* Gabrieli, who told us very much the same story as we had heard at Chisuna, viz. that a single huge bull elephant had been frequenting the gardens for several days, and even chasing the inhabitants out of their *shambas*.

On our suggestion Gabrieli went off at once to tell his people to scout round for fresh news, and we wondered if our luck, almost too late, was really going to turn.

At five o'clock there appeared a breathless native, who declared that the said monster was even then close by near the gardens of his *shamba*; that he had, in obedience to our request, been looking about for his tracks, when a sudden trumpet in his very ears made him take to his heels. It was close enough, he said, for us to get there and possibly back again before dark.

There was a good deal of scepticism in the reception of his news, but he stuck to his story under cross-examination; and as it wanted forty minutes to sunset, there was nothing to be lost, at any rate, by following the spoor for twenty minutes or so and then, if nothing transpired, returning to camp.

It took us just twenty-five minutes to reach the spot, but only to find that—with the best intentions, perhaps—we had been fooled again. There were tracks, it is true, but they were of a cow and one or two calves, and certainly some six or seven hours old.

Now there was an interesting contribution to the study of Bantu psychology. Our informant had obviously not seen or heard the beasts just before he had come to tell us. It is more than probable that he had not seen or heard them at all, and that he had only just begun, in obedience to Gabrieli's orders, to look for the tracks of the notorious bull. While looking he comes upon traces of *some* elephants: he does not stop to investigate: he is looking for the traces of a big bull elephant who is a constant marauder and who is credited with ferocity towards any human being who crosses his path, and he immediately jumps to the conclusion that the tracks he has seen are those of that bull and none other. The mental process by which he brought himself deliberately to state that he had actually seen and been put to flight by the animal is harder to analyse. It could not have been a mischievous attempt to deceive; for all he knew, condign punishment might have been meted out to him then and there for his falsehood, and, further, he took an obvious pride in being given the opportunity of proving the accuracy of his account.

Little use in either reasoning with or revenging oneself upon such. One can only dismiss it as an unusually striking instance of the deficiency in the power of association that is a characteristic of the negro intellect.

Naturally we did not waste any more time on the spoor, and retracing our steps reached camp again just before dark.

Some, if not all of us had been in considerable danger on the way out to those gardens, though we only found it out just as we got there. Our amiable old "*munyampala*" (or headman of the carriers), who was allowed a badge of office in the shape of an old Snider rifle (without ammunition), apparently elated at the possible prospect of a second elephant in one day, or at his unique opportunity of being in at the death, accompanied us on our sally, brandishing his weapon and executing a silent but fantastic war-dance round us, or prancing along with the weapon at the "present" as if facing some tremendous beast.

As we were on the point of turning back, somebody happened to look closely at his gun. It was loaded—he had got a cartridge from somewhere—and at full-cock. For something over a mile, mostly through tangled grass and creepers, he had been carrying it thus. The slightest thing might have sent it off, and goodness only knew where the thing had been pointing all the time.

The next day, while waiting at Gabrieli's for the tusks, a note reached us from Captain Place saying that he hoped to be able to get us what carriers we needed in four days' time, and further encouraging us with regard to the prospects of finding elephant on the Kole River on our way to Nimule.

Under these circumstances we decided to spend no more time in the Masindi district, although another herd had been reported close, but to go on to Palango at once.

Leaving at about seven o'clock we reached the ferry in two and a half hours. The river proper here is some four hundred yards broad, and is fringed on the western side with a broad belt of swamp.

The crossing occupied each boat-load half-an-hour, the tedious part of it being the negotiation of the muddy and tortuous passage through the fringe. A canoe arrived at our landing-place just at the right moment, and others were hastened from the opposite side as soon as we reached the open water. The canoes that took us over were some of the hugest dug-outs we had ever seen. That in which we crossed comfortably held a dozen of us with a few loads and our bicycles, while there were others which were used for transporting sheep and cattle. One of these we met when half-way across carrying a few of both kinds of stock, tethered by rope passed through holes near the top of the gunwale.

On the farther bank we found some unusually good specimens of the conical basket in which the local natives catch their fish, but had not an opportunity of seeing it used.

Three miles on a straight road up a slight incline brought us to Palango station; the last mile led through a regular belt of borassus palms, with practically no other trees, and the last few hundred yards between flourishing cotton plantations.

The offices are placed on high ground at the foot of a bunch of huge stony kopjes. At the top of a pass through these is built the resident official's house, with a stupendous dome-shaped rock on its south-eastern side. It was hot, but there was a pleasant breeze. The view from the station was spacious, but monotonous and flat, broken only by a clump of low hills to the south-east and the low range beyond the river towards Port Masindi to the south-west.

Captain Place was still away, but had kindly sent word that we were to make ourselves at home, so we pitched our tents in an open space amongst the rocks near his house.

Our Mubendi carriers were paid off, and returned to their homes the following day. Our Wawemba had by this time made up their minds that they had come quite far enough—if not too far—already, and nothing would induce them to contemplate the prospect of coming the rest of the way to Gondokoro and returning by the Nimule-Butiaba route by boat. We tried to convince them that it would entail their being but very little longer away from home, but did not press the point.

With Musa and the two servants we had engaged at Hoima, as well as the boy Kasonde, who was to come right through, we were, of course, quite adequately staffed.

They had done an exceptionally long journey and in —to them—exceptionally strange lands, and they had really done remarkably well. The Central African native is not a traveller by nature, and adapts himself less easily to new conditions and altered modes of life than the white man. Added to their bewilderment at strange coinage, strange languages, and strange foods was their conviction that, at the best, it was going to be nearly half a year before they saw their homes again. Striking as was their confidence in us generally, they found it difficult to believe that a journey on which we had spent nearly five months could be accomplished by direct routes in less than ten weeks.

As we had made arrangements for their passage on the lake steamer from Entebbe to Mwanza, and for their maintenance should they be delayed while waiting for connections *en route*, there was little likelihood of their meeting with any difficulties on the way; and, as a matter of fact, we heard in the course of time that they reached their homes without mishap in nine and a half weeks, having drawn without any hitch the ration allow-

Preparing to cross the Nile.

Fish Basket on the Victoria Nile.

ances we had deposited for them at Entebbe, Mwanza, Tabora, and Abercorn.[1]

Captain Place returned two days later, and lost no time in procuring carriers for our journey to Gondokoro, meanwhile making us his guests.

[1] They have now rejoined us once more in Northern Rhodesia, and are none the worse for their long journey.

XV

THROUGH THE LANGO AND ACHOLI COUNTRY

The Lango—The system of governing through Baganda agents—Description of the clothing, ornaments, accoutrements, villages, and huts of the Lango—Start from Palango—Our escorts and carriers—Travelling in the Lango country—Two swampy rivers—Mount Moru—Reception at Mwaka's—The Lango at work—Mwaka's "army"—Gulu—The Acholi—A hunting party—Oliya's village—His cadet corps—More trouble with the bicycle—Nimule.

ONCE across the Victoria Nile we had left behind us the better known regions of Uganda with their advanced and partly civilised inhabitants, and had entered a wilder region—one concerning which very little is known, and which is peopled by races as yet untamed and unsophisticated. It was the beginning of a section of our journey that was rich in ethnographical interest, and over which we would willingly have lingered had we not had to hasten our steps to catch a steamer at the other end.

Geographically, too, interesting and useful work might have been done, for though the district commissioners at Palango, Koba, and Nimule have entered the country, no European had passed through direct from the first-named station to the last, and but little mapping has been undertaken in any direction. However, the making even of sketch-maps takes time, and having to cover about two hundred and seventy-five miles in sixteen or seventeen days, we decided that it would be hopeless to attempt it.

In the study of the interesting races through whose country we passed we were a little more fortunate, as we had continual opportunities for observing them in spite

Ferrying cattle on the channels abutting on the Victoria Nile.

THE LANGO AND ACHOLI COUNTRY

of the short time at our disposal. Not only did we live amongst them all the time, but the friendly nature of our reception enabled us to gain a fairly close insight into the nature and habits of the Lango and Acholi at home. Both Captain Tufnell and Captain Place warned us that after the first two days we should probably see no natives at all in the villages, and certainly no women, as they would all flee into the bush at our approach. As it turned out, at no stage in the journey did any natives show less concern at our arrival—not a soul allowing our presence to interfere in any way with the ordinary tenor of his life. This was all the more remarkable not only because no other travellers had passed that way, and the advent of two Europeans might consequently be looked upon as a novelty, but also because the relations between the administration and the Lango are not yet free from occasional differences of opinion. Indeed it was only while we were at Palango that Captain Place returned from taking steps to avenge the death of one of the Baganda agents and his followers. Accompanied as we were, therefore, by a police escort, the natives might easily have suspected us of being concerned with these reprisals, but our presence amongst them aroused neither fear nor curiosity.

The Lango and their northern neighbours the Acholi are allied to, and speak practically the same tongue as, the Jaluo Kavirondo in the westernmost province of British East Africa, and the Bakedi (which only means Naked People) who live to the north of the Ripon Falls. This group appears to come of a different stock to the races around them, their language not being a "Bantu" tongue, but, apparently, a guttural mixture of Nilotic and Gala origin tinged with West African phonology.[1]

---

[1] According to Sir Harry Johnston (*The Uganda Protectorate*, vol. ii.), the Nile negroes—including Shiluk, Dinka, Acholi, and Lango, &c—were probably driven from the north by the first determined Hamitic invasion of the Egyptian Soudan and Abyssinia, and in places were checked by the thinner stream of Hamitic immigrants (Gala) who were continually entering negro Nile-land from the north-east. This created the Masai and Sūk types, and the temporary successes of this powerful blend carried the modified Nile languages westward as far as the Bari country, where the language became tinged with West African

To start the administration of the Lango country[1] recourse has been had to native "agents" who are recruited from the Baganda. This system was apparently inevitable owing to local conditions, but is generally admitted to be an unfortunate necessity, and the obvious disadvantages of such a system appear to have been aggravated by the inadequate scale of pay allowed to these agents. There are ten of them in the Lango country, and they are scattered about in small stockaded forts, in which they live and from which they control the inhabitants, getting them in for road work, which, as the poll-tax has not yet been introduced, is the only form of taxation to which they are at present subjected. Each agent has a staff of fourteen armed followers, Baganda like himself, and—excepting the head agent, who receives Rs.30—is paid Rs.10 per month.

Theoretically the agents are all chiefs whose followers accompany them for nothing on account of their position, but we gathered that only two out of the ten have any pretensions to that title, and that therefore their followers do not come to the Lango country without expecting to benefit financially by so doing. As Rs.10 is of course quite inadequate pay for fifteen men, they add to their salaries by keeping trade goods for the purchase of sheep. This stock of trade goods tends to become a mere cloak for illegal confiscation or for appropriating to themselves stock that has been confiscated in the name of the Government. In other words, they are tempted either to steal

phonology. The constant stream of Nilotic negroes following one another in waves of immigration, carried this negro type and dialect to the north-east of Victoria Nyanza (Jaluo Kavirondo). South-west of the Victoria Nile and west of the Bahr-el-Gebel (except for the Aluro to the north-west of Lake Albert) they were checked by the Bantu, who sprang some three thousand years ago from a horde of West African natives that poured into these parts, driving out the pygmy—prognathous group—whom they found there. Sir Harry Johnston classes the group of languages spoken by these people as the "Masai-Turkana-Bari" group, which, he says, "constitutes a very loosely knit group of languages, each of which, perhaps, resembles the other slightly more than it approaches dialects outside this grouping." He adds that "there is an obvious relationship between the Masai and Nilotic tongues—Dinka, Shiluk (Shwolo), Dyur, Shangala, Acholi, Aluro, Lango, and Jaluo."

[1] This system of government by native agents has not been introduced into the Acholi country, but it is in force, we believe, among the Bakedi and also in the Elgon district.

BORASSUS PALMS.

WEIGHING OUR THIRD PAIR OF TUSKS IN CAMP.

from their employers or from those over whom they rule—the inevitable result with any agents, white or black, who are underpaid.

If the rate of pay accorded to these agents were on a more liberal scale, irregular additions to their incomes and the trading which cloaks them could be entirely prohibited, and the extra expense entailed would be to a large extent counterbalanced by the reduction in the numbers of Government cattle and sheep that are now returned as "dead" or "lost," as well as by the benefit that would ensue from the removal of many causes of friction at present existing between the governors and governed. We were favourably impressed with the agents whom we met, who appear to be wonderfully little disliked considering their anomalous position; but though the men chosen for these posts may be well selected, the system is a bad one, and, if it is inevitable, it should be rendered as innocuous as possible by the adoption of an adequate scale of pay.

During our stay at Palango we met Dora, one of the principal and most friendly of the Lango chiefs—a man who has very considerable influence over his people, and rules them directly without the assistance of an agent. When a few more chiefs of his type and standing follow Dora's example, and cease their hostility or opposition to the Government, the services of the Baganda agents will doubtless be dispensed with. Dora kindly told off a sub-chief, Mwaka (or Kelomwaka), to accompany us on the first stage of our journey, and doubtless much of the smoothness which marked our passage through the country was due to this man's presence. He was accompanied by two buglers and an escort of armed men, supplementary to the police provided by Captain Place.

Dora brought up two of his wives as well as several other ladies to pay us a visit. The wives were clothed in cotton cloths—though one of them removed hers when facing the camera—but the remainder were in the national costume, consisting chiefly of tattoo marks—which are more numerous and more pronounced than any we have seen elsewhere—a small girdle round the waist, from which hangs, in front, a diminutive apron—sometimes made of native wrought-iron chain-work, and sometimes simply of strands of grass or hair—and behind a short "tail" sticking out at right angles to the body, from which, in the case of married women, a long tail, made of hair, hangs down to the ground. Their ornaments are necklaces, anklets, wristlets, rings, and earrings of native iron, or, more rarely, copper from the Congo, or imported brass, while the neck, forehead, and ears are often further adorned with shells and fish bones. The hair is plaited and is worn long.

The men, who are of fine physique, occasionally wear a small skin loin-cloth, but more often a small skin apron is suspended in front from a girdle or corset of strands of twisted grass. Some of the young bloods affect very tight lacing with these grass corsets, which gives them a ridiculous appearance, while most of them have a habit of binding the upper arm, when young, with an iron wire bracelet, which causes a shocking distortion of the muscles of the biceps. In one case that we measured, we found that what should have been the thickest part of the biceps measured only $8\frac{1}{2}$ inches over the wire, while below, between the "ornament" and the elbow, the measurement was no less than $13\frac{1}{2}$ inches. Their hair is allowed to grow long and is welded in a cone—something after the manner of the Mashukulumbwe, but not to such an exaggerated extent—which is often supplemented by a warthog tush, fastened in the hair behind the cone, the whole head being encircled by a band of fish bones or cowrie shells. Iron earrings are frequently worn, and necklaces of iron, iron and copper, or beads from which is suspended a small antelope's horn or other charm.

Perhaps the most striking feature in the Lango's remarkable, if limited, wardrobe is the crescent-shaped glass ornament worn in the lower lip. This is inserted through a hole at the base of the lip, and is made from pieces of glass bottles carefully filed down. As there is no centre of civilisation near, bottles have not yet become

"Costume consisting chiefly of tatoo marks, a small girdle round the waist from which hangs, in front, a miniature apron . . of iron chain-work . . or strands of hair, and behind . . a long tail hangs down to the ground."

THE LANGO AND ACHOLI COUNTRY 223

common, and we found that no present was more acceptable among these dusky dandies than an old bottle. They have rather striking features, and some have quite aquiline noses, and lips of only moderate thickness. The colour of the skin is the chocolate hue usual in this part of Africa.

They all carry sticks, and mostly use a rough spade instead of the almost universal African hoe. All are armed with spears and bows and arrows, and many have guns, which have come in from Abyssinia, though they are not so plentiful as among the Acholi.

There is a somewhat peculiar difference between these people and the kindred Wakavirondo, in that while the latter show no inclination to adopt clothing of any kind either European, or the ordinary blanket or coloured print, the Lango seem quite pleased to wear anything they can get hold of. Reference to the photograph of Mwaka's "army" will show that half of them are clothed, while all the chiefs that we encountered were wearing European clothing of some kind or other.

The usual Lango village is surrounded by a stockade of poles, and contains from ten to fifty huts built close together side by side with the grain stores. The huts are shaped like beehives, with low walls and high, steep-pitched roofs on which the thatch is laid in step-like ridges. The doorways are more or less circular and very low, those in bachelors' huts being so small that the occupants can hardly squeeze through them,[1] while even the benedicts have to crawl on their hands and knees when entering or leaving their abodes. This is, of course, a great convenience to raiding parties, as they can spear the inhabitants between the shoulder-blades as they crawl slowly and awkwardly from their huts.

The Lango appear to regard raiding as one of the

---

[1] Although we searched diligently for them we failed to find in any village we visited, either among the Lango or Acholi, any of the bachelors' huts raised on piles like a grain store or pigeon-cote in which it is said the bachelors are shut up at night—the surrounding ground being covered with sand every evening so that any night excursions on the part of a gay young spark would be patent to his elders.

chief pleasures of life, and it is because he interferes with this pursuit that the white man's presence is rather resented, as would be the domination in England of a race that made illegal cricket, football, and other national sports. A happy, unsophisticated crowd, they are in reality very friendly and well-disposed, and their outbreaks are really due to their innate exuberance of spirits which is liable to get out of hand at the beer season. This is the season at which they generally raid each other, a neighbouring tribe, or even one of the Government agents, but as is natural with such a light-hearted people, they appear to bear no ill-will for reprisals taken after a raid.

Their staple food consists of the small red millet, supplemented by sweet potatoes. Bananas, which form the main dietary of the Baganda and Banyoro on the other side of the Nile, are not grown except at the forts of the Baganda agents, who have also introduced the cultivation of cotton.

On December 11th, our quota of carriers being completed, we said good-bye to our host and chief Dora and set out for the North. We had fifty-seven carriers for ourselves and three for the police. Kasonde, the sole remaining Rhodesian, two local personal servants, a cook's boy, Musa, a local headman to boss up the loads, two Lango gun-bearers, Mwaka and another representative of chief Dora, and an escort of nineteen armed men, six of whom were police, the rest being irregulars, including two buglers.

The orders issued to the police, in our presence, were as follows:—

    I. To escort us and our carriers to Gondokoro, and to escort our carriers back to Palango.
   II. Not to loot.
  III. Not to allow the carriers to loot.
  IV. In the event of the local natives failing to provide food, to escort the carriers, when instructed by us, to the village gardens, so that

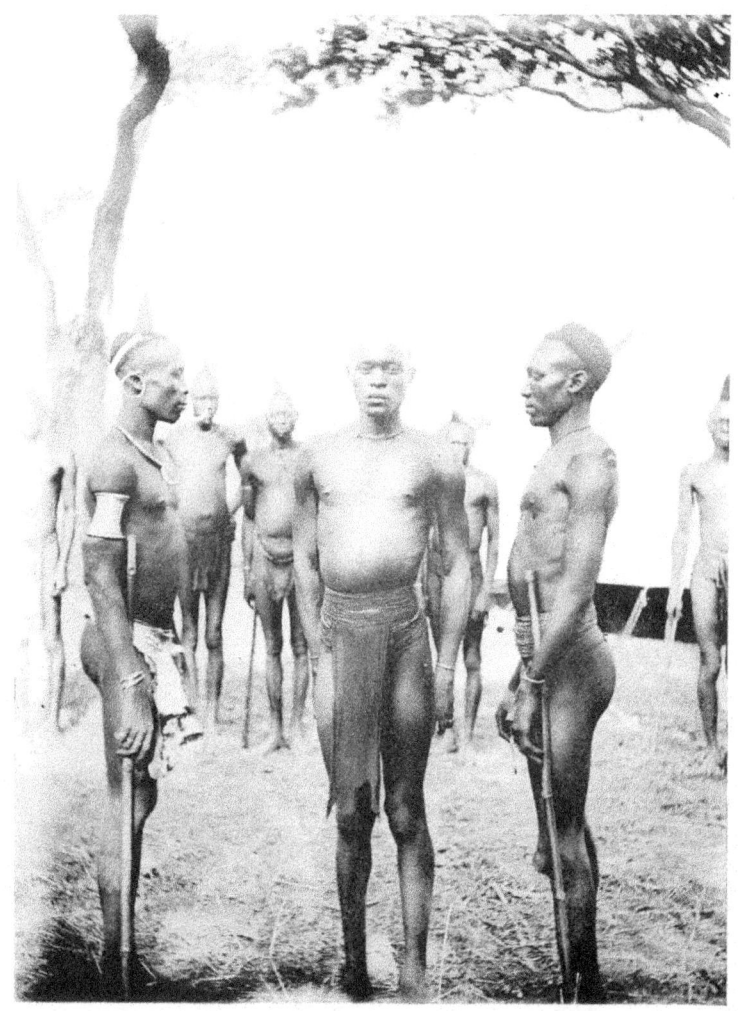

"THE MEN .. OF FINE PHYSIQUE, OCCASIONALLY WEAR A SKIN LOIN-CLOTH, BUT MORE OFTEN A SMALL SKIN APRON IS SUSPENDED FROM .. A CORSET OF .. GRASS."

THE LANGO AND ACHOLI COUNTRY

they could dig sufficient sweet potatoes for their needs.

V. Not to fire at any natives except by our instructions.

The *raison d'être* for this escort was twofold. Firstly, no carriers would have consented to travel a day with us without them, as had they attempted to return alone few if any would have reached home again in safety. Secondly, although the chances of an attack on a caravan headed by Europeans was extremely remote, obstacles might have been encountered, and had anything happened to us punitive measures would have been necessary, so the provision of an escort was really a preventive measure.

We did not leave the station till 2.15, though our loads had gone ahead at noon; and as we had fourteen miles to cover we were unable to halt at Dora's village, as we should have liked to have done, to witness a big dance that was in progress.[1]

The path soon led over a rough piece of dried swamp on which the footmarks made earlier in the season had dried in such a way as to leave a surface like that of badly laid cobble-stones.

As the track was but nine or ten inches wide, very erratic, and fringed with high grass which prevented the rider from seeing what lay ahead of the numerous curves and twists, we soon gave up the attempt to cycle.

On dismounting we discovered that one of the two savages engaged to accompany the bicycles had vanished, so one of the policeman shouldered the machine—an earnest of the manner in which, throughout the journey, all the members of our escort cheerfully undertook any odd job that came their way. After a short walk we arrived at the Parosa, a swampy tributary of the Nile

[1] As so little is known of the country through which we were about to pass, the description of the next ten days will be given in rather greater detail and in more exact chronological order than that in which the other stages of our journey have been described; and, for the same reason, the illustrations are more numerous.

P

which has earned a niche for itself in our memories through the shortcomings of its canoes. That in which we were accommodated let in water at the rate of some three gallons a minute, though some energetic baling, coupled with a paddler's dexterity in placing his heel over one of the principal apertures, enabled us to reach the other side without actually sinking. Here we struck the road, which though bumpy in places was, on the whole, rideable and had no gradients sufficiently steep to make it necessary to dismount.

A fine open camp with a big, airy *banda* marks the first halting-place near Kelodaki's village, close to which is the fort of a Muganda "agent." The latter greeted us on arrival with a present of a sheep, and later produced the food we required for our carriers. In a perfect plague of mosquitoes, due to the proximity of the Kole River, the corporal mounted the guard, and our two buglers—one of whom was clothed in a blue jersey, white trousers, and a fez cap, while the other had nothing at all except his bugle—sounded "Officers' Mess," and we sat down to dinner, but we were soon driven to our tents to shelter inside our mosquito nets.

"Réveillé" went at 4.25, but it was seven o'clock before we made a start, as our carriers were new to the game and had muddled up the loads, while three, more faint-hearted than the rest, had decided to bolt before further advance into the country of their exuberant neighbours rendered unescorted return a somewhat unsafe form of recreation. After half-an-hour's walk our road crossed the Kole River, which was of greater breadth and volume than the Parosa, but luckily boasted a more trustworthy canoe. The carriers went on foot, and by making a detour were able to avoid the deepest parts. We two, together with Musa and Mwaka, sat in the canoe, which was pulled and pushed across by two swarthy Lango. For the most part the water was barely waist-deep, but once or twice it reached their shoulders, and on one occasion proved too deep for them, so the "bow" man swam across, and when he reached a shallower spot the

MWAKA'S ARMY.

"THE DOORWAYS ARE MORE OF LESS CIRCULAR AND VERY LOW."

THE LANGO AND ACHOLI COUNTRY 227

"stern" ferryman pushed us over to him, and then followed himself. After a quarter of an hour we reached the mud on the far side, which was deep enough to get comfortably over the tops of our boots.

About eleven o'clock we arrived at the next camp at Kelobong's, near the Toshi River, fourteen miles from Kelodaki's. Except for one strip of uncleared thorny bush the track had been quite good for cycling—the only incident being the explosion of a back tyre, and the discovery that one of the two spare covers supplied with the bicycle did not fit the wheel: yet another chapter in the long list of catastrophes that had befallen this machine.

In the early afternoon we visited two of the neighbouring villages and took some photographs of the huts and their owners and their cattle. The latter seem to thrive throughout this country, and are the principal source of wealth among the Lango. On our return we were visited by Kelobong, whom we had met with Captain Tufnell between Hoima and Masindi. He greeted us as old friends, and expressed his pleasure at seeing us in his country. After talking about the wonders of civilisation at Hoima, he took his leave and returned to his home.

The next day we were surprised and amused to find that no less than forty local Lango had been impressed to fill the four vacancies in our caravan, and imagined that the necessary four would be chosen and the rest dismissed. Not a bit of it; they were all told to come along, and so far from minding, they began cheerily fighting for loads. We did not interfere, for with two men for each of the heavier loads it meant more rapid progress. Moreover, it was apparently the local custom, and the Lango seem to have no objection to carrying a load gratis for one day, though, as we discovered later, nothing will induce them to go for two, nor will such local substitutes go beyond what they consider is the day's trek, even if the rest of the caravan is going on.

Our route lay in a north-easterly direction along the left bank of the Toshi, and as the road ended abruptly soon after passing an agent's fort at Wini, we had a hard bit of tramping through a half-dried swamp on a tussocky track like a sheep walk. This only lasted an hour, and then the road began again, so we remounted our cycles and reached the agent's fort at Zakayo's at 12.40, having covered sixteen and a half miles, ten of which had been on foot, and all of which had been intersected at frequent intervals by swamps. The country differed somewhat from that which we had been passing through recently, being a moderately open, undulating land clothed with a few scrubby trees and bushes, and short, fine grass not more than four feet high—a good example of the unreliability of rumour. At Hoima we had spoken feelingly of the elephant grass around Muhemba's at the south-east of the Albert Nyanza, and were assured that the grass there was nothing compared with what we should find in the parts we were going to visit. In the twenty-three days during which we wandered about between Hoima and Palango we found nothing half as bad as the grass round Muhemba's, and up here it was, as we have said, rarely more than four feet high.

The soil here is fairly fertile, but the country is poorly watered. It carries large numbers of cattle, sheep, and goats. We saw no game, and only a little old elephant spoor. Judging by the skins the natives wear, the bush buck is the commonest animal, or at any rate that which is most easily killed.

The following day, one of us was suffering from a touch of fever, so we decided to make a short trek to Yusufu's ($9\frac{1}{2}$ miles).

Our *corvée* of the preceding day had returned home, but we had no difficulty in securing others to take their place. There were not more than half a dozen invalids among our gang, but no less than fifty-six local Lango were produced to relieve them, and not one of them would be denied. So far from showing any disinclination to oblige us by carrying our gear for a day, they seemed to regard it as the chance of their lives! Drawn up in a line at the side of the road they quietly awaited the word, and then threw themselves as one man upon the surplus baggage.

As there was obviously not enough to go round, the most lively scrimmage ensued. Jostling, grabbing, scratching, punching, and even using their sticks on each other's skulls and ribs, they fairly fought for their loads, and had it not been for the interference of a couple of police with a couple of serviceable *viboko*[1] the process of selection would probably have been terminated by the survival of the fittest. Hostilities, however, died away quite as suddenly as they had begun. A few more of the old gang affected temporary indisposition and gave up their places to meet the sudden demand, the heavier packages were shared by two, three, or even four of our cheerful substitutes, and all the new-comers were eventually accommodated. There was no sign of any inclination to run away or abandon their loads once they had started, and there was no doubt that, as long as too sustained an effort were not demanded of them, they thoroughly enjoyed the novelty of a little work—though load-carrying, with their elaborate head-dress, was rather an awkward occupation.

At Yusufu's, Mwaka asked leave to go ahead of us to his village (which we hoped to reach the next day), so as to be there to receive us; and we took the opportunity of sending a note to the Assistant District Commissioner, who was engaged in building a new station at Gulu to ask him if he could give us some idea of the distance to Nimule. Our friendly chief promised to send out men to see if there were any elephants in the neighbourhood, and, should the search prove successful, to send a man to meet us *en route* with the news.

Kelo Mwaka and Kelobong were good examples of what their subjects may become when they have been in longer and closer contact with the white man and his government. Their cheerful, playful but good-tempered and good-natured characteristics carry with them the conviction that, properly handled, the Lango will before long be as loyal a tribe as any in the Protectorate. It is to be hoped that there will be no attempt to civilise them too rapidly. That a tribe of genuine savages should be able

[1] Hippo-hide whips.

to assimilate civilisation as the Baganda—a nation with a culture and a history of its own—are assimilating it, is manifestly impossible. The result of precocious aspirations could only be the acquisition of a thin and offensive veneer in place of the best qualities that they now possess, and it would be folly to encourage them.

To us, who had lived for some years amongst natives but little further removed from their former savagery, our visit to these people, after rather a surfeit of the educated Baganda and Banyoro, was an unmixed pleasure. It is impossible not to appreciate the work that is being done in assisting these latter to absorb what is most suitable in civilisation, and the almost unique opportunity for the development of a cultured and highly organised African community, but there is something undeniably more attractive in one's intercourse with tribes that have not yet reached even the primary stages of transition and are still in a condition of untouched and primitive simplicity.

Nothing could have exceeded the obliging courtesy that we enjoyed at the hands of the Baganda and Banyoro chiefs, but it lacked the childlike and open frankness of our intercourse with the Lango.

They were as free from the cadging or grovelling spirit as from any awkwardness or bashfulness, and greeted us as welcome visitors with a friendly equality that was as refreshing as it was surprising.

The sick man being rather worse than better the following day he was carried to Mwaka's—fourteen miles—in a *machila* or hammock improvised from a game net provided by the Muganda agent Yusufu, who was the last agent that we were to see.

The track was bad and rarely fit for cycling. It was crossed by a dozen small swamps, most of them ankle deep, and two up to the knees, and neither of us was sorry, after four hours of it, to reach our camp.

On our way we passed several granite boulders, on which the Lango had gathered to watch us pass. Many of them were standing on one leg after the manner of the Dinka and kindred tribes.

THE LANGO AND ACHOLI COUNTRY 231

Some four miles from our destination stood the hill known as Mount Moru (3900 feet), near which the remnants of the Soudanese mutineers had made their last camp. These numbered about a hundred, and as they caused trouble by raiding the neighbouring villages, were finally overthrown by an expedition under Major Radcliffe about the year 1901.

Mwaka met us with an apology of engaging naïveté.

"I am sorry," he said, "that I have not got a better camp for you, but I only got here early this morning, and this is all I have been able to do in the time."

"This" consisted of a clean and freshly built *banda*, with two doors and three windows, and measuring twenty-four feet by twelve, a hut for a kitchen, and others for our staff, all standing in a level open space which he had chosen for us near his village, and from which his natives were still zealously clearing the grass and undergrowth that remained! All this was for our use for one afternoon and night, done gratuitously and unasked.

We had seldom seen natives putting their hearts into their work as these Lango were doing. They hardly paused to look at us when we arrived, but concentrated all their energy on the wielding of their quaint spades, chaffing and bantering one another the while in the highest good humour.

After lunch we went down to the village and took a few photographs of the inhabitants. A baby that ran to its mother and howled vigorously when it caught sight of us was the only member of the community that seemed even interested in our presence. We might have been Lango ourselves for all the notice that was taken of us.

At three o'clock Mwaka brought us a present consisting of 127 bundles of food, two sheep, some milk, honey (which was tasted by the bearer before being handed to us), twenty eggs, and some beer. We had a good hour's entertainment photographing some of the sportsmen who brought up this profuse offering. They were "clothed" in typical Lango fashion, and were quite delighted at being photographed, as well as at the interest taken in their ornaments, of which some were very proud.

We had heard with some interest that the "body-guards" or corps of irregulars maintained by the Lango and Acholi chiefs were accustomed to drill in the manner of the regular forces of the Protectorate, and, gathering that Mwaka would be only too willing to hold a parade for our benefit, we expressed a desire that he should do so. He assented with alacrity, and in less than a quarter of an hour the martial strains of bugles and side-drums announced his approach, and he appeared at the head of his "army." They were some thirty strong, comprising two drummers, three buglers, and twenty-five rank and file, who had discarded their firearms and provided themselves with stout sticks in their place.

The front ranks were made up of the buglers, drummers, and some others, all more or less clothed, with the exception of one of the buglers; the other two ranks were in the orthodox national costume—consisting, besides a few ornaments, of an apron averaging two inches by ten.

They marched on to the scene in perfect time, the buglers blowing a really creditable march, reached the end of the short stretch of road that formed one side of our camping-ground, halted, and "marked time." This was done standing firmly on the right leg with the body thrown gracefully back, brandishing the left foot in the air and bringing it down with a well-timed thud.

It was really a moving spectacle. At first it was all we could do to get into our shelter before bursting into laughter. When we had pulled ourselves together and emerged we were really not sure whether we wanted to laugh or cry. Our police escort did not move a muscle, and their example helped considerably our self-control.

After marking time for a space in the same position they turned about. The scantily clad rear ranks, who were now the front ranks, were as solemn as judges, and evidently deadly keen on doing the thing seriously. A minute or two later they marched back to the corner of the "parade ground," marked time, "abouted," marked

THE LANGO AND ACHOLI COUNTRY 233

time again, and so on *da capo*, three or four times, sometimes in ranks and sometimes in fours. The buglers changed their tune more than once, and Mwaka marched at their side carrying his stick like a sword, issuing the words of command and watching their every movement like a young captain who has just got his company.

It was an amazing thing to find this keenness on civilised methods of soldiering amongst a primitive and untutored African tribe like the Lango and Acholi. [For we were to see an even more astonishing manifestation of it among the Acholi a few days later.]

They are instructed apparently by time-expired members of the police or military forces, who spend their leisure on their return to their villages in forming a nucleus of an army out of their fellow-enthusiasts. It would be interesting to know if this voluntary adoption of European drill and European music has been noticed amongst any other uncivilised African people.

We congratulated ourselves once more on having taken the overland route instead of the river journey by Butiaba, but felt sorrier than ever that we had no time to wander farther afield and learn more of these entertaining folk. Their language was a collection of the most uncouth and strangely inarticulate sounds, and sometimes was extraordinarily like the chatter that English children may be heard inventing when pretending to be foreigners.

It was nearly always spoken in a high-pitched and forcible tone, which, unless one was watching the speakers, suggested that they were on the verge of coming to blows. Mwaka spoke the local Ki-Swahili fairly well, as did Dora at Palango, but it was probably known to but few or any of their staff, and certainly to none of the populace.

Mwaka expressed himself as quite willing to accompany us as far as Nimule, though his instructions had only extended to the Palango district boundary, and further left us three delightful young sons of his. They, he said, would "come on" with us—more or less permanently, apparently. We wondered whether they meant

England, Cairo, or only Gondokoro, but forbore to ask. One was attired in an abbreviated waistcoat and practically nothing else. The others were similarly clothed, but without the waistcoat.

In the evening we heard from Mr. Sullivan at Gulu, who told us that it was two days to his camp—Mwaka's runner had taken five hours—and added that it was seven good days on from Gulu to Nimule; but as he added that it was seventy-five miles, we reckoned we could do it in four, which we did.

The journey to Gulu the next day, which turned out to be a matter of eighteen miles, we accomplished in five hours. There was no road, and the track was for the most part beyond what even we considered possible for cycling, and we only managed to use our machines for about five miles, in stretches of half a mile at a time. During the last of these, one of us collided with a tree with such force that the regulator of the two-speed gear was driven some way into his knee, causing a nasty little wound that became rather troublesome later on.

Mr. Sullivan made us very welcome, gave us lunch, and then showed us the beginning of the new "boma" which he was building. It is well situated on a hill commanding a fine view of the surrounding country, which, though timbered farther away, is, in the immediate neighbourhood, bare except for a few borassus palms.

We got off at a quarter to six the next morning after an early breakfast, and started for Lakor's—17 miles distant. Our host had provided us with thirteen carriers, but they bolted after travelling an hour and a half, as they considered that was a day's march. Luckily it did not cause us much inconvenience, as we soon obtained a fresh gang at a wayside village. We were in the Acholi country by this time, and noted that they cultivate a good deal of millet, sorghum, ground nuts, and sim-sim. The country was fairly open, and fine clear streams replaced the disagreeable swamps that had been a prominent feature of the Lango country. As no game was visible, our shooting was confined to an occasional brace of guinea-fowl, generally secured in the evening after a couple of hours' hard tramping in the grass.

At Lakor's we struck a road of sorts. It was a narrow, bumpy track, but it was a good deal better than nothing, and as it was twenty-one miles to Adulla's, where we had decided to camp, we were glad enough of it. Five miles after starting we passed a spot known as "Baker's camp," being the place which Sir Samuel Baker had made his temporary residence many years before. It was a good spot for a rest, among small hills with some fine trees and a beautiful stream of clear water flowing lazily over some rocks close by.

We reached Adulla's at a little before midday, but had to wait another hour and a half for our chairs and food, while the rest of the loads did not arrive till about four. There were some lounges in the village of most original design, constructed of logs laid horizontally on parallel sloping poles. Four of them were built facing one another so that the bases formed a small square, in the centre of which a small fire was kept burning. On them were sprawling and chatting some young Acholi bloods—even more tightly laced than their Lango neighbours.

Before arriving at the village we had an opportunity of watching a party of Acholi hunters at work. Some days before they had burnt a strip of grass in the bush, leaving a large unburnt area up wind, and the day on which we passed they had placed game nets about six feet in height on light poles, studded with rough pegs, all along the burnt strip of ground. The grass was then fired about three-quarters of a mile away, and the hunters arriving with bows and arrows, waited for any game that might be driven into the nets by the flames. We arrived there at the right moment, but unfortunately the drive was fruitless and no game forthcoming. We saw three Jackson's hartebeeste a little farther on, the first game—other than elephant—seen since Kishilisi.

Mwaka reported in the evening that a chief named Wo, who lived close by, had refused to send us either food for our men or any extra carriers for the next day.

As he declared that he had spoken very nicely to Wo, and that the latter, having plenty of food and a big population, had no excuse for his boorishness, we sent along for Wo, Wo's food, and some of Wo's people. They all turned up—at about nine o'clock at night. Wo was most apologetic. His mistake had been due, he said, to the fact that we were travelling just outside his own particular sphere, and he did not think that the message could really be for him.

The next morning, after walking two miles, we crossed the Nyame, a fair-sized river which rises near Gulu and flows into the Nile at Nimule. The day was then enlivened by the third collapse of the bicycle that had been patched at Hoima. Its latest manifestation was an obstinate tendency to free-wheel in both directions, which made progress a trifle spasmodic. This meant walking to Oliya's, but as it was only fourteen miles, it was not immediately disastrous, and we arrived at half-past ten.

The camp was one of the most ideal spots we had seen. A huge tree with dense foliage stood at one end of a cleanly swept square, enclosed with a fence of old crotons. Some years before it had been the site of the village. The new village was a few hundred yards away, and contained six or seven hundred roofs, of which perhaps two hundred and fifty were huts, the remainder being grain stores. Each group of a dozen huts or so was separate, yet the village is continuous, though small hedges divided off the groups from one another and there were many open spaces in between them.

Oliya himself, one of the most important Acholi chiefs, was absent at Nimule, but we were courteously received by his younger brother, who appeared shortly after our arrival bringing a dozen eggs and a bugler. The latter greeted us with an almost faultlessly blown "general salute." When visiting the village later we were shown round with unassuming civility by some headman, who met us at the entrance of the village, and, immediately appointing himself our cicerone, said, " This is the way to the chief's house, will you please come this way." We followed, taking a

OLD LANGO WOMAN.

THERE WERE SOME LOUNGES . . . . OF MOST ORIGINAL DESIGN.

THE LANGO AND ACHOLI COUNTRY 237

photograph here and there, and while doing so a graceful damsel leading a picanin by the hand emerged from a hut.

"This is Oliya's daughter," said our guide; and as the young lady seemed bashful, he added: "Come and have your picture taken; don't be shy."

She braced herself up and, holding her younger sister by the hand, approached and stood for her portrait. Her clothing consisted of a necklace of fish bones, two rows of beads round her waist, and a heavy ornament consisting of some forty strands of copper-wire round each ankle.

Our guide then produced the chief's son, whose attire consisted of a goat-skin and a walking-stick. His portrait also was added to our collections. We then visited the different parts of the village, and were shown everything there was to see, after which our guide escorted us back to our camp.

Most of the rest of the afternoon was devoted to the broken-down bicycle. It was taken to pieces three times in all, being put together again on each occasion in an atmosphere of equally hopeless despair. How it had run the four hundred miles since leaving Hoima was a small mechanical miracle. The cones—wonder of wonders—were intact, but the split cogwheel-casing had gone on splitting, and apparently the only reason why it had not started its impartial free-wheeling a month before was that the fragments of broken metal had got so generously distributed in the mechanism that everything was bound to "engage."

But a redistribution had now taken place and natural propensities had begun to reassert themselves. The task of restoring the disintegrated atoms to their original pattern being dismissed as too sublime, it remained to be seen whether by any means at our command we could persuade the "damthing" to resume its functions as a bicycle for another hundred and thirty miles. After fourteen different kinds of diagnosis and remedy had suggested themselves and had in turn been discarded, it seemed possible that a cunningly placed rivet or two might succeed in temporarily arresting the next stage of decay. But the drilling of case-hardened steel is a poor amusement, even in the quiet seclusion of camp life in tropical Africa. First one drill and then another blunted and broke without making the slightest impression where it was needed.

When on the point of giving up the attempt in philosophical despair, our prospecting operations suddenly succeeded; we thought a soft spot must exist somewhere, and—we found it! Feverishly amputating the tails of three files—the only hard metal we had (and soft was useless under the circumstances)—we tapped the improvised rivets cautiously into their places and got the machine together again before it could strike out a new line of resistance. "Now," we said, "if it does not miss-fire right away, it may conceivably hold together till Gondokoro." It did miss-fire right away, and for a few minutes there was an eloquent silence. Then: " Let's give it one more chance. If it fails, into the bush with it and we'll finish up with one machine as we began." We gave it another chance, and, for some unaccountable reason, something gripped and only the right wheels revolved. And to anticipate and cut the story short, though during the last two days into Gondokoro it was going just as if both brakes were on, it actually held together till the end.

It was just before sundown that we had quite the biggest surprise of our whole journey. We had heard of Oliya's "army" and band as being superior to those of any of his neighbours, and, after seeing Mwaka's contingent, we learnt with regret that, with the exception of a bugler, he had evidently taken all the members of the force with him to Nimule.

But we were not altogether disappointed: his "cadet corps" gave us a show beyond our wildest hopes. We had had our first glimpse of them a few minutes after arriving in camp, when half a dozen naked infants who had been standing staring at us, suddenly—on observing that a camera was being turned on to them—at the word of command of a youngster an inch taller than the rest,

"Young Acholi bloods ... even more tightly laced than their Lango neighbours."

THE LANGO AND ACHOLI COUNTRY 239

formed up and proceeded to go through nearly all the details of squad drill.

But this was merely a preliminary canter. Just before sundown, when the afternoon's occupation had driven most other things out of our heads, we were startled by the strains of martial music coming nearer and nearer from the direction of the village. Evidently the chief had returned, and we were not after all going to miss our parade. Our feelings may be imagined when the "army" which marched two deep on to the camp square turned out to be not Oliya's picked men-at-arms, but a company of some forty youngsters, from eight to fourteen years of age, all but two as naked as on the day they were born, and commanded by the same picanin that had been drilling the "squad" at midday. Armed with sticks for rifles, and headed by a band consisting of two battered old side-drums, an equally battered old cavalry bugle, and a still more decayed pair of cymbals, they swaggered along in perfect time, passed us with an "Eyes left," and came to a halt a little beyond where we were sitting. After "dressing" his company the captain gave the order "Form fours," and then proceeded to put them through most of the company drill. Their movements and their music were astonishingly correct, and their discipline and seriousness as striking as in the adult force that we had seen a few days before.

The words of command were given with a clear enunciation that could scarcely have been improved upon. Evidently the English language did not present the same difficulties to those young savages that it does to the southern Bantu, some of whose happiest efforts are "Bunner murrer," "Reffut incleon," and "Cutty note, cutty chain," for "By numbers," "Left incline," and "Guard turn out, Guard 'tion."

After the performance had reached its zenith in the "bayonet exercises" the company re-formed two deep once more and retired whence they came.

With such enthusiasm for military discipline and military training shown at all ages from infancy upwards one cannot help feeling that here, at any rate, is exceptional material for the formation of a valuable native force.

Having some twenty-five miles to do into Nimule we made an early start, though not so early as we had intended, as after waking us first at 2.30 the guard, who had been instructed to rouse the camp at 3.30, left us severely alone till nearly half-past four. We were off in less than an hour, walking for the first mile or so until it was light enough to ride.

The road was a good one up to the last two or three miles and the trek comparatively uneventful. The Nyame River was less than knee-deep, and the broken bicycle, though running stiff, held together for the first twenty-two miles. Then a miss-fire occurred in the old spot, followed almost immediately by a bad puncture, and it had to be wheeled the rest of the way.

At a little before eleven o'clock we reached Nimule station, and enjoyed a hearty welcome from Mr. B. L. Baines, the District Commissioner, and Mr. Hart, the District Superintendent of Police. Our loads were all in by four.

Nimule is an unlovely spot. It is built on and among hot, dry, and stony barren ridges and hillocks, from which can be seen one of the "S"-like curves of the Nile, just below its junction with the Nyame. Across the river to the west the eye rests with some relief upon the face of the escarpment leading up to the plateau of the Lado province of the Soudan, but to the east is baking and desolate unloveliness.

The houses are substantially but roughly built of stone, and rather conspicuously free from the comforts that might well be added to make life worth living in such unattractive surroundings.

The staff consists of a District Commissioner, an Assistant District Commissioner, a District Superintendent of Police, and a Doctor, besides an Indian telegraphist and Indian clerks.

The day's trek had aggravated the inflammation of the knee that had been cut near Gulu, and the after-

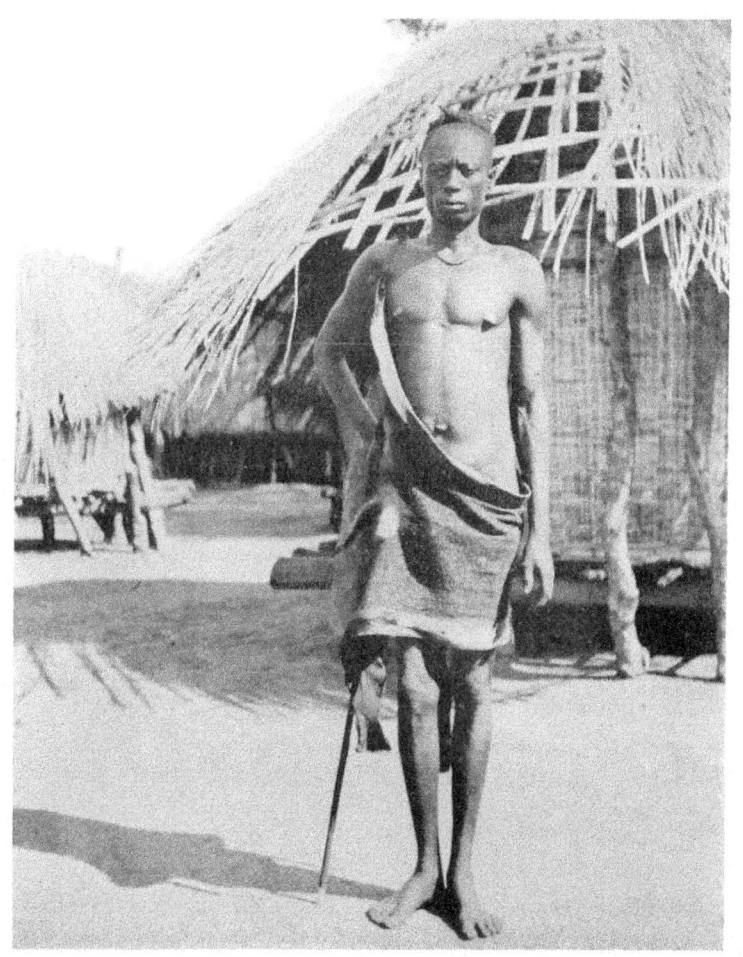

"OLIYA'S SON, CLAD IN A GOAT SKIN AND A WALKING STICK."

THE LANGO AND ACHOLI COUNTRY 241

noon was spent in poulticing and resting, and reading a belated mail.

Our letters included one from an old friend, Captain C. H. Stigand, formerly of the King's African Rifles, now in charge of the Lado province and stationed at Rejaf, expressing a hope that we could visit him at his station.

At tea-time we made the acquaintance of Oliya, the Acholi chief whose village we had just left, and another and more important chief of the same tribe named Agwok.

The latter was a most interesting old character. He stood well over six feet, and was attired in a spotless if not exactly well-fitting suit of white duck, with yellow boots and bright plaid socks—one of his many costumes, which, we were told, comprised several varieties of fancy uniforms as well as of native finery.

He and his territory, which lay to the east, were as yet quite unadministered, but he was willing and even anxious to be included in the Protectorate, and meanwhile, in the intervals between his own little raiding operations, nothing pleased him better than to co-operate with the Government, to which he was a staunch and loyal ally. He had recently carried out a small punitive expedition in his sphere, chiefly on his own behalf, and having confiscated some hundreds of cattle from his refractory subjects, had somewhat embarrassed the Government by offering it eighty head as its share.

Oliya was more like the true Choli. Scantily, but not nationally, clad, he looked what he apparently was—a cheerful, unspoilt, more or less untamed, but intelligent and well-disposed nigger, with a fine figure and a sprightly gait. He complained of the lack of fighting in these days, and looked as if he might thoroughly enjoy any that might be going.

The natives of the Nimule district were largely Soudanese, a plucky and a warlike race, who had more than once routed and scattered the fighting Dervish "armies" sent against them from the north.

They have not, however, given much of an account of themselves in their occasional passages with the Government. In spite of their greatly superior numbers and the fact that they are fairly well armed with a variety of comparatively modern weapons imported from Abyssinia, they are apparently quite unable to withstand the discipline and steady rifle-fire of a few trained men.

It was fortunate that we had obtained carriers at Palango to take us through to Gondokoro. The District Commissioner, under the impression that our request through Mr. Grant at Hoima was holding good, had obtained what men he could for our last stage, but they were no longer available. A first supply he had been unable to persuade to wait more than two days for us, and a second he had been obliged to commandeer for urgent Government business. Temporary substitutes for about a dozen weak members of our gang could be provided without much difficulty.

Once more we could not suppress a smile at the common estimate of a day's journey in Uganda. Our journey from Palango—161 miles in ten days—was voted extraordinary. It was a little over 100 miles from Nimule to Gondokoro, and astonishment was again expressed at our intention to get there in six days. The orthodox allowance was ten; and we had a short time before met a man who, in perfect health, had travelled $74\frac{1}{4}$ miles in ten days! And it was the custom, we learnt, to start on these journeys at the strenuous hour of three or four in the morning.

With the majority of office work performed by Indian clerks, the tax collection in parts where taxes are enforced and minor administrative duties by the native chiefs, it must, one would suppose, be something of a problem how to spend the rest of one's day, if one starts on a seven to ten mile march at 3 A.M.

After the disposal of our third pair of tusks to the local branch of Alidina Visram at the reduced price of Rs.5.25 per lb.—the manager declaring that the price of ivory had gone down during the last month—and the purchase of one or two necessities such as flour and sugar, we left Nimule on the 21st of December for the last section of the journey to Gondokoro.

A HEADMAN OF THE LANGO CHIEF AND ONE OF MWAKA'S SONS WHO CAME THROUGH TO GONDOKORO WITH US.

XVI

NIMULE TO GONDOKORO

Uninviting country—The Assua River—Arrangements for food supply and extra carriers—Christmas Day—Ledju, the rain-maker—Rejaf—Arrival at Gondokoro—Sale of our camp kit—Arrival of the *Gordon Pasha*—Notes on Uganda and its administration.

WE left Nimule on the 21st of December. Messrs. Baines and Hart, who were going out on duty, and whose route was the same as our own for the first day, left early, but we, detained by sundry small matters, did not get off till nearly ten.

For the first two or three miles the road wound in and out amongst the stony hills at the back of the station and led through the barest, thirstiest, most scorched and repulsive bit of country we had seen. After a while the Congo hills showed up again to our left, but to the right the landscape melted away through a smoky haze to bare, hot, and vacant desolation. The scanty patches of vegetation had mostly been burnt by a bush fire, which was still blazing at both sides of our path.

Later the road became quite good for bicycling, but the natives who were carrying the machines had lagged so far behind that we decided to walk the rest of the eleven miles to camp. Fortunately there was a steady breeze which made the heat just bearable.

At one o'clock we reached the Assua, a broad and picturesque tributary of the Nile which rises near the borders of the Rudolph province, and refreshed ourselves by wading across, though we should have been pleased had it been waist instead of but knee deep. Baines and Hart were camped a few hundred yards down stream, and we established ourselves at a rather decayed camp on the road near the ford. The posts of the *banda* bore a notice to the effect that this and the remaining camps on the road were free from the *spirillum* tick, which struck us as being a trifle sanguine, though as a matter of fact we found no traces of it.

The following morning we rose at 4.30, just in time to see the tail-end of the Nimule caravan disappearing into the shadows ; Agwok and Mwaka, who brought up the rear, saluted cheerfully as they passed. We had bidden farewell to the latter the day before, with thanks for his assistance, under the impression that he was going back home, but apparently he intended to see a little more life first.

We left at six and reached the Vuni stream, where we camped, at ten. It was a rough, stony trek of sixteen miles. The river bed was dry where the road crossed it, but there was water—of a kind—quite close. Some neighbouring headmen were found and persuaded without any difficulty to produce food for our carriers and extra men for some of our loads for the next stage, the Nimule contingent having returned home. The feeding and transport system had changed. The natives along the route were supposed to bring what food might be required by travellers, but it was paid for at a fixed rate. Carriers were similarly paid (at twelve cents a day), but would not travel more than a single stage at a time. In fact it was quite an unusual thing on the Nimule-Gondokoro road for a single gang to be going right through.

. The next day's journey of fifteen miles was equally uninteresting. We crossed three or four watercourses, only two of which boasted a little water in pools, the others being dry sandy beds.

A small herd of elephant had crossed the road earlier in the day, but there was apparently nothing big in it, and we had no time to waste in investigation. We reached camp at Gombiri's at half-past ten. Some of the carriers took eight hours to get in. Food and spare carriers were again obtained without much difficulty, though the first supply of the former was a little modest and had to be repeated by request. For our wants we could get nothing beyond half a dozen bad eggs.

The natives along our route were Bari. They were mostly tall, shifty-eyed, unprepossessing and unattractive folk, singularly unlike the Lango we loved.

The penalties of wading in the Assua had begun to make themselves felt by one of us the previous evening, and during the day acute rheumatic pains, somewhat complicating the problem of equilibrium on a bicycle, threatened a possibly serious delay. Fortunately they wore off after three days, and the victim, but for the memories of intermittent torture, was none the worse.

From Gombiri's we went to Tombe Musa, fourteen miles. The road was quite suitable for bicycling most of the way, and watered with three fairly good streams, but it was an unattractive country, and peopled by unattractive folk. Our twelve local natives from Gombiri's were some of the lowest types we had ever seen.

Five minutes' delay occurred on the way to attend to a carrier who was rolling on the ground, doubled up in agony and complaining that he was dying of a snake. It was not, as we at first believed, a snake bite that was afflicting him, but merely his descriptive manner of alluding to a pain in his inside. We had hardly grasped the delicate distinction when Musa arrived on the scene, and, unrolling the victim on to his back, proceeded to administer the most drastic abdominal massage. It seemed to make him no worse, and he turned up smiling later at camp. A carrier who the day before had been suddenly and unaccountably attacked by almost total though painless paralysis of a leg also had—quite as unaccountably—almost recovered.

The food supply was nearly as readily obtained as before, though as it did not arrive till night we were afraid at one time that we should have to go and fetch it. It had been promised by a representative of the *Mwami* who had brought us a supply of highly flavoured milk shortly after our arrival, but at seven o'clock there were no signs of it, though the village was only a couple of miles away.

Half-past eight and there were still no signs, so the corporal was instructed to take half our escort and make polite inquiries. As they were starting they asked if they were to be allowed to fire if they were attacked by the population or had spears thrown at them from the high grass. The population, they declared, was not at all a pleasant-spoken crowd, and they were quite sure that there would be violence. We were quite sure that there would not, but as they were in that frame of mind it was obviously risky letting them go alone. With difficulty persuading Musa that something less than our combined battery was indispensable, one of us was starting off when, rather to our disappointment, torches appeared in the distance, an obliging and apologetic *Mwami* appeared with a couple of sheep for us and meal for the carriers, and the " expedition " was " off."

The following was Christmas Day: we had detected it the previous evening, but rediscovered it at daybreak with some surprise. Our first three days' journey had necessarily been at rather a low average owing to the disposition of camps, on which, in our ignorance of the route, we had to depend for water and supplies. We had now to begin making up for it, and for a start made twenty-two miles to Ledju's, passing another camp at Lokko-Legga's at eight and three-quarters.

We passed a quantity of elephant spoor on the way—some of the previous day, some of the same morning. Any elephants that live in those parts must be hopelessly enamoured of the simple life. Nothing in the way of sustenance but the scantiest and most ragged of thorn trees, and not very many of them—though they had been making the best of them. The carriers astonished us. Our lunch was in before noon, and the whole *safari* by 2.25.

Another alarm with regard to the food supply turned out to be quite a false one. A messenger to the village, which was close to our camp, reported that not only were the chief and all his representatives away, but that the people found at home sullenly refused to give any intimation of their whereabouts. The appearance of Ledju in person less than half-an-hour later, coupled with the exceptional courtesy of his greeting, was a pleasant surprise, and dispelled all our fear. His method of salutation was as charming as it was rare. He was a thin, spare man of medium height, with an unusually thick shock of hair standing out like a mop, a large, mobile, but not very thick-lipped mouth, and quiet, benevolent expression. Doffing his fez cap, he first halted and saluted at some twenty paces and again at ten feet, then advancing to where we sat he saluted us one after the other, grasping the right hand in both his own, bowing over it till he touched it, first with his lips, and then with his forehead, and then again with his lips. He was quite a graceful old gentleman and eager to do our bidding. He told us that he and his tribe were " Barrrri," with an imperceptible final vowel and a rolled " r " that would have done credit to a Scottish comedian.

In the evening we visited his village. The male inhabitants were mostly strolling and squatting about in a state of absolute nudity that scorned even the simplest ornament. The women generally affected the aprons back and front that we had seen among the Lango and Acholi, though some wore ephemeral confections of fresh grass. Among the women's ornaments we first noticed the necklaces and waist-belts composed of tiny and slightly concave shells fitting closely into one another and strung upon a cord, giving the impression of spangles.

Ledju himself is a rather famous "rain-maker." It would appear to be comparatively simple to acquire and retain a reputation as a rain-maker. Not only may the magician refuse his services—and frequently does so if rain is not imminent—but when he consents to act, he does not bind himself to the observance of any time limit, simply contenting himself with claiming the next shower that falls as due to his powers.

In former times it is possible that the position was somewhat less of a sinecure, as we are told that in the case of a persistent drought it was not exceptional for the people to assemble and kill the rain-maker.

Seventeen miles more brought us to Kiriba—our last camp before reaching Gondokoro. We were not altogether sorry to be reaching the end of the trekking part of our journey. A hundred and sixty-one days passed largely in camp life had not, *per se*, been anything of a surfeit, but the last few days had been rather trying and quite the least pleasant part of the trip. The country was dull, thirsty, and uninteresting, the natives apathetic, sullen, and unattractive, and the heat, even in the first three hours of daylight, bordered on the oppressive.

Our camp was a mile or two from the Nile and nearly opposite Rejaf, Captain Stigand's headquarters. Hoping to find him in residence we made our way to the river bank and inquired of the natives what they knew of his whereabouts. Absolutely nothing, they declared. He might be there or he might not, but they had no dealings of any kind with the natives on the other side.

It was not intentional discouragement, for a couple of them were quite ready to paddle across with a note, after a few gunshots had failed to elicit a sign of any particular activity from the settlement.

Our efforts were however merely rewarded by a reply to the effect that the Governor was away on tour. So we returned to camp—not in a very merry frame of mind, for it was past one o'clock. We had breakfast at half-past four, and for the last two hours, especially while waiting in a little village on the bank, the heat had been infernal. A fairly strong and constant breeze took the edge off it, but the breeze itself was so hot that it was only from the evaporation of one's own perspiration that one could gain any relief.

The village headman, an attenuated man with an attenuated voice, had saved our lives, we felt, by the gift of a bowl of milk—which was actually fresh and untainted. The latter was not a common luxury. Kiriba brought us about half a gallon of milk the same day, once in the afternoon and again in the evening; the latter was

LOOKING ACROSS THE NILE TO REJAF.

THE D.C.'S HOUSE AT GONDOKORO.

NIMULE TO GONDOKORO

at least twenty-four hours younger than the first, but it was, as usual, strongly flavoured with the cow urine in which the local natives wash their vessels.

Seven of our carriers from Ledju's we found had gone back without waiting for pay. We photographed the remainder as comprising some of the ugliest faces we had seen during the whole trip.

The heat right up to eight o'clock at night was astonishing. There was still quite a stiff breeze blowing, yet it seemed every bit as hot as it had been in the middle of the day. It was difficult to say whether the breeze now made it cooler or hotter than it would have been without it, but it felt like the breath of a furnace.

Making an early start next morning we put behind us the sixteen miles into Gondokoro by half-past nine, mending a final puncture on the way.

After learning at the Post Office, where we rescued some mails, that the "post boat" due on the 28th would be perhaps a week late, and that one of the Soudan Development and Exploration Company's vessels would be in on or about the 1st of January, we wended our way to the office and made ourselves known to Captain Henry, the Assistant District Commissioner in charge.

Gondokoro is but a little less desirable resort than Nimule. The heat is excessive, the soil dusty and poor, and the vegetation consists mainly of a few scorched and distorted palms.

The principal buildings, the office and the resident official's house, which are of very inferior brick, and falling to pieces, do not contribute much to the alleviation of their unattractive surroundings.

The station has perhaps little in its favour besides its position on the high banks overlooking the Nile, but it has much greater possibilities than Nimule, and a good deal might be done to make it a more desirable place to live in.

We were lodged in a roomy brick tenement that had once been the official's house, the other half of which was occupied by Captain Hutchinson, Superintendent of Uganda Marine, who was proceeding on leave and awaiting the "post boat," and our four days' stay was made exceedingly pleasant by Captain and Mrs. Henry's hospitality.

We were almost tempted by the proximity of the Gondokoro herd of elephant to try and make up our full number, but eventually, though they were so close that Captain Henry had heard them three days in succession when taking an ante-breakfast stroll, decided that they were not worth the trouble. They had been constantly seen, were fairly well known to comprise no big bulls, and to be nasty tempered; while their habitat was a particularly treeless bit of flat country with long grass and a few but small thorns. So we contented ourselves with the refund, on one of our licences, of the £20 that may be claimed in the case of a second elephant not having been killed.

The second day after our arrival, with the assistance of the District Commissioner's Indian clerk (who, incidentally, was the only one of his kind whom we had encountered in the Protectorate whose name was not Sousa) we held a rather successful sale of our superfluous kit. The buyers were the two or three local traders, Greek and Indian, and the Indian telegraphist.

Our bicycles were bought at £5 *each*, in spite of the persistent honesty with which we pointed out that one of them, as a bicycle, was practically useless without a new back wheel. For though it had actually got there, it was obvious, from the terrific labour that was required to propel it the last few miles into Gondokoro, as well as the fantastic oscillations of the wheel upon its hub, that final disintegration was painfully imminent. Our tents fetched about the same price, and the rest of our camp gear went at varying sums. Uganda coinage was changed without difficulty into English sovereigns and Egyptian silver.

The Soudan Development and Exploration Company stern-wheeler *Gordon Pasha* arrived from the north on the 30th of December and proceeded the following day to Rejaf, after having landed Mr. Shaw, of the Church Missionary Society station at Malek, and a Mr. Blain, who was visiting Uganda for a shooting trip. The boat's return was delayed by the various sandbanks that impede the river above Gondokoro, and she did not make her reappearance till four o'clock on Saturday afternoon. To our surprise and delight, Captain Stigand was on board and intending to accompany us as far as Lado.

We embarked at once, and at a little past five on the last day of the year we had said good-bye to our host and hostess and, turning our backs on Uganda, were steaming down the Nile. Since leaving our stations in Rhodesia we had covered altogether 3020 miles, of which 1720 had been walking and cycling, 607 by lake steamers, 520 on the Uganda railway, and the balance by motor vans in the East Africa and Uganda Protectorate.

During our seventy days' visit in the Uganda Protectorate we had been unable to visit the Toro, Ankole, Elgon, Busoga, and Rudolph districts, but we had seen and learnt something of the Buganda province and a good deal of the Bunyoro, Lango, and Nile districts.

Of these sections the Rudolph district is as yet quite unadministered, the Nile province (Lango, Choli, and Bari) only partially controlled, and till 1910 was unadministered except for a narrow strip along the river. Buganda, Bunyoro, Toro, and Ankole are not only thoroughly administered, but show in some respects a higher state of advancement than any other part of tropical Africa known to us.

While tempering our admiration for this by the reflection that there was already existing among the native population an exceptionally high social and political organisation on which the present enlightened and more civilised system has been grafted, it is only fair that adverse criticism should allow that the very existence of this organisation may have involved certain difficulties of adaptation which are, in a measure at any rate, responsible for present defects.

It may be, in short, that the system's defects are those of its qualities.

The administrative system of the Uganda Protectorate

is largely one of decentralisation. Immediately after the Governor come the Provincial Commissioners, of whom there are two, though there is provision for four ; under the Provincial Commissioners are the District Commissioners and Assistant District Commissioners. All communications between headquarters and district officials have to pass through the Provincial Commissioner (or Senior District Commissioner acting as Provincial Commissioner), and, if from an Assistant District Commissioner, through the District Commissioner first.

There are, of course, excellent reasons for the adoption of a general policy of decentralisation, and we have an especially interesting manifestation of it in Uganda, as here, where their intelligence and organisation admits of it, it is carried right down into the administration of the natives. Now the dangers of this are potential rather than inherent, but certain of the conditions under which it is worked (though at the same time it is just the existence and operation of it that make those conditions possible) seem bound to bring out its worst faults. We refer to the practice, apparently general and deliberate, of constantly moving the district officials at short intervals from post to post.

With the exception of the two Provincial Commissioners every member of the district staff is liable to be moved from one corner of the Protectorate to the other, and is rarely, if ever, more than two years—frequently not more than a few months—in charge of the same station.

So far as the junior members are concerned, the practice has much to recommend it, but when it is carried up to the higher grades its disadvantages begin to be apparent, and the frequency with which even a Senior District Commissioner may be moved from, say, the Northern Province to Elgon, and then after a short interval to Ankole, and again to some post in Buganda, is a feature that has already lent itself to a good deal of criticism.[1] Let us briefly examine the system of native

[1] Even in cases of junior officials it can be carried too far. One Assistant District Commissioner, in charge of a district, had been at nine different stations in the space of two years.

administration and the effect on it of this practice of constantly changing the district officials.

The official administers his district and derives his information mainly through the chiefs, by means of a system of regular and complete reports. It is through them largely that he knows his people, and there is consequently a risk that he derives relatively little information from any other source and that he contents himself with seeing everything through their eyes.

The powers in the hands of the chiefs are judicial as well as administrative and exceptionally wide. They have their own civil and criminal courts, their own gaols, the right to imprison therein, and within limitations the power of life and death.[1]

As to the manner in which these powers are exercised for the management of their internal affairs we had no means of learning. But the extent to which, apart from the administration of purely internal affairs, the chiefs are depended upon as the medium through which the District Commissioner rules is sufficiently obvious.

To rule through the chiefs should be the aim and object of all native administrations, and it would be folly not to maintain as far as possible the efficient machinery that already exists in Uganda for this method of government. The system is an ideal one, but without relentless supervision and checking it is inevitable that it must result in corruption and abuse.

The District Commissioner need not take the work out of the hands of the chiefs, but he and his assistants might yet take an active and independent part in the administration and see things for themselves as well as through the eyes of the "Kabaka" and "Sasa" chiefs. Nor is there any doubt that they would do so, and efficiently, were they left long enough in one district to master more than the mere details of routine. As it is, a District Commissioner, on taking charge of a new district,

---

[1] The "Kabaka" can condemn and sentence to death, though the sentence has to be confirmed by the High Court. The "Sasa" or "county" chiefs as well as the Kabaka have their courts and gaols. The former is a considerably greater power than those exercised by the District Commissioner.

finds the old machinery running smoothly, the chiefs apparently doing their work efficiently and reporting regularly, and knowing that he is unlikely to remain long enough to acquire a thorough insight into things, naturally accepts them as they are.

The system in force demands an impossibly high standard of integrity as well as mere intelligence from the native. That abuses are not more frequent or more flagrant is due no doubt to a standard that is exceptional, but even the enlightened Muganda is but an African native, and cannot be regarded as free from the weaknesses, common to all inferior races from the Bushman to the Egyptian and the Hindu, that prove him to be as yet unfit for self-government.

The irregularities connived at, or perhaps even encouraged by the chiefs of which the District Commissioner knows nothing[1] may at present be trifling, but given an ambitious, unscrupulous chief capable of taking advantage of the existing conditions, considerable harm might be done before the official became aware of it. The possible irregularities, after all, are not everything. There is the effect upon the officials themselves. It amounts practically to this, that there is a risk of excellent material running to waste. Native administration is robbed of half its pleasure when it is carried on by an indirect system of deputies. It becomes narrow and uninteresting, and it

---

[1] Only the more important chiefs are allowed to hunt elephants (two each year) and the ordinary native is forbidden to kill any of the animals even when *damage feasant*, but in reality a good deal of elephant hunting is surreptitiously indulged in by the population. A native frankly told us that he and his friends had wounded six within two months. One had already died, and some of the others were sick and he wanted us to go and finish them off for him.

These elephants eventually die and are then reported as found dead, and the "finder" receives a percentage of the value of the ivory. The average chief—even if he does not get a share of the spoils—can hardly be expected to court unpopularity by reporting the delinquents. The above case occurred within forty miles of an important station. It is a minor case, but it shows that if the Government is to know what is going on there must be other sources of information than the chiefs alone. If breaches of the game regulations can be concealed, other irregularities may also be committed without detection. That the suppression is wilful may be deduced from the fact that the District Commissioners boast, and not without reason, that few, if any, breaches of the game regulations by Europeans go unreported—simply because it is not to the interest of the natives to conceal them.

is *ipso facto* unlikely, if not impossible, that the official will put his best into his work.

Relying as he does upon his chiefs' reports, it is natural that the District Commissioner's personal visits to his people are restricted and perfunctory. They tend, in short, to be but formal tours of inspection. He does not, in the ordinary course of things, leave the beaten tracks to visit outlying villages or groups, but passes from centre to centre, and from one big chief's to another's, keeping to the principal roads and generally without varying his route. Should the natives of any other villages besides those of the important chiefs have any case or complaint to bring before him they must go to his camping-places, and, as a rule, be introduced by the local chief.

It is obvious that if the District Commissioner were able to make a point of travelling about amongst the people and off the beaten tracks, he would rapidly become *au fait* with many things of which at present he is bound to remain in ignorance, and be able to keep in closer touch with his subjects. Considering the fact that the staff at the central stations consists of a District Commissioner, an Assistant District Commissioner, a Medical Officer, a Police Officer, and a Public Works Engineer, besides Indian or Goanese for clerical and postal work, it is clearly not overwork that prevents a more thorough system of district travelling. It is the fault of the machinery; and yet not of the machinery alone, but of the extent to which, owing to his constant transfer, the official is unable to do more than make use of the machinery as it exists, or to test by personal knowledge the efficiency of its working.

He is unable to master the local language and is forced to rely entirely on the official Ki-Swahili, which is only understood by the chiefs and more advanced natives and *not* by the rank and file of the population. Hence in the hearing and settlement of native cases and complaints, either at his station or on tour, he is largely at the mercy of an interpreter, while in the latter case probably only those plaintiffs whose application is approved by the chief succeed in gaining a hearing.

Even where the official has been keen enough and has had time to acquire a working knowledge of the language in one district, his removal elsewhere would, in nine cases out of ten, result in him being too disheartened to begin upon another.[1]

One of the most important factors in the satisfactory and successful administration of natives is thus eliminated, viz. the ruler's knowledge of and sympathy with the ruled. No matter how keen or efficient a man may be he will not be able, in such spasmodic intervals, to acquire more than a superficial and second-hand knowledge of the people in his charge, or of the inside working of his district.

Further, there can be little doubt that the personality of the official is of considerable value in the management of native races. It need not necessarily be a very strong one, but the actual acquaintance with and influence of their white ruler's personality is of real importance to the natives. They take an interest in him, want to know him, and, making tremendous allowance for his faults, even if they notice them, are far more amenable when they do know him.

The official who is constantly moved from post to post has no chance of becoming a living personality to the greater number of his people. He cannot become a friend, counsellor, and trusted head-chief as he should be.[2] He is little more than a figurehead, the representative for the time being of the abstract Government. Their chiefs the natives know, but the District Commissioner—who is he? Here to-day and gone to-morrow, seldom penetrating into the corners of their country, he is and must be, under this system, more or less of a stranger. Consequently the position of the chief becomes stereotyped as that of the "middleman"; there is little or no direct intercourse between the official and the people, and no encouragement or opportunity for them to talk to him of things that do not meet the eye.

---

[1] *e.g.* We only met one district official who could converse with the Baganda in their own language, and he was in a district where a knowledge of Luganda was absolutely useless to him except for conversing with his personal servants.

[2] " Native administration should be more paternal than official: the seat and centre of authority should be visible, permanent, and accessible" (*Report of Natal Native Affairs Commission*).

A not uncommon source of information is provided by the missions. The teachers and catechists, who are working in or constantly visiting all parts of the country, naturally hear much of what is going on, and retail *some* of it to the missionaries, who, if their communications be of sufficient importance, pass them on to the official. But though perhaps occasionally of value, such information must be often discounted by the same considerations as those that apply to the revelations of the interested chief, and at the best, information from such a source is slipshod, irregular, and unsystematic.

Where independent information is obtained the tendency seems rather to keep it in reserve for use should it bear upon other matters, than to act upon it for the correction of existing irregularities. This, of course, is no sort of policy, and none know it better than those who adopt it. " But what is the use of worrying ?" they ask. " We may be here a year, we may be here less; is it worth while upsetting a system that we may not have time really to readjust ?"

The surprising thing is that under the circumstances the results are not more pernicious than they are. But the fact that they are not does not seem a sound enough argument for continuance of the system. Presumably the attitude is: " Things work pretty well really, we know of no serious irregularities, we can afford to overlook a few trifles." Very well ; but what, after all, is the object of this game of "general post" among the district officials ? What is the vast consideration for which administrative anomalies are to be tolerated and the apathy of the best officials reckoned of no account ?

The only reason we heard put forward was that there were some stations in the Uganda Protectorate at which no official could be expected to remain a long period, *e.g.* that it was not fair to keep men in unhealthy districts like X. or at hot stations like Y. for more than a short spell or to send them back there on their return from leave. We happened to mention this to the official at Y. and he replied that he would rather remain at Y. all his life than be moved again and again—most of all moved to such stations as

R

A., B., or C., which were considered at headquarters to be the most desirable stations in the country.

In other words, if, as we were given to understand, consideration for the officials is the sole reason for the policy of moving them so often from place to place, it is based on misapprehension of their wishes. They would far rather have an opportunity of learning one district well, and administering it efficiently.

Granted that there are stations like X. and Y. at which the conditions are such as to preclude a protracted residence, they are probably not the majority. Why, then, should the whole service be affected by the desire to give the official at an unhealthy station a change? Why, too, should there be a desire to make this change so complete that in many cases when an official has spent one term at one of these stations and, incidentally, has begun to get a grip of local affairs and an interest in his work, he is never sent there again?

It would not seem to be a matter of much difficulty to devise a system by which the official at an unhealthy station is given his change, and at the same time that station be generally, if not always, in the charge of one who has already acquired some knowledge of its working.

(In "unhealthy stations" we purposely do not include those which from their mere remoteness are frequently but erroneously considered undesirable.)

At the most it would require the addition of one or two more officials to the staff of the district in question so that there might always be one of previous local experience to take the place of the official to be relieved. The extra expense would be probably more than balanced by the advantages both to the administration and to the officials themselves.

It is a little surprising that in a highly organised native administration such as that of Uganda there should be no attempt at the compilation of a native census. With the existing machinery it would be a matter of little or no difficulty, and would prove of immense utility in every branch of the administration, as has been aptly demonstrated in those parts of Africa where a complete census has been made and kept up to date. In Uganda, with the present migratory system for officials, it would probably be of even more use than elsewhere. For a good census soon includes much more information than lists of names, and its perusal would give the strange District Commissioner some idea of the individuality of his subjects.

The "agent" system of the Eastern Province has already been commented upon. For the rest all seems admirable. The general administration ; the orderly behaviour of the population in the administered parts, and the courtesy of the chiefs and people ; the network of excellent roads which are justly famous through half Africa ; the encouragement given to agriculture and the development of the country's natural resources—these leave a deep and lasting impression. The natives are industrious and steady workers, and earn a regular income from the cultivation of cotton, coffee, and sim-sim, and thus have ample opportunities of earning the money required for the payment of the poll-tax (Rs.3) and the rent (Rs.2) which they have to pay to their chiefs.

The fact that in the previous year the actual revenue was £40,000 more than had been estimated is a sufficiently convincing proof of the prosperity of the Protectorate. Half of the surplus so earned goes automatically towards the reduction of the grant-in-aid, and the other half is devoted to the development of the country by improving the communications, and so on. The total revenue for the last year for which figures are available (1910, 11) was £191,000, the expenditure £252,000, and the grant-in-aid £96,000, compared with five years ago when the figures were (for 1905, 6): revenue £77,000, expenditure £173,000, and the grant-in-aid £103,000. To a planter with a capital of about £2000 it holds out excellent prospects. After three years he should be getting good returns : first from coffee, later from cocoa, and finally from rubber. And those responsible for the Government seem as intent on making the best of the unrivalled material in the native population as on developing to their utmost the agricultural resources of the country.

XVII

THE SOUDAN

The *Gordon Pasha*—New Year's Eve at Lado — Mongalla — The Dinka tribe—An old friend—The sudd—Bahr-el-Ghazal and Sobat—Kodok—The White Nile railway bridge—Khartoum—Omdurman—Khalifa's palace, Mahdi's tomb, and market-place—School and hospital—The Gordon College—The Nubian Desert—Wady Halfa.

THE *Gordon Pasha* is an example of the best type of stern-wheeler and one of the newest and finest boats on the Upper Nile. The main deck contains a roomy saloon, cabins and accommodation for eight passengers, including a *cabin-de-luxe* at the stern. The latter we were fortunate in finding available for our use. It measured fourteen by sixteen feet, was furnished with comfortable bunks, four windows and two doors, one of the latter leading into the bathroom. The windows and main door were, as throughout the boat, fitted with mosquito screens. After the limited conveniences of camp life this was the height of luxury.

The second and third class accommodation was provided by a two-storied lighter, or barge, lashed to the port side. On this was also piled the stock of fuel, replenished from time to time from wooding stations *en route*, while sundry cargo was stowed in the shallow hold.

The upper deck was devoted to the second class (Greek and Egyptian traders and such), the lower to negroes. Their cooking was done in a bucket in the bows, in which a fire was constantly kept burning.

Occasionally these Nile steamers carry two or more barges—sometimes two lashed together and pushed in front of their bows.

The cool breeze on the river, heightened by the motion

of the steamer, was delightfully refreshing after the stifling heat on land, and the next hour to Lado, spent mainly in talking over old times with Captain Stigand, whom we had not seen for some years, had gone by almost before we realised that we had started.

Lado is a desolate encampment on the left bank of the Nile, which, we were not surprised to learn, is shortly to be abandoned in favour of some more salubrious spot. Messrs. Done and Bruce, whom we found in charge, welcomed Bimbashi Stigand and ourselves and invited us to see the New Year in at their mess. We had previously been sceptical about the necessity of dining under a mosquito-net even on the Nile, but our evening at Lado succeeded in completely converting us. In spite of its protection and the added precaution of wrapping a coat and a bath-towel round our legs and covering the perforated chairs with copies of the *Field*, we were in considerable misery the whole evening. There were swarms of them, and they bit through shirt, trousers, socks and everything. We were assured that we were really fortunate—that it was nothing to Lado at its worst, but even as we saw it we have no compunction in assigning it one of the places of honour among the pest-ridden spots of the earth. The conversation during and after dinner mostly turned upon the affairs of this, the most recent addition [1] to the provinces of the Empire, and it was good news to hear that in spite of the depredations of hunters during the interregnum preceding its absorption in the Soudan there are still large numbers of elephant, white rhino, and other game. Indeed, while we sat under that mosquito-net a herd of elephants could be heard trumpeting in a *khor* quite close.

Shortly before midnight, after exchanging wishes for a happy New Year, we took our leave and returned to the steamer, where we were relieved to find our cabin comparatively free from mosquitoes.

Weighing anchor at dawn we reached Mongalla, the

[1] It had been leased to the King of the Belgians during his lifetime, though actually belonging to Great Britain.

headquarters of the province of the same name, at eight o'clock. Owen Bey, the Governor of the province, came down to greet us, and we regretted that having already been longer than we had intended over the first part of our journey, we were unable to spend some time in his district, for we learnt from him, as we had already done from Bimbashi Stigand, that His Excellency the Sirdar, who had been advised of our coming, had kindly issued instructions that every facility be given us by his officers with whom we might come into contact during our visit to the Soudan. We would gladly have availed ourselves of this opportunity to study the conditions prevailing in the country, and would especially have enjoyed an excursion into the Mongalla province and a tour in Kordofan. The riverain population forms but a small proportion of the whole, and a real insight into the country cannot be gained without penetrating into the interior, of which we heard (especially from a fellow-passenger, Mr. Brownsworth of the Kordofan Trading Company) a rather tempting description.

After anchoring at a wooding station principally notable for its mosquitoes, we started at half-past five and at nine o'clock reached Malek, where we dropped Mr. Shaw, after going ashore with him and visiting his station and the Dinka villages close by.

With the exception of a few of the inland cattle-rearing members of the tribe, who were sharing huge beehive huts with the herds in their charge, the whole population consisted of the riverain Dinka, who are chiefly fishermen. Like the Bari farther south they live in a state of complete nudity, only smearing their bodies with cow-dung ash as a preventive of mosquito bites. They complete their toilet by dyeing their hair with cow-urine to a reddish-yellow.

We learnt some strange and interesting facts about these people. One of their prophets, Mr. Shaw told us, had not only foretold the coming of Halley's Comet seven months before its appearance (which, after all, he might have learnt from some ordinary source), but had impressed upon his people that its appearance, so far from being a signal for war or strife, must be marked by universal abstention from any kind of violence. The population of a whole village had subsequently been thrown into a state of terrible anxiety because, during this millennium, one of their number had so far disregarded the prophet's warning as to clout his wife over the head and cut it open. A still more striking circumstance was that the said prophet had identified his own general precepts and teaching with those of the Christian religion as propounded by Mr. Shaw. The latter had been more than surprised when an audience of his remarked at the end of a discourse that they had been taught just that kind of thing by their own fellow-countryman. Mr. Shaw put it to the test by visiting the man, and found him astonishingly in accord with his own teaching.

An agreeable surprise awaited us at Bor, which we reached at noon the same day. The Bimbashi in charge proved to be an old friend, in the person of Captain C. V. Fox of the Scots Guards. Fourteen years had elapsed since our last meeting, but the twenty minutes' halt was made the best of for a stimulating discussion of old times.

Nine hours after leaving Bor—a dull spot populated with the lowest type of Dinka—we arrived at Kerissa, and after spending nearly another two hours taking in fuel, continued our journey through the night—the previous wooding station having been the last place at which we had to tie up when darkness fell.

In the morning we found we had entered that waste of wastes—the sudd—through which we were to steam for two days and another night.

The sudd is a thing one must see to realise. Once the last tree of the upper reaches is left behind, it becomes an endless sea of green monotony, reaching apparently to the ends of the earth, and unbroken by even a leaf or a twig one inch above the level of the feathery papyrus tops. Seen from the deck of a comfortable Nile steamer, with a cool breeze blowing and practically no discomfort but the constant shifting of the sun's rays as the river winds and winds again, one feels it to be fairly innocent and even beautiful with its gently swaying, soft, unchanging green. But those who have had any experience of the drudgery of making one's way in a small boat along the narrow waterways through this clogging pest-ridden vegetation—as we had both had, to a small extent, in the Bangweulu swamps—can guess at its possibilities, and we were reminded of the terrible four months spent in this region by Dr. Milne and Captain Gage when finding a channel through the sudd in 1898. This courageous and perilous achievement, like too many brilliant exploits in African history, is in danger of lapsing into oblivion. Mr. E. S. Grogan, in his *Cape to Cairo*, alludes to "this successful attempt of Captain Gage, of the 7th Dragoon Guards, and Dr. Milne, as one of the most daring feats ever accomplished in the history of African travel. They suffered indescribable hardships for nearly four months, during all of which time they hardly slept one night on land, but were compelled to see the long hours of darkness through, night after night, cramped up in a small boat or lying on the vegetation, tormented by myriads of mosquitoes, and with very little more substantial than native porridge to keep their spirits up. Day after day, nothing but that vast expanse of weed, of a hopelessness beyond civilised conception; day after day dragging their boats through and over stinking bogs and spongy masses of weed tenanted by a thousand crocodiles—not knowing where they were, nor, in characteristic British fashion, caring, yet ever keeping their face forward, strong in the knowledge that perseverance must succeed. Their food ran short, and to return was impossible. Had they not come unexpectedly upon Major Peake's steamers they would probably all have perished. Very few people can ever have any conception of the magnitude and apparent hopelessness of their task."

Though bumping first on one side and then on the other as the current swings the steamer back and fro in the winding and narrow channels, the passage is now free from discomfort, but one cannot help thinking of the hard-

GONDOKORO POST BOAT GOING UP STREAM.

INLAND DINKA HUT.

ships of the men who first forced their way through those channels, and whose daring and tenacity made possible the luxurious travelling of the present day.

On the morning of the 5th the Bahr-el-Gebel was left behind and we were steaming east towards Taufikia and the junction of the Sobat, which we reached at 10 A.M. The White Nile—as the river is called after the junction of the Bahr-el-Ghazal and Bahr-el-Gebel—is here a broad waterway, dotted with islands of floating vegetation that have broken loose from the sudd. The land on either side is flat and uninteresting, a few villages of the Shiluk tribe—from which some of the finest fighting material in the Soudanese regiments is drawn—forming the only break in the monotony till the mission of the Austrian Fathers is reached. Kodok, famous under its former name of Fashoda, we reached after dark, and from which, after a halt of a couple of hours we steamed in the peaceful light of a starlit sky. Two days were passed during which we met occasional *nuggars*, their sails and rigging reflected with wonderful clearness in the calm river, and we reached Costi at about midday on the 7th. Here the Nile is crossed by the magnificent new bridge that carries the railway from Khartoum into Kordofan. After tapping this province, with its rich gum-producing forests, the line will eventually reach Darfur, one of the wildest and least known areas of Northern Africa. The bridge consists of nine spans—eight of one hundred and twenty feet, the ninth (the centre span which revolves to allow the larger craft to pass) being two hundred. All along the river banks we saw native boats being laden with the produce of the country, and realised that a tremendous future lies before this fertile land so suited for the cultivation of cotton, gum, grain, and many other valuable products.

On the 9th of January, at 3 A.M., after a most comfortable journey through what a dozen years previously had been one of the "darkest" stretches of the continent, we turned up the Blue Nile and moored alongside the river bank at Khartoum. The trip had been, thanks largely to Mr. Archer, the engineer in charge, his management and his catering, a most comfortable one. The only excitement was caused by the things and passengers that fell overboard. The first had been the Indian cook's infant brother—he could swim like a fish. The second was a sheep, which was nobly rescued by one of the crew just as it was sinking—to be our dinner the following day. The third was a native passenger who slipped off just as we rounded the corner into the Blue Nile, and, in spite of the prompt measures that were always taken on such occasions, was never seen again.

At Khartoum we were once more among friends. The Governor of Omdurman, Mr. Moore, had been contemporary with one of us (Melland) at Oxford, while his chief assistant, Mr. Arthur Asquith, was a relative of the same. Mr. Harold Hall, the manager of the Soudan Development Company, we knew of as a brother of a colleague of ours, and yet another friend and former pupil was found later on in the King's Own Scottish Borderers.

The river at Khartoum is like an inverted Y, the tail of the letter pointing north, the eastern branch being the Blue Nile (Azrak), on the south bank of which lies Khartoum, and on the other, connected by the railway bridge and a ferry, is Khartoum North. The western branch is the White Nile (Abiad), and on the left bank of the united river, just below the junction, lies Omdurman, connected with Khartoum by a steam ferry-boat service.

After the battle of Omdurman and the downfall of the Khalifa's power in 1898 an effort was made to abolish this settlement and to unite the whole population at Khartoum, but prejudice was too strong, and Omdurman still remains the centre of the native population, both permanent and transitory. It is an enormous mud city, with approximately 45,000 inhabitants, partly composed of Arabs and Berberines, partly of almost every tribe in Africa north of the Equator, besides generally including many pilgrims to Mecca. Among those at the time of our visit were 3000 Hausa from Nigeria.

The shipping firms and construction workshops are in Khartoum North on the opposite bank of the river, while

Ash-covered Dinka.

Dinka woman making mats.

Khartoum itself contains the palace standing in its beautiful gardens, all the residences of the official and civil population, the Government offices, the Gordon College, barracks, cathedral, mosque, commercial houses, and hotel.

There is only one hotel, "The Grand," and there we took up our quarters. It is a pretentious and roomy building on the embankment. Dinner is served in an electrically lighted garden; lunch and breakfast are equally good, and second helpings can be obtained on extra payment. No objection is raised to their own servants attending to visitors' modest requirements when the hotel staff is otherwise engaged. For three meals and a bedroom a charge of twenty-four shillings a day and upwards is made.

A telephone message from Mr. Asquith invited us to Omdurman for lunch, and crossing in Mr. Hall's convenient little launch, we found our host and his sister in a comfortable mud-house which had formerly been the mess of one of the Soudanese regiments. He had migrated thither during his sister's visit, as the Khalifa's old palace in which he had been living was hardly adequate to the accommodation of a lady. After lunch we visited this interesting relic of the Dervish dominion which had been his former quarters, and were taken all over it, noting with interest the various semi-civilised contrivances, including a fine bath with which the Khalifa had, with the aid of European prisoners, fitted his residence. From the topmost turret a clear view is obtained of the half-demolished Mahdi's tomb, which was shelled at the battle of Omdurman, and which, in the opinion of many, should have been levelled to the ground.

All round us lay spread the city of Omdurman, with the Kereri hills (at which the battle of Omdurman was fought) eight miles north-west, and beyond—the desert. Omdurman straggles about six miles along the riverside—three miles each side of the Khalifa's house—and two or three miles inland. There are a few stone houses, some finished and some not; the remainder are built of monotonous brown mud—some of it dignified by the name of "sun-dried bricks." It consists of a variety of streets, parallel and at right angles, and of buildings that are, doubtless, of a variety of sizes, though from a distance it is a brown sea of mud dwellings all about the same size and shape; flat-roofed, verandahless and shadeless, separated by streets and alleys of baking sand, and backed by the baking desert. Except here and there near the water's edge, not a leaf or a blade of grass is to be seen. The palace stands at the corner of a huge square enclosed by a seven or eight foot wall of stone. A second wall, of which only parts now remained, enclosing a much larger space, originally contained the residences of the Khalifa's particular followers. Most of the buildings occupied by them, originally covering some acres between the palace and the river bank, are now mere heaps of sand and clay and broken mud walls, the unpopularity of the original residents being so great that none will build or live upon the site.

After leaving the palace we visited the native market, which is one of the largest congregations of buyers and sellers in Northern Africa—a maze of crowded burrows, some ten feet broad, between rows of tiny booths in which all manner of native work—carpets, brass ware, pottery, food, scents, soap, cloth and wearing apparel—was being sold by Greeks, Syrians, Armenians, Cretans, Arabs, and natives. The roofs over the shops and alleys were in an indescribable state of disrepair, though the booths themselves were clean and well arranged. The whole formed a picture as typically "Eastern" as could be imagined, and emphasised, more than anything else we had seen, the fact that we had left negro Africa behind and had emerged into the northern part of the continent, which seems to have been so cut off from the centre and the south as to form a different land.

The two most interesting types were the makers of fringes on cotton cloths, and the bead turners. The former were tiny urchins who worked at a primitive loom with tremendous rapidity, their feet in a pit, supported by a rail against their stomachs. The latter used a lathe that

PRIMITIVE IRRIGATION ON THE NILE.

WHITE NILE BRIDGE, THE CENTRE SPAN SWINGING.

was equally primitive, on which they fashioned wooden beads, turning out, so they told our host, a string and a half a day. One worker told us that he cleared a profit of about 40 per cent., but the outlay was so small the gain cannot have been more than a few millièmes a day.

Our own purchases were confined to a few ostrich feathers at 4s. each—the Omdurman market is famous for these, and the presence of our host and hostess prevented us from buying inferior feathers at ridiculous prices—and a couple of pairs of red morocco leather shoes of the local boat-shaped pattern. In spite of the courteous and ready manner in which the merchants and salesmen gratified our curiosity on any matter which excited our interest, it was difficult to carry away more than a confused memory of the bewildering variety in each alley-way of this warren of buyers and sellers, hawkers and their wares.

A closer inspection of the town itself was postponed to another day, and at sunset we re-crossed the river to Khartoum.

The following morning was spent quietly in visiting the sights of Khartoum, notably the lifelike statue of General Gordon in the main street, the nearly completed cathedral, the War Office, Law Courts, and the Sirdar's palace, where we had a stroll in the beautiful gardens, which were particularly refreshing after the glaring dust of the streets.

The next day was rather more strenuous. We rose early and caught the 7.30 tram to the ferry, reaching Omdurman in time for breakfast with Mr. and Miss Asquith, after which we went to visit Mr. Moore at his office, and chatted over old times. Then, armed with letters of introduction from our host, we proceeded to pay a visit to the Omdurman Primary School.

The headmaster is an enthusiast. He was obviously delighted at having an opportunity of showing us the establishment, and we spent something like an hour and a half being treated to a thorough inspection and examination of each class, and of almost every pupil in it. It was all very interesting, the tiny nippers learning "the three R's" being especially attractive, while the admirable discipline and keenness throughout was not the least striking feature of the entertainment. We felt a little sorry for the ushers who were teaching English, for they had to expose the weak points in their knowledge of the language. All these teachers were Egyptian, and the pupils were of every shade from black to nearly white.

With only twenty-five minutes to spare after our tour of the school, we had to abandon the idea of visiting both the hospital and the survey office, and decided in favour of the former. The Egyptian doctor in charge received us with an eagerness that equalled that of the headmaster. He took us into every corner of the establishment and explained with great thoroughness every case of any interest or importance.

The hospital was of mud, the various wards being similar in style and construction to the native houses. This, it was explained, had been found advisable, even though funds might be available for a more pretentious building, as not only were the natives unable to appreciate the luxuries of better appointed quarters, but positively preferred and had more confidence in an establishment that gave them accommodation more or less of the same style as exists in their own homes. Though crudely constructed the hospital was scrupulously clean, excellently managed, and apparently well equipped.

We had to hurry away so as to catch the 12.30 ferry to Khartoum, for we had a good deal to do after lunch.

The rest of the day was spent in a little photographic business, a visit to the gymkhana of the 1st King's Own Scottish Borderers and dinner at their mess, at the invitation of one of the officers, who turned out to be an old pupil.

January 12th was our last day at Khartoum. Though sufficiently impressive as a testimony to the conquest of the Soudan, the town can hardly be called either particularly beautiful or particularly attractive.

The metamorphosis that has taken place during the last ten years is striking enough. Trees are already giving or promising grateful shade where all was once the glaring sunstruck sand. Some of the buildings would be no discredit to Whitehall, but it is—and must always remain—that uncomfortable conglomerate, a painful hybrid 'twixt the East and West. The Gordon College, which we visited after obtaining permits from the Civil Secretary for the export of our guns, may be described as the finest monument of the British occupation of the country. Carrying with us a letter to Mr. Simpson, the Assistant Director, we were first introduced to Dr. Andrew Balfour in the magnificent Wellcome Research Laboratory, in which he takes such pardonable pride.

Everything of importance was shown and explained, and, interested as we were in tropical diseases, their causes, their symptoms, and their cure, we were particularly grateful to him and his staff for giving us the opportunity of learning something of the resources and achievements of so well equipped and efficient an institution of tropical medical research.

We next visited the Museum, and then were placed in the hands of one Artiah Effendi, an Egyptian member of the college staff, who proved a capable and lucid cicerone as he piloted us round the educational parts of the college, and concluded with a visit to the workshops, where young Soudan is learning various simple handicrafts and the practical uses of machinery for the advancement of his country.

The work is not altogether unprofitable, for the pupils in one section were busy pressing and baling cotton for export, while in others they were engaged in making useful articles such as doors and window frames. Any one interested in the practical work that is being done in this institution should read the annual reports or some of the articles that have been written on the subject.[1] Lord Kitchener could not have thought of a finer or more suitable memorial to the great Englishman whose name will always be associated with Khartoum, and the Soudan owes him a debt of gratitude for the conception as well as the successful execution of his idea.

---

[1] For instance, Mr. Hamilton Fyfe's article, entitled "Educating the Sudanese," in the *National Review* for October 1910.

After dinner we drove to the station and boarded the ten o'clock train for the north. The rolling-stock is built on the same pattern as the Indian railways, with mosquito screens and sun-hoods, and but for the constant head-bumping that the inexperienced traveller suffers from the latter, are comparatively comfortable.

At half-past five we awoke to find ourselves at Atbara, and at eleven reached Abu Hamed. Here the railway leaves the river and plunges into the Nubian Desert.

It is an awful thing merely to look at. The last sign of life is quickly left behind, and for miles and miles there opens out on either side a waste of hot nothingness glaring into infinity.

At midday the mirages between the track and a ridge of rocks to the east were so perfect an illusion that it was almost impossible to believe that there really was not a clear sheet of water something less than a mile away.

But these mocking phenomena hardly compensate for the vacant dreariness of a tract in which even the railway sidings are known by numbers instead of names, and sunset was greeted with a sigh of relief.

At a quarter to ten we ran into Wady Halfa, the border station of the Soudan and Egypt and the terminus of the Soudan Government railways. The next stage was by river to Shellal; and the mail-boat *Soudan* was alongside and awaiting the embarkation of her passengers from the train.

The train had been divided into two, one part preceding us, as we thought, to Halfa. We were therefore rather alarmed to find on arrival that this half, in which the boy Kasonde was ensconced, had not arrived. The alarm was a false one, however; the missing portion had after all been awaiting us, and appeared in due course.

We were scheduled to leave the same night, but owing to the vagaries of certain sandbanks down stream our departure was postponed till dawn.

XVIII

EGYPT

Down the Nile to Shellal—Philæ and the Dam—Asswân—Luxor—The temples of Thebes and the tombs of the kings—Karnak and Luxor temples—Abydos—Cairo—Tura—The Pyramids in sleet—Port Said — End of our journey— Retrospect — Notes on clothes, rifles, cameras.

THE *Soudan*, a stern-wheeler several sizes larger than the *Gordon Pasha*, and proportionally more splendid, seemed the last word in luxurious travelling. She had three decks, several excellent single-berth cabins, saloon, promenade, and smoking-room, and a delightful lounge for'ard enclosed on three sides with sliding glass doors, giving a shelter from the keen north wind.

We sailed at dawn, and at eight passed close to the first relic of ancient Egypt that we were to see, the temple of Abu Simbel, hollowed from the cliffs of rock on the Nile's right bank. Nothing of course was visible to us but the doorway and the sixty-five foot Colossi on either side. Though reckoned one of Egypt's finest temples, we had, as yet, seen none of them, and in spite of feeling a little tantalised, we had no idea of what we had missed. The scenery for miles was grandly rugged, the sandstone ranges bordering the banks now and again broken by patches of fertile and occupied land, and here and there on either side an ancient temple standing sentinel over the buried past.

Our passage was to be but a hurried one. We could scarcely hope for more than a fleeting impression of Egypt's varied treasures, and each hour that passed brought with it the suspicion that we might feel quite dissatisfied with ourselves for not making a long stay.

We reached Shellal between three and four in the

morning. As the train which was to take us on our next stage to Luxor and Cairo did not start till after ten o'clock, we seized the chance of a hurried visit to the temple of Philæ, within a hundred yards of which the boat had come to anchor, and the Asswân dam. Philæ, as all the world knows, is one of the minor gems of ancient Egyptian architecture, and will soon, in all probability, be no more visible to the tourist. Standing as it does but a mile or so above the dam, and being even now at high-water partially submerged, the raising of the dam will, sooner or later, mean its end.

In January—as yet—it is high and dry, and despite the prohibitive efforts of a hoary native custodian whom we failed to convince of the retrospective properties of " antiquity-tickets " to be obtained the following day, we saw most of it, and probably were more impressed than those who, coming from the north, have already seen the finer and older specimens of Egyptian architecture. Its preservation and its unique position—occupying an isolated islet in a miniature bay—tempts one to think hard things of the Asswân dam, but, after all, the fertility and prosperity of Upper Egypt are of some consequence compared with the saving of a single relic of the past.

The dam itself we had no time to more than skirt, and we could not have gone along it, in any case, owing to the construction work in progress, but the view we had was enough to leave the impression that while for the magnitude of its conception it is worthy to rank with any of Egypt's ancient monuments, for its utility it stands in a class of its own.

Our train left a few minutes before eleven, and after a brief halt at Asswân, continued its journey with but short stoppages to Luxor.

It was dusty travelling, though pleasantly cool. The railway here runs close to the river again—between it and the desert—and the contrast between the two sides of the line is as marked as it could be. On the right the desolate desert broken by shaly shingle foothills and a barren and stony escarpment that seemed to mark the flood-

river banks; on the left a strip of cultivated land between the railway and the river, green and gold with crops, some sprouting and some ripening, and gradually becoming broader as we moved along. But the journey was, on the whole, lacking in interest; the narrow gauge line is not conspicuously comfortable, and we were glad when just before sunset we caught our first glimpse of the temples of ancient Thebes in the west and presently drew up at Luxor station.

Though our time was short we had no intention of merely passing by all the gigantic glories of the past, and had decided to break our journey and see what we could in two or three days.

Luxor has a choice of hotels, and, ignoring the jibes of certain of our friends at our reckless sybaritism, we chose the Winter Palace. Its uniformed myrmidons could barely hide their scorn at our travel-stained and battered baggage, wondering no doubt what manner of vagabonds they were who had the nerve to enlist their services to handle and transport such dubious-looking articles. But they made no audible comment, and leaving them in their care we contrived to assume a creditable amount of self-assurance and walked to the hotel. When we reached it, with its enormous gleaming white front, its broad terrace approached by a double flight of steps, all in a soft blaze of electric light, bougainvillæa, and pointsettia, we really wondered for a moment whether our assurance was equal to it. Luxury for ourselves did not perhaps appal—coming from the wilds we rather hankered after it—but for the pagan with us—where on earth in this brilliant mansion could a home be found for a Mid-African mud-hut dweller?

Our fears proved groundless. Equally suitable accommodation was forthcoming for all of us, white and black, in contrast to our experience at Khartoum; and it only remains to say that in every possible respect—attention, civility, *cuisine*, and comfort—our sojourn in the Winter Palace Hotel left nothing to be desired. A quite exceptional string band, which played before and after dinner, reminded us with a thrill that we had not heard any orchestral music for four and five years respectively.

Securing antiquity-tickets and the services of an intelligent dragoman, who was to show us what he could of the cream of things in two days and a bit, we started off at nine next morning across the river to the city of Thebes. Our experience of the Soudan donkey-saddle had led us, in our ignorance of the different type in use in Egypt, to adopt some other means of transport, and we engaged for the first day a two-wheeled trap with broad flat tyres and drawn by a mule—known as a "sand-car"—which was awaiting us on the other side. Shamandi Ahmed, our dragoman, followed on a donkey, and Kasonde, to be shown what he might see of man's ancient handiwork, on foot.

Passing the Colossi of Memnon seated in solitary grandeur in the midst of a beautiful broad plain, green with waving wheat, we proceeded to spend our first day among the temples and the tombs of the queens.

Of the former we visited all but Der-el-Bahri; of the latter Shamandi took us to what he considered the two best, as well as to the Gardener's and another tomb.

Needless to say, we shall not attempt in these pages a description of things that are already so well known to the travelling world, and have been described again and again by a hundred expert pens. In our innocence we thought that perhaps a day or two would give us a surfeit of mouldering antiquities and massive blocks of stone, but each step served but to whet the appetite and make keener our regret that our stay must be so short.

The exquisite bas-reliefs, of which the weathering of four thousand years had hardly dulled the edge, the crowded hieroglyphic records that one aches to know and read, the stupendous egoism personified in the gigantic statues of the kings, the baffling problem of how and why these pagans learnt to rear their mountains of perennial masonry to shelter and to satisfy their cult—these are things that must arrest and stupefy the most apathetic and perfunctory sightseer.

Out of a multitude of wonders the fallen and shattered statue of Rameses II. in the Ramesseum, owing to its stupendous grandeur and the marvel of its transport from Asswân and of its destruction by Cambyses, and the dark-blue star-spangled sky in the ceiling of Queen Nefertari's tomb, owing to the perfection of its colouring, were perhaps the hardest to forget.

Shamandi, besides his varied if somewhat superficial knowledge of the different objects most worthy of attention, took a keen interest in our photographic ambitions, and was full of useful hints as to the light and position that would be best for the various objects; and on our return he surprised us by suggesting that we should curtail our stay at Luxor by a day and devote the third day to a visit to Dendra or Abydos, or both. He was evidently an enthusiast, and, realising that we were not so unappreciative after all, he did not want us to miss even the treat that he generally kept in reserve. It meant a hard day for Tuesday, but he had inspired us with confidence, and we decided we should gain more than we should miss by carrying out his suggestion.

The next morning, therefore, we started at sunrise with the intention of "finishing" the other side of the river in the morning and seeing Karnak and Luxor in the afternoon.

A couple of excellent donkeys besides Shamandi's own were awaiting us on the farther bank, and before eight o'clock we were cantering across the plain towards the foot of the hills that hide the tombs of the kings.

Some declare that to gain the most vivid impression of the gaunt desolation of the approach to the tombs, the visit should be made at noon on a hot and cloudless day, but the ride along that pass in the cool of a glorious morning is sufficiently impressive.

The hills tower on either side of the road, amidst gleaming and glaring red and yellow masses of forbidding rock and sand showing no single sign of life—not a leaf nor a stalk of vegetation, not even a solitary lizard basking in the sun. It is, in fact, an ideal place in which to be dead.

On winds the road, trodden by countless funeral cortèges of old, till rounding a corner one reaches the mighty cul-de-sac, hidden away in the corners of which are the burial-places of kings. Only when the entrances of the tombs are seen does one fully realise to what extent seclusion and concealment were the object of the choice. No purpose here of gratifying the eye of inquisitive posterity or of leaving a monument of art or labour for all time. Proving by their very exclusiveness their belief in the after-life, these old barbarians were so intent on preserving the privacy of the dead that the craftsmen and artists of the tombs were summarily executed on completion of their tasks lest they divulged to others the place where their bodies and their treasures had been entombed.

The tombs themselves are gems in an appropriate setting: appropriate from its very contrast. Gallery after gallery with their colours undimmed by the ages that have passed, panel after panel of minute and close-writ hieroglyphics telling the history and the virtues of the dead, shelf after shelf that once bore the lurid mummy-cases of the embalmed remains of those who dumbly waited for the after-life, and, crowning all, the tremendous labour of excavation in the solid rock.

One sarcophagus, and one only, still rests undisturbed —that of Amenhotep—and it is with a feeling that it is something akin to sacrilege, as the light is switched on and floods a chamber whose existence had been almost unsuspected, that the visitor gazes through the glass cover on the features of one who has been dead three thousand years. No photograph, lacking colour, could, even were there light within, give an adequate idea of the mural decorations of the tombs; and an additional regret is felt when one learns that in all probability the exposure to the air will sooner or later make them grow dim and fade.

We felt, as we had before, that each tomb wanted days or even weeks to see it, with perhaps just one enthusiastic and reverent antiquary at one's side ready to answer every question that one wanted to ask, and keep silent when one wished to ask no more. Our early visit had one charm to recommend it—we were the only visitors at that hour, but even our dragoman and an apathetic custodian or two tended to spoil the effect. In such places, when sympathy is lacking, one wants to be alone.

On leaving the last of the four tombs which we visited, we took another way back across the hills. Climbing a steep and stony path winding up the side of the eastern slope, and peering over the edge of a precipice near the brink of which our way had led, we found ourselves looking back into the barren depths whence we had come. The change of route is well worth the climb. A little more scrambling, climbing, and ascending, and an inimitable panorama greets the eye. The Nile, with Karnak and Luxor on the farther side, and in the middle-ground, on the edge of the vivid green plain, the Ramesseum, the Colossi, the Roman remains, and at one's feet the temple of Der-el-Bahri. The latter, with the tomb of Queen Hatishu, was once completely buried by the falling débris of the cliff at whose base it stands. Excavated and partially restored, though a building of plain design, it gives a glimpse of what Egypt in her glory may have been.

After a brief rest we hastened back across the river and rode out to Karnak, that wonderful mass of ruins where amidst the wreck so much has withstood the ravages of spoilers and of time. The pylon, the obelisks —standing and fallen—the sacred lake with the new-found granite scarab at its edge, and, grandest of all, the mighty hypostyle hall which every visitor should worship by the light of the full moon. Then, on our return to Luxor temple, where, after a first feeling of impatience at the modern buildings crowding on two sides, and of disgust at the crude Coptic church in its very midst, we drew comfort from the glories of its colonnade and the cynicism of the yet another statue of Rameses with the figure of his wife *en miniature* half-hidden behind the calf of his colossal leg.

Weary but not sated we returned to our hotel to find a bathetic if suitable antidote in preparation in the shape of an impromptu dance.

Half-past five the next morning found us once more on the move, and, swallowing a hurried breakfast, we caught the 7.20 train to Baliana for the temple of Abydos: for the railway service did not admit of a visit to Dendra in the same day. In a little more than four hours, one of which was spent driving over a flat and wind-swept plain, we reached the village of Abydos; and leaving our Jehu struggling vigorously though not vainly to prevent his steeds backing over a small precipice at the foot of the dusty gangway that did duty for one of the main streets, we proceeded to a leisurely enjoyment of the finest example extant of the Ramessean period.

If only for its better preservation it has established its claim. Within are covered bas-reliefs almost as vivid as those in the royal tombs, while on the outer weather-beaten walls the paintings still give a hint of their early splendour. Massive portions of the flat slab roof are still in their place with their wonderful deep-blue ceilings, and the exquisite figures, scenes, and symbols covering the limestone walls are as sharp and clear as the day the chisel ceased its work. In parts the masonry is blackened for several feet of its height, stained by the accumulated rubbish of generations of a later age. Part has been used as a Coptic church, of which little but some rough red frescoes and inscriptions now remain, while here and there obliterated profiles and crude erasures bear witness to the early Christians' mischievous intolerance of pagan art.

There was one detail in the scheme of decoration that especially caught the eye. In two panels representing the heads of beasts there were an oryx and reedbuck and a reedbuck and sable respectively. There was no mistaking the last-named beast any more than the other two, and in view of the present zoological distribution, it would be interesting to know what trace there is of a sable antelope being found in the latitudes under Egypt's influence or sway.

At about five we drove back to Baliana to await our train. As it was not due till after ten o'clock we had about four hours to squander somehow, and adopted Shamandi's suggestion that we should hie to a buffet of which he knew, and at which he said we could obtain a decent meal. We found his buffet in an hour's time—a grubby wine-shop in a grubby street on the banks of the river Nile. Its accommodation was a trifle dingy and unsavoury, and it was crowded with noisy and not particularly attractive natives of various costumes, ranks, and shades of colour, but an inoffensive Greek proprietor, who spoke intelligible French, promised us a meal within an hour, and, preferring the open air to the atmosphere of the cabaret, we seated ourselves in a sort of decayed bandstand across the road. It was bitterly cold, we were annoyed by repulsive mendicants and abusive boot-blacks, and every passing minute brought a deeper conviction that we were going to get nothing fit to eat. However, just when we were beginning to suspect that we had been entirely forgotten and were going to get nothing at all, dinner was announced, and following Shamandi into an inner parlour, the existence of which afforded some relief, we were served by the proprietor with a respectably cooked meal that dispelled our fears.

We still had an hour to wait at the end of it, before there was any object in going to the station. It would have been a very dull wait had not Shamandi nobly risen to the occasion, and after presenting his account passed away the time by an entertaining sketch of some of his experiences. He had taken a great interest in the boy Kasonde, and was scarcely able to believe that he was really going to England. He had estimated him to be an infant of ten or twelve, and when he had got over his astonishment at learning his true age (which was nearly twenty-four) he regaled us with reminiscences of his own early and brilliant youth. He had never been to England, he had to admit, but he had very nearly been to France, and as nearly to America. In the first case it was a royal princess who had expressed a desire to add him to her staff, and had offered his parents £250 for their consent. The infatuated party from across the Atlantic had been an heiress, who had come but a little later, and had been willing to give £700 for the privilege of taking him home and giving him an education. In both cases Shamandi's father had been only too ready to let him go, but his mother had thwarted the old man's greed for gain, and had hidden away the young Shamandi till the danger had passed, so he was still Shamandi Ahmed, dragoman of Luxor; a highly accomplished dragoman, no doubt, with all the certificates for proficiency in his work, but without the Western polish that might so easily have been his. His mother, he added sadly, was a good woman, but her attitude had tried the old man too far, and his father had divorced her, and had taken to himself another wife.

When he dropped for a time the serious note and became a humorist, the transition was so gradual that at first we did not notice the change. He confided in us that his patience was sorely tried by a certain class of visitors who would protest airy incredulity at his facts and dates, and would brutally declare that the paintings in the tombs and temples were not more than six months old. In relating the delinquencies of one party who had tried him more than most, he described it as consisting of "One young gennleman and one young leddy, one old gennleman, nineteenth dynasty, sixteen hundred years before Christ, and one old leddy, twentieth dynasty, fourteen hundred years before Christ"; and whenever the characters recurred in his story he never failed to give them their full description.

His account had been a little heavier than we had expected: he had charged us for four days, some of them at double rates, but as he had shown us things that occupy the usual visitor seven to ten days, we did not complain, and the presentation of this big account showed us a new side of his character. When he learnt that if we paid him in full we might be short of cash for railway charges to Cairo, he not only readily consented to our suggestion

EGYPT

that part should be remitted by post on our arrival there, but tried to persuade us to leave the whole amount in abeyance as long as it suited us.

The loading of baggage on to the *train-de-luxe* in its five-minute halt at Baliana station seemed to be a quite unprecedented service to ask of the railway staff. In fact, with half-an-hour to spare, it seemed at first more than doubtful if we were even going to get ours weighed. Eventually, however, we managed to circumvent the obstructiveness of the station-master, whose attitude afforded a considerable contrast to the courtesy with which earlier in the day a senior colleague had relieved us of 10s. for an accidentally broken window-pane, and we got successfully away. Kasonde was in luck. The conductor of the train had been in Nyasaland, Madagascar, and Zanzibar, and still retained a smattering of Chimang'anja and Ki-Swahili. There were no third-class compartments on the train, but his kindly interest secured for the boy the luxury of having a second-class carriage for his exclusive use. For ourselves the *wagon-lit* provided what is generally considered to be the acme of railway comfort, though greater convenience might be secured by the sacrifice of a little less room to massive gaudiness and show.

At eight o'clock on an icy cold morning we arrived at Cairo and betook ourselves to Shepheard's Hotel and a welcome fire. Despite the warmth of our reception by an almost lifelong friend, Mr. Maurice Moberly, Governor of the Tura convict prison, our memory of Cairo will always be one of cold. It was bleak, windy, sleety weather, and about as unlike the Cairo of one's fancy as could be imagined. This is an example of the climatic changes that began to take place on the opening of the Suez Canal, and, helped by the ever-increasing irrigation of Lower Egypt, has been since growing more and more marked. The rainfall has already increased nearly sevenfold, and the mean temperature has become appreciably lower.

The wealth of antique treasures in the Museum—one of the best designed and best lighted in the world—was enchanting, but needed much more time than we had at our disposal. The Pyramids we visited in one of the most poisonous blizzards that man would venture out in. It was raining fast and blowing a gale, and the rain and wind-whirled sand stung us like whips and penetrated everything we wore. It was impossible to enjoy or appreciate anything. We had intended to climb up the Great Pyramid, and explore it to its depths, but in that weather it was impossible, and after a perfunctory tour half round it, a visit to the temples of the Sphinx, with their marvellous corners dovetailed in granite, and five minutes with the Sphinx itself, we abandoned the effort, and forced our way, shivering, against the hurricane, to seek tea and warmth in the Mena House Hotel.

One of the most enjoyable incidents of our stay was a visit to the Tura prison, the central penal settlement of the country. The buildings, which cover a large area, stand on the eastern bank of the Nile, a few miles out of Cairo. They accommodate 1700 convicts, with a staff of 350, of whom the only European is the Governor himself. We were privileged to enjoy a complete tour of the establishment, visiting every corner of it, and much admired the economic management of its varied and self-supporting departments. Before we took our leave we witnessed an admirably executed performance of musical drill by the sons of the warders, who are provided with a school and free education on the premises, and we were at once reminded of the somewhat similar performance—the parade of the Choli cadet corps—that we had enjoyed some weeks before.

On January 22nd we took our departure, sailing from Port Said for Europe the same evening on board the Orient liner *Orvieto*, having covered in all a distance of 5688 miles in a hundred and eighty-eight days. The journey had even exceeded our anticipations in enjoyment and interest, and we felt no regrets at having spent our leave in this manner, travelling through the continent. Apart from the interest of seeing the various countries passed in the stage of evolution that they have at present reached, the experience gained in such an extended trip

EGYPT

cannot but be of use to us if we should be able to carry out another journey through less known stretches of Africa.

With the exception of one carrier dismissed in the first week of our journey through German East Africa, and the abortive strike of our Baganda carriers near the Victoria Nile, we had no trouble with any of our carriers. We never had occasion to punish any of them, nor to report any to their district commissioners. Our relations with the chiefs, headmen, and people of every tribe were equally satisfactory, and throughout the journey they assisted us in every possible way, besides treating us with friendliness and courtesy.

Every traveller has his own ideas as to outfit, so we do not intend to add to the numerous lists of camp equipment that have been published in other books, but will content ourselves with brief notes on a few items such as clothing, rifles, cameras, and cycles, as these may prove of some value. We both wore drill shirts—without coats—and shorts when trekking, and though many may disagree, we consider this to be the most comfortable kit in which to walk or cycle. On the shirts, which had short sleeves, we wore spine-pads of *solaro* cloth, and our double terai hats were lined with the same material (neither of us wore helmets). Except in the bad elephant grass we had bare legs, wearing no covering on them above our socks, but for the two months during which we were in such rough country, we supplemented these with puttees, or wore stockings. One of us wore thin chrome leather boots, one pair of which lasted throughout the journey, while the other was shod in rubber-soled canvas boots.

Our battery consisted of, for one, a double-barrelled .450 by Rigby, and a .350 Rigby Mauser, a shot gun, and a .22 rook rifle; for the other, a double-barrelled .360 by Evans, a .310 by Greener, and a ball and shot gun; and, in our opinion, the .350 and .360 bore rifles are the most useful for all-round work in Africa for everything from elephant, rhino, and buffalo to small buck. With both these weapons we have on more than one occasion dropped elephants with the frontal shot, which for a long time was considered an impossibility. The possessor of the .450 has now changed that weapon for a double .350, and now relies entirely on this weapon and the magazine rifle of the same bore, while he has substituted a double .310 by Greener for the .22, as the latter is too small for practical purposes, and the former is as good for small buck as it is for guinea-fowl. The other has made no change in his battery except to substitute a double-barrel .310 for the single-barrelled rifle of the same bore and make.

Our cameras deserve a passing notice. We carried, first, a half-plate stand camera by Chapman of Manchester, fitted with a Ross R.R. lens working at F8, which had been in use since 1893, and is as good to-day as it ever was (with this, Paget XXX glass plates were used, and out of six dozen only one was broken); secondly, two 5 in. by 4 in. kodaks, one of which had been in use in Africa since 1901; and, thirdly, a panoram kodak, purchased in 1905. For these kodaks N.C. films were used, and out of some seventy-five dozen exposed, we had not one bad or deteriorated film. We found the light in British East Africa and Uganda weaker than in Rhodesia and in German East Africa, and considered it advisable to work—for snapshots—on an average at F11 instead of at F.16. In the Soudan and Egypt the light was again more powerful, and to start with, especially with time-exposures with the half-plate camera, we were inclined to over-expose; but considering the fact that our exposures varied from $\frac{1}{100}''$ to .75" we were, on the whole, very lucky. All the plates and films were always in airtight tins, carried in wooden boxes, as in tin trunks the heat is often more than they can stand.

The only other items in our kit that call for any comment are the bicycles and the acetylene lamps. For the former we would recommend any one contemplating cycling in Africa to take a *light* roadster of a reliable make, with a first-class saddle, thorn-proof (pneumatic) tyres, or roadster tyres with chrome leather bands, spare nuts, washers, bolts, and balls, and some extra tubes and outer covers. Heavy bicycles are a mistake, and so (we think) are two-speed gears. As for lights, for camp life as well as for life on an up-country station we both swear by acetylene, and throughout the journey we relied on a couple of miner's hand-lamps, burning the ordinary rock carbide. Though a *little* more trouble than paraffin, we have found it more economical, and the light is infinitely superior.

XIX

SOME AFRICAN PROBLEMS

The rapid opening up of Africa by rail and river, and some reflections on the problems that this development is presenting.

A JOURNEY through Africa in 1910 cannot be compared with even the shorter journeys of the great explorers. The difficulties encountered are nothing compared with theirs; they are far less than they were even twelve years ago when E. S. Grogan first travelled from the Cape to Cairo. The line of the great lakes and the Nile is no longer an unknown country—the slave raiders have gone —the barbarous rule of Mwanga in Uganda is a thing of the past—the Dervish power in the Soudan is broken. Railways and telegraphs, steamers and motor cars are replacing the old caravans. Well-built brick and stone towns lighted with electric light and supplied with the luxuries of civilisation, well-tended farms and plantations exist where recently was nothing but savagery. But Africa has not ceased to be interesting because it has begun to be civilised; on the contrary, it can be stated without much fear of contradiction that tropical Africa is more interesting at the present date than it has ever been, and the problems of its future are more complex than those of its past.

We have tried in these pages to convey some idea of the country as it is to-day, to show something of the life of the resident as well as that of the traveller, and to portray the centres of civilisation as well as the still unspoilt wilds. The reader may well ask, "What of it? What of this huge country that you have traversed? Is it well with it? What are *we* doing there, and what of the future? What are these complex problems to which you refer?" A subject that might well occupy a whole volume can be but touched upon in a single chapter, but a brief survey may serve to indicate the main problems, and provide some food for thought. As recently as ten years ago there were many who wondered whether the statesmen responsible for our imperial policy in the decade from 1885 to 1894 had not made a great mistake in assuming for Great Britain heavy responsibilities in tropical and unhealthy Africa. To-day there are found but few who doubt the wisdom of their action. The results of the past ten years have more than justified our protectorates; there is, in fact, an ever-increasing number who regret that greater advantage was not taken of the vast opportunities that then presented themselves. Not only have peace, prosperity and liberty, both religious and civil, taken the place of war, devastation, and slavery, but England is beginning to realise that these tropical dependencies are a profitable investment; and that the possibilities of Rhodesia, Nyasaland, British East Africa, Uganda, and the Soudan have as yet only been hinted at.[1]

Tropical Africa is developing at a tremendous rate. Those of us who live in it can hardly grasp the changes: the average Englishman at home does not form a picture of the new conditions till they have already given place to newer ones. How many realise that already one can travel from Antwerp to within a hundred miles or so of Tanganyika by rail and steamer? or that, but for three small stretches (Ujiji–Tabora, Bukoba–Entebbe, Nimule–Gondokoro), there is direct telegraphic communication between the Cape and Cairo? Yet not so long ago this was considered a wild-cat scheme. When we left Rhodesia in July 1910 we had not heard of Elisabethville, the Belgian town over our borders—probably it did not exist. On our return (June 1911) we find that it has a population

[1] "We have arrived at a new era in the history of the White Man's burden. The problem of the present and near future is the active and scientific exploitation of the tropics. The Colonial Secretary is trustee for one of the greatest undeveloped estates in the world."—Noel Buxton in *The Nation*. "The struggle for the control of the tropics during the later years of the Victorian era proved our tropical colonies to be of political and commercial necessity to the Empire."—*The Broad Stone of Empire*, by Sir Charles Bruce.

of 1200 and boasts a daily newspaper! In the eastern half of the continent the rapid construction of railways is not only an indication of progress and enterprise, but it is pre-eminently the most notable feature of the present day, and is probably almost unparalleled. It may be years before there is a through line from the Cape to Cairo, but the basis of the scheme that Cecil Rhodes first propounded to a sceptical world is already nearly a *fait accompli*. Nearly two-thirds of the main route has been covered, while connecting links with the coast are coming in at every side,[1] and the day of the branch line has already begun—from Port Soudan to Khartoum, from Jibouti to the heart of Abyssinia, from Mombasa to the Victoria Nyanza, with a branch to Fort Hall, the German lines from Tanga and from Dar-es-Salam, and the Shire Highlands Railway. From the West Coast the Lobito Bay line is being pushed on to Katanga to meet the northern extension of the Rhodesia Railways which are already creeping on from Elisabethville to Kambove, and these will connect before long with the Congo route from Boma to Albertville. Later there is little doubt that the whole system will link up with Tanganyika, Victoria and Albert Nyanzas, and form a continuous network of railway and steamer routes connecting every place between Elisabethville and Mahagi with the coast. In the interior the Jinja–Kakindu Railway is linking up Bunyoro with the East Coast, and will soon be part of a through communication between Alexandria and Mombasa. The Soudan Railway has advanced up the Blue Nile to Sennar, and has now cut across the White Nile and is pushing on into Kordofan. Steamers run on all the great lakes: the White Nile is navigated by stern-wheelers to Rejaf, the Blue Nile to Roseires, the Sobat to Gambela, and the Bahr-el-Ghazal to Wau. From Butiaba to Nimule, and from Kakindu to Foweira, steamers also ply.

It is a long list, but it is not complete, and before

[1] In 1900 Rhodes wrote, "The object is to cut Africa through the centre, and the railway will pick up trade all along the route. The junctions to the east and west coasts, which will occur in the future, will be outlets for the traffic obtained along the route of the line as it passes through the centre of Africa."

one has grown accustomed to the prospect of all these lands being thrown open to civilisation and development it will be out of date. Africa has been moving fast since the century began—a glimpse at the experiences of the first traveller from the Cape to Cairo is sufficiently convincing of that—but the rate at which it has already advanced is nothing compared to that at which it is going to advance during the next few years. No effort should be spared, therefore, to understand and master the various problems that face us. We Europeans have taken upon ourselves to govern Africa; we have made ourselves responsible for the country. Are we doing our best for it and with it? Are we going to continue to do so, and on what general lines should its development proceed?

In a discussion on the future of this part of Africa we may exclude the questions involving political problems of international interest, such as the future of Abyssinia, and the "storm-centre" of Darfur and the Senoussi. The questions that are imminent are those touching the regions already under definite control and awaiting development— the settlement of a European population, the labour question, the relations between black and white, the treatment and use of the natives, and our right to, and rights in, the territories we are administering. With regard to the first, enough is already known of East and Central Africa to dispose of the old fiction that it is necessarily and inevitably the white man's grave. The greater portions of Rhodesia, the Belgian Congo highlands, and the western parts of British East Africa at any rate are suitable for European settlement; they are, indeed, more suitable than many parts of South Africa. The climate is admirable, the soil fertile, and the rainfall adequate. Their accessibility grows each succeeding year, and their healthiness is, with one exception, rapidly becoming only a matter of experience and care. The one exception that must be borne in mind is the Sleeping Sickness. There is, however, a reasonable hope that the discovery of a remedy is but a matter of time, and may quite conceivably soon be an accomplished fact. There is also the consolation that, whether or not the scourge has been effectually checked, there is a considerable choice of territory that is either free from suspicion, or where a reasonable amount of care can avert the risk.

The prospects of stock-raising are also at present complicated by the existence of the tsetse fly (*Glossina Morsitans*) in some districts that are otherwise eminently suitable for cattle, but this has already yielded in many instances to the effects of progress and civilisation, and, although possibly slow, its extermination may also in time be effected. The possibilities of the land have already been touched upon. The prospects of cattle-raising and cotton and rubber cultivation in Northern Rhodesia, of cotton, tea, and rubber in Nyasaland, of sisal and rubber in German East Africa, are more than good. Forest timber and rubber, as well as the great mineral wealth in the Congo, are attracting deserved attention. Uganda has proved beyond dispute its eminent suitability for plantations of rubber, cocoa, coffee, and cotton. The highlands of the East African Protectorate have a future for the cultivation of wheat, sisal, wattle, and other crops, as well as for raising cattle, sheep, and ostriches, while the lowlands are being successfully exploited for the production of cotton and rubber. The Soudan already produces great quantities of cotton, gum, and other valuable products. The development of the Congo has been retarded, but if the indication that its future is going to be regulated on sound lines is a true one, its progress will be one of great rapidity. Every section of its eastern system of communications will soon be linked not only with each other but with the ocean at Boma, Lobito Bay, and Beira. The opening up of these profitable territories will attract a large population, and involve the settlement of a variety of problems.

In the selection and admission of the settler himself the greatest care will for many years have to be exercised. Men of little or no experience or training, and with an insufficient capital, will only be encouraged to their own

SOME AFRICAN PROBLEMS

ruin. Africa is essentially not—except within narrow limits—a country for unskilled white labour ; this is and must always be to a large extent the province of the indigenous population. It offers rather an opportunity for men who are trained artisans, or who are capable of the rôle of overseer—men who can manage, teach, and extract work from others.

The allocation of land, and the terms on which it is to be held, must be reasonable, equitable, and encouraging. Land should be granted as far as possible as freehold—the disadvantages to the serious ambitions of the settler of leasehold property in a new country are sufficiently patent without labouring the point. Huge grants of land to syndicates and companies who intend to wait for the rise of land values and then speculate should be as rigorously discouraged as the system of granting strips along the line to railway companies in lieu of subsidies.

The birth of the Union of South Africa has brought a factor into the consideration of the future of the continent that may possibly make itself felt even beyond the Zambezi River. The extension of the North American Union from a beginning of thirteen small States to its present dimensions was originally neither foreseen nor intended, and it is quite possible that those who are concerned in the preservation of the identity of the South Central African dependencies will have a considerable force to reckon with in the future.

With the opening up of these new lands will arise the question as to what extent is the future of an exclusively European settlement justified. The Indian immigration problem has already proved acute in parts of South Africa, and there have not been wanting indications that other and almost equally habitable portions of pacified Africa have been regarded with covetous eyes by a section of the public which apparently holds that because something that we have is good most of it ought to be given to some one else. The service that a portion of the population of India has done in the opening up of the East Africa and Uganda Protectorates is considerable, and is denied by none. Their employment on the Uganda Railway rendered possible an achievement that without them would probably have had to wait for years, while their highly developed trading instinct and ability to live on almost as little as the natives themselves have paved the way for European trade in the interior to a very valuable degree. But at the same time it is a most unnecessarily altruistic policy that would, in return, offer them the unrestricted immigration into and occupation of a country that they have, either for attractive pay or for their own ends, incidentally helped to develop. The bricklayer or mason is a valuable and indispensable factor in the construction of a palace, but the most philanthropic of owners could hardly be expected to offer him, except indirectly, a share in the joys and luxuries of the completed edifice. The claim of the Indian population to unrestricted settlement on equal terms to those granted to Europeans cannot be seriously considered, and it is difficult to see that they would have any just cause for complaint if they were to be entirely prohibited from acquiring land, at any rate in such parts as are suitable for European settlement. The immigration of Indian races to the lower and more tropical regions is on a different footing. If there should be sufficient reason to maintain that overcrowding in India calls for some outlet, then parts of British East Africa might be found for their settlement. But such a step should not be hastily decided on, for it must not be forgotten that as it was the British and not the Indian taxpayer who has borne the expense connected with acquiring these lands, it is he that is entitled to a prior claim. The European, too, is beginning to make good his claim to the fertile coast belt on the Indian Ocean, and to the tract known as Jubaland, which promises to become a miniature Egypt. The assistance to trade rendered by Indians is due to the fact that they can dispense with the comforts that are a *sine qua non* to European settlers in Africa, and as they come to the country to make money, and spend less in it than their European rivals, sending all their money home to India, it is difficult to see that they have

SOME AFRICAN PROBLEMS

any claim beyond that of not being hampered by special regulations and restrictions relative to trading.

The problem of paramount importance, however, is the native problem, though it is by no means universally assigned its proper place. That the stay-at-home student of African affairs should be unable to realise the actual position and exigencies is not altogether surprising, but it is also not uncommon to find residents in the country whom it seems to have escaped, that the native problem not only even now affects every phase of African life, but is one that in the future is likely to become rather more than less acute. When the subject of the development and settlement of Africa is under discussion it is not unusual to hear the question put, " What right have we to the land? What right have we to take it from the natives whom we found in possession, and to use it ourselves? What benefit is our occupation conferring upon them?" Some even go further, and, on hearing it urged that at any rate our administration means peace and comparatively sound government where formerly there was nothing but bloodshed and grotesque injustice, uncompromisingly deny the right of any nation to impose upon even the lower grades of humanity any form of government other than that which they have already chosen to adopt. Abandoning the task of correcting by argument a dogma that would deny to every unhappy section of humanity, white or black, the opportunity of amelioration afforded by the assistance or interference of their more fortunate and enlightened fellows, and would deprive a nation of even its cherished mite of altruism, let us examine for a moment the right by which Britain and the other European powers claim a share in the wealth of Africa. It is, in fact, so simple that to those who have any knowledge of the history and traditions of the African tribes it is a wonder that it is ever asked. The right of the European nations is very nearly the same as that of the natives whom they found in possession : only very nearly, because in reality it is better. Every tribe that has on the advent of the European powers been found in possession or claiming possession of any portion of African territory, except a few like the Pygmies of the Semliki and Congo forests, the Watwa of the swamps in Northern Rhodesia, and the Bushmen, has based that claim on comparatively recent conquest and on nothing else. Force was everything; might was right. The further conquest by the European nations has been sometimes accompanied by bloodshed, but to a very large extent by none. Are they to be denied the rights of conquest because their victory has been a peaceful or a peace-producing one?

The native conqueror either arrived because of pressure from outside—the pressure that gives rise to migration—or else owing to motives of greed. The white conqueror has generally invaded their country primarily in the interests of humanity,[1] but even when he has extended his possessions with less unselfish motives he has brought liberty, security, and peace, where he found slavery, rapine, and war. There can be no question about the white man's right; the admission of it by the natives themselves could not be more frank or complete: and even Britain, the greatest criminal of all, if the annexation of African territory is to be called a crime, earns no worse title than that of "Land-grabber" amongst the rivals whose energy or enterprise or altruism has proved itself a shade less profitable. The claim of the civilised conqueror is strengthened by another fact: the native population is, almost without exception, an unprofitable proprietor of the land. Their wants are simple, and the area huge out of all proportion to their numbers, and even such portions as are cultivated are generally treated in such crude and ignorant methods, as hardly to redeem them from the condition of waste lands. They need but a fraction of the land, and they are quite unable to make the best as yet of what they have, or to trace and develop the hidden resources of the country. When they have learnt to make the best of what they have they will be able to do with

[1] This was especially the case in Nyasaland and in Uganda : and when there was some talk of abandoning the latter country in 1892, the Anti-Slavery Society was amongst those who protested and urged its retention.

even less than they now occupy. Is it reasonable that huge tracks of fertile land to which the former proprietors had no better claim should be abandoned by its present conquerors to indolent and unprofitable occupation by savages who cannot appreciate, utilise, or absorb? The very idea of such dog-in-the-manger occupation must surely be Anathema Maranatha to the legislator of the present day. And yet—such is their paradoxical inconsistency—it is chiefly the supporters of recent legislation (under which the owner of unprofitably held land is to be so heavily penalised that he is obliged to give it up) who descant upon the iniquity of the settlement of "native" lands.

We have, however, maintained that our claim is even better than that of the former conquerors of the land, and we base this superiority of claim on the premise that our dominion is, in effect, for the good of humanity, and for the benefit of the natives whom we have brought under our sway. To make this good we have a duty to perform.[1] Our duty is to help and advance the country, raise the level of morality of its inhabitants, and give them the advantage of so much of our civilisation as they are able to absorb. How much that is, is a matter of considerable controversy. It is, however, beyond question that the African negro is, and perhaps must be for centuries, incapable of a standard that is anything but low. His nature has been described as that of a child, and it has been described as partly that of a woman and partly that of a child, but, although there is truth in both similes, it also largely approximates to that of an adult of arrested and even distorted development.

Before comprehensive schemes are formulated for the civilisation of the negro, facts must be recognised, or failure and confusion are bound to result. Like the domesticated animal, he is an admirable institution in his place, but those who have failed to realise his limitations are obviously

---

[1] "It is incumbent on him (the white man) to see that his influence is not destructive only. . . . He should do his utmost to direct into the right paths the force which he is unloosing."—*The South African Natives*, by the S.A. Native Races Committee.

unqualified to adjudicate upon the question of his destiny. Not only does it stand to reason that animate beings who, since their evolution from protoplasm, have been guided by little but the most distorted principles of justice and humanity, must of necessity be unable to emerge at a bound, and take their place with those whose enlightenment has been progressing for some two thousand years, but there is actually scientific proof that the negro is at present physiologically incapable of more than a limited moral and intellectual development.[1] The conformation of the negro's skull shows that it is as obviously futile to expect him to attain a European standard of civilisation and culture as to require a crew of paddlers to propel the latest Dreadnought, or a fretwork machine to do the work of a steam-saw. Within limits everything that is possible should be done, and it is indeed as much to the advantage of the white colonist as it is to that of the native that it should be done. The simple virtues of honesty, industry, and reliability can and should be diligently instilled, but in the attempt to raise his moral status it should be borne in mind that he is in a sense *in statu pupilari*, and that he needs careful and unremitting supervision and discipline to an even greater extent than does the schoolboy of civilised nations.

Even at his present stage of development the native as a worker is invaluable to the development of his country. Purely manual labour is largely his monopoly, and will probably have to remain so, though training and discipline should make him far more efficient. In the lower branches of skilled labour he is already beginning to take a useful place. Here again we tread close on controversy, but without entering into a discussion of the extent to which, even for economical reasons, he should be encouraged to do work at which the white man can earn a living wage, one may draw attention to the departments in which he is already being profitably employed, and in which his employment might with excellent results be still further

---

[1] " A negro cannot by any amount of civilizing be evolved into a European."
—Dr. Keltie in *The Partition of Africa*.

extended. In Nyasaland and Northern Rhodesia his service as clerk, typist, and artisan is an invaluable asset. He is imitative rather than initiative, but he is capable of getting through a protracted amount of mechanical copying and drudgery that relieves the white man to a considerable degree of the dull tedium of his work. In Uganda and the East African Protectorate this work is still mainly performed by Indian and Goanese. It is especially surprising that in so advanced a country as the former little use has yet been made of the local material in this respect. From the general standard of the native population it is reasonable to suppose that the necessary training would be a matter of but little difficulty. The results would be more economical and presumably of greater benefit to the country than the employment of aliens, and the substitution of natives for Indians would be free from the objection that has been made in other parts, that the employment of native clerks and artisans is taking the bread out of the white man's mouth.

For the formation of a native army there may at present seem to be but little need, but it might conceivably occur, and it is a question whether we are not wasting our opportunities of making the best of the material at our command. France is utilising to a remarkable degree the fighting forces in her West African possessions, and we might well consider the advisability of following her example. Military training is a thing that the African native takes to with considerable readiness—as has been proved in the Soudanese regiments, the King's African Rifles, and the Northern Rhodesia Police—and the discipline itself would be an educative influence that is not to be disregarded. The Baganda are, by treaty, under an obligation to serve as a militia when called upon, but though they have on one occasion shown a striking readiness to fulfil their contract, they are quite untrained, while the resources of many another warlike tribe have as yet been scarcely tapped. But it is in his capacity as an unskilled workman that the native is at present, as he will be for all time, attracting and demanding the most serious attention. The development of Africa, given capital and enterprise, depends upon the native labour supply, and upon relatively little else.[1] The chief difficulty in the labour problem consists in the obstinate and patent fact that the native requires to-day so little for his maintenance that, left alone, he has neither need nor desire for employment. The obvious remedy is not to leave him alone, and there are a hundred reasons, many of which have already been touched upon, why he should be taught and encouraged to work.[2] If this can be done without creating too hurriedly a variety of new and purchaseable wants, so much the better. His wants need developing gradually, so that he can begin to feel the need for things that tend to raise him in the social scale rather than things which only lend themselves to incongruous adornment. The evolution of efficient methods of stimulating, organising, and regularising the labour supply of the eastern half of the continent is a problem that is exercising Governments and employers from Egypt to the Cape. Great progress has been made in the last few years, and from large districts, the very boundaries of which the inhabitants were too timid or too unenterprising to cross, gangs of labourers are now proceeding to the mining, railway, and agricultural centres that depend so largely upon their aid.

But the real work is only beginning, and great care and foresight must be exercised if the best is to be extracted from the material at hand. A very large degree of parental supervision must for an indefinite time be necessary during the whole period of the natives' employment as well as while travelling to and from the place of employment. The task of equitable distribution to the various centres of industry is no easy one, and may well grow in difficulty as development proceeds. But

---

[1] "The core of most problems connected with the opening up of Africa is cheap labour."—Sir H. H. Johnston in *George Grenfell and the Congo*. "Without labour we cannot develop the continent, and if we cannot get the native to work, what is to become of Africa?"—Dr. Keltie in *The Partition of Africa*.

[2] "Labour is good for the people, but only if they find some satisfaction in it . . . a healthy commerce should be fostered."—*George Grenfell and the Congo* (1894).

the possibility of a distribution of labour leading to a redistribution of population must be for many reasons rigorously guarded against, and repatriation must be regular and unfailing. An almost equally important consideration is the restriction and equalisation, as far as possible, of the rates of pay. The situation has not yet become generally acute, but it requires careful handling, or there will be a risk of a variety of scales of wages coming into existence as widely divergent as the localities at which the labour is employed. Especially is this risk apparent where rapid development or a promise of rapid development attracts a sudden influx of capital, and creates an abnormal demand for labour. The township of Elisabethville is a case in point. Here, in a settlement barely twelve months old, wages and consequently prices are ruling as high as if not higher than in the notoriously expensive city of Johannesburg, although the surrounding country has enjoyed for years rates of pay which are as low as any in Africa. To obtain this equalisation of wages as well as the distribution of labour, highly organised and well-managed Labour Bureaux have already been found indispensable, and their institution might well be extended to other of our African dependencies—for instance, the East Africa Protectorate, where labour is largely in demand by two distinct classes of employer, and the precarious nature of the supply is beginning to be seriously felt.

The Labour Bureau cannot be an independent commercial undertaking; it must either be a recognised department of the Government, or the Government must keep it very largely under its control. An independent institution cannot be expected or allowed to exercise the influence necessary to gain its ends; its action must within limits be arbitrary, or a highly important branch of national industry is liable to be shelved. Mineral wealth is a huge and undeniable asset. Mine development attracts capital and population, and brings with it the construction of railways, but it must be regarded as a means to an end rather than the sole ambition of a fertile country, and precautions should be taken lest its temporarily higher paying power hamper or overwhelm the agricultural enterprise on the fruits of which the final and lasting prosperity of the colonies must rest. As Rhodes remarked in 1893, "There is a bottom to every mine!"

The methods and principles of native administration form a subject of inexhaustible interest and vast importance, on which all, from the hurried visitor to the oldest resident, are almost equally prepared to dogmatise, and almost equally certain to be met with contradiction. The government of the African natives is not a difficult task, but the study of the natives themselves is so complicated, and their attitude such a fantastic mixture of frankness and reticence, innocence and cunning, that every succeeding year spent amongst them serves but to convince the student of the shallowness of his knowledge and the depth and difficulty of all there is left to learn. That they are easy to govern in spite of it may be taken to be largely due to two facts—that though they understand the white man quite as little as he understands them, they accept him, as they have always accepted those who have proved themselves stronger or superior, as something in the immutable order of things, and even more—they accept him as something superhuman, something almost divine. Their readiness to submit to authority, then, predisposes them to docility, and if the white man's rule is conducted on principles of justice and humanity—even though his ideas of justice may be at variance to their own, as they often are [1]—the difficulties of government are already largely overcome. But this condition must be strictly and conscientiously fulfilled: there must be sympathy and understanding as far as may be between the rulers and the ruled: [2] justice must be strictly dispensed and the dignity of the white man rigorously upheld. The latter is not difficult while the numbers of the governing race are few, but the influx

---

[1] "Our administration of justice can never appear to the Kafir as satisfactory."—Dudley Kidd.
[2] "An Administrator must understand the native point of view."—Andrew Lang.

of a population of all grades and principles brings complications, and it is then that the discipline has to be, if anything, more rigorous, and a just balance firmly maintained.

The chiefs and any existing organised system of control should be utilised to the greatest possible degree, but it should be under the guidance and supervision of the white man, who should keep in touch with the populace and rigorously avoid the rôle of a mere receiver of revenues and an administrative figure-head. That the benefits to the natives themselves of European occupation—if not the right of conquest—justify the imposition of a monetary tax can scarcely be open to discussion. The principle of foregoing its collection just so long as a people can govern itself and manage its own affairs in an orderly manner without assistance or interference is sound, but there are few if any such cases now in existence, and it follows that the payment by tribes who are brought under the control of civilised nations, and whose welfare and good government is consulted, of a contribution towards the working cost of the administrative machinery is merely a matter of course. If any are disposed to cavil at the justice of this we would remind them that very few—and those the lowest types—have ever at any time enjoyed immunity from some sort of tribute or tax; that as a rule their enforced contributions entailed considerably greater hardships and were based upon far less obvious rights than are their present obligations;[1] and that the relaxation or abolition of all tangible sign of their submission would be as demoralising for them as it would be suicidal for us.

Native administration is complicated at present by the variety of languages or dialects spoken by the different tribes. It is to a considerable extent also the reason of the incapacity for combination, which has rendered the pacification of African territories so rapid, and so little hampered by insurrection and revolt. At the same time,

[1] "They sacrifice their own private gains and private ideas for the good of the State. . . . The people readily and willingly pay their way, they support their chiefs and even glory in the self-sacrifice it entails."—Dudley Kidd.

though the knowledge of its own particular language is indispensable for the present to the man who is devoting himself to the administration of any particular tribe, there is little doubt that a *lingua franca* or two or three *linguæ francæ* for general purposes must come sooner or later. The hybrid jargons growing daily in popular use, such as "kitchen Kafir" or the Ki-Swahili of the interior, are as repugnant in nature as they are limited in range, but as communications improve and civilisation proceeds a more or less general medium must and will in the natural course of things eventually be evolved.

It would not be fair to conclude a book which deals, however briefly and inadequately, with some of the features and problems of parts of Africa without some allusion to the past and present services of that body of men whose pioneer work amongst the savage inhabitants has been of such invaluable assistance in the pacification and regeneration of the continent. It is easy to criticise the work of Missions in Africa; it is easy, and too common, to pick out isolated instances of failure in their ambitions, to ascribe to their direct influence the recrudescence in the sophisticated and half-educated native of the unregenerated traits which their most patient training has not quite eradicated or subdued; it is easy to hold up to ridicule and contempt an instance here and there of not quite unselfish devotion to the cause; and it is not difficult to point a comparison between the ease and comforts of the lives of some of the African devotees and those of their fellow-workers in the slums of our great European cities. But it is as impossible to deny the general and almost universal good that is now being done as to belittle the heroic and self-sacrificing enterprise that has in many quarters smoothed the path and opened the door to pacification and good government. The influence of Christianity in Uganda, for instance, has been of immense value, not only for its intrinsic worth and its improvement of the morals of a most immoral race, but as a barrier against the encroachment of Mohammedan propaganda. The Church Missionary Society, the Universities Mission, the

Pères Blancs, the London Missionary Society, the United Free Church, and other denominations have done and are still doing patient and valuable work in the continent. There has at times been friction, and there has at times been a tendency to step beyond a purely non-political sphere, but the present situation is generally marked by broad-minded tolerance, consistent with the maintenance of the highest principles, and a willingness to assign spiritual and temporal matters to their proper provinces.

But there can be no hard and fast line between a sound and rational missionary policy and a sound and rational administration among the African natives. Every European in Africa is a missionary, and though he may not be engaged in preaching the gospel, his high example and jealous guardianship of the dignity of his race must have an elevating and civilising effect, and serve to justify his claim to regenerate and enjoy the conditions and resources of the vast territories upon which he has imposed his sway.

IN SOUTH CENTRAL AFRICA

BEING AN ACCOUNT OF SOME OF THE EXPERIENCES AND JOURNEYS OF THE AUTHOR DURING A STAY OF SIX YEARS IN THAT COUNTRY

By J. M. MOUBRAY, F.R.G.S.

Demy 8vo. With Map and Photographs by the AUTHOR.
10s. 6d. net

DURING a residence of some six years in South Central Africa (1903-1908), where I was engaged in the work of a mining engineer, much of my time was spent in visiting new districts in what was in many cases almost unknown country. I thus accumulated of necessity a good deal of novel and miscellaneous information. Having since been repeatedly asked by various friends to put this into book form, I have endeavoured to do so now.

I have found the task of recording the events of my sojourn in Africa much harder than living the life itself there, and must ask the kindly reader to bear with the many shortcomings in style to be found in the following pages. Against this he will perhaps bear in mind that the record is that of one who has lived year in year out among the natives of those little-known climes, and not merely the impressions of a passing traveller.

CONSTABLE & COMPANY, LIMITED

LAND AND PEOPLES OF THE KASAI

By M. W. HILTON-SIMPSON
F.R.G.S., F.Z.S., F.R.A.I.

With Eight Full-page Plates in Colour by NORMAN HARDY, who accompanied the Expedition, and Seventy-five other Illustrations. Price **16s.** net.

SOME PRESS OPINIONS

"We get a very vivid picture of the Southern Congo region . . . many problems of great interest are touched upon . . . a most interesting book on a region hitherto unknown."—*Morning Post.*

"A valuable supplement to the monumental work published by the Colonial department of the Belgian Government . . . though it may be described as popular in style, it is fraught with scientific interest. . . . Mr. Hilton-Simpson's photographs of the negroes of South-Central Congoland will be of much interest to anthropologists and ethnologists."—*Nature.*

"This book is something very different from the ordinary record of big game shooting, and we congratulate the party not only upon what they acquired both of fetishes and folk-lore, but on the fact that they came out of their perilous expedition with comparatively whole skins . . . they are able to say that they spent many months in perhaps the savagest part of the whole world and never shed a drop of human blood."—*Globe.*

"A journey which was full of strange and adventurous experiences; the record of a scientific expedition which resulted in large additions to knowledge of geographical conditions, the native manners and customs, and the animal life in the Kasai Basin. No more important book of travel in the heart of Equatorial Africa has appeared for a long time."—*Field.*

"A solid contribution to geographical knowledge, a first-rate story of geographical adventure through country so unhospitable that no white man had ever traversed it before."—*Daily Graphic.*

"The reader will not find a dull page in the whole book. . . . The book is well illustrated with photographs, and contains several excellent full-page colour illustrations."—*African World.*

"About the peoples of the Kasai . . . there is much fresh and often curious information."—*Illustrated Sporting and Dramatic News.*

"A very informing and interesting volume."—*Daily News.*

Full Prospectus on application to

CONSTABLE & COMPANY, LIMITED
10 ORANGE STREET, LONDON, W.C.

www.ingramcontent.com/pod-product-compliance
Lightning Source LLC
Chambersburg PA
CBHW070525090426
42735CB00013B/2870